Organizational
Learning
at NASA

Public Management and Change Series
BERYL A. RADIN, *Series Editor*

Titles in the Series

Challenging the Performance Movement: Accountability, Complexity, and Democratic Values, Beryl A. Radin

Charitable Choice at Work: Evaluating Faith-Based Job Programs in the States, Sheila Suess Kennedy and Wolfgang Bielefeld

The Collaborative Public Manager: New Ideas for the Twenty-first Century, Rosemary O'Leary and Lisa Blomgren Bingham, Editors

The Dynamics of Performance Management: Constructing Information and Reform, Donald P. Moynihan

The Greening of the U.S. Military: Environmental Policy, National Security, and Organizational Change, Robert F. Durant

How Management Matters: Street-Level Bureaucrats and Welfare Reform, Norma M. Riccucci

Managing within Networks: Adding Value to Public Organizations, Robert Agranoff

Measuring the Performance of the Hollow State, David G. Frederickson and H. George Frederickson

Organizational Learning at NASA: The Challenger *and* Columbia *Accidents,* Julianne G. Mahler with Maureen Hogan Casamayou

Public Values and Public Interest: Counterbalancing Economic Individualism, Barry Bozeman

The Responsible Contract Manager: Protecting the Public Interest in an Outsourced World, Steven Cohen and William Eimicke

Revisiting Waldo's Administrative State: Constancy and Change in Public Administration, David H. Rosenbloom and Howard E. McCurdy

Organizational Learning
at NASA
The *Challenger* and *Columbia* Accidents

JULIANNE G. MAHLER
with **Maureen Hogan Casamayou**

Georgetown University Press
Washington, D.C.

Georgetown University Press, Washington, D.C. www.press.georgetown.edu

The image used for the cover is of the Mission Control Center (MCC) Flight Control Room 1 (FCR 1) taken shortly after the landing of STS-30 Shuttle *Atlantis*, May 4, 1989. The flight controllers shown are Kevin McCluney and Bob Doremus.

Library of Congress Cataloging-in-Publication Data

Mahler, Julianne.
    Organizational learning at NASA : the Challenger and Columbia accidents / Julianne G. Mahler with Maureen Hogan Casamayou.
        p.   cm.
    Includes bibliographical references and index.
    ISBN 978-1-58901-266-0 (pbk. : alk. paper)
    1. United States. National Aeronautics and Space Administration—Reorganization. 2. Organizational learning—United States.   3. Organizational change—United States. 4. Columbia (Spacecraft)—Accidents.   5. Challenger (Spacecraft)—Accidents. I. Casamayou, Maureen Hogan.   II. Title.
TL521.312.M32   2008
658.4′038—dc22

                                                                                        2008033982

⊗ This book is printed on acid-free paper meeting the requirements of the American National Standard for Permanence in Paper for Printed Library Materials.

15 14 13 12 11 10 09   9 8 7 6 5 4 3 2
First printing

Printed in the United States of America

For the *Challenger* and *Columbia* crews and their families

Contents

Illustrations

FIGURES

TABLES

Preface

JUST AFTER 9 A.M. on February 1, 2003, the shuttle *Columbia* broke apart and was lost over Texas. This tragic event led, as had another catastrophic shuttle accident seventeen years earlier, to an intensive government investigation into the technological and organizational causes of the accident. Chilling similarities appeared. The shuttle elements that caused both accidents had failed on numerous previous flights. Erosion of the seals between the joints in the shuttle's solid rocket boosters and tile damage to the orbiter from foam debris from the external tank had been recognized as undesirable but "acceptable" conditions despite the fact that each violated specifications. In both accidents, investigators found that decision makers were isolated and failed to listen to either in-house or contract engineers who expressed concern about the problem elements. Before both accidents, flight managers had been under extreme pressure from Congress and the public to maintain launch schedules, and they had not followed established procedures for clearing unresolved problems. Based on these and other observations, the Columbia Accident Investigation Board concluded that NASA was not a learning organization.

Organizational learning, especially in public organizations, is an idea that is often promoted but seldom studied in any particular detail. This book hopes to remedy that deficiency by examining a case in which it is charged that learning did *not* occur. Using a detailed operational definition of organizational learning and its component processes, this book looks closely at the conditions and actions that did lead to learning and the circumstances that blocked learning or led to the loss of earlier lessons. The book also assembles evidence about the learning process at NASA to refine the general theory of organizational learning to account for the pressures and constraints of learning in public organizations.

Organizational learning is not one but several processes by which organizations seek to improve their performance by searching out the causes behind what they judge to be unacceptable results. What counts as unacceptable is often problematic, however, and may range from public disasters to less dramatic opportunities to correct or enhance agency programs. In the core learning process, members compare past actions with consequences to make cause–effect inferences about how to achieve the results they want. Finally, what makes learning organizational as opposed to personal is the process of institutionalizing new knowledge in rules or professional norms so that other members have access to it. Like social learning, organizational learning means that lessons are passed on from person to person rather than gained independently through direct experience.

Despite the frequency with which organizations are encouraged to adopt learning practices, it is certainly not easy to do so. Many of the features of the public organization environment produce special challenges for learning, as this case demonstrates. Nevertheless, organizational learning can be a particularly valuable tool for public management. It offers a model for an indigenous, self-correcting organizational process that makes use of the agency-specific experience of professionals to solve problems, in contrast to many recent reforms and movements in the field that rely on some form of external intervention. Learning also represents a change in focus about how agencies improve, from a view that meaningful change only results from outside political pressures or strategically designed rules to a view of change that rests on knowledge-based enhancements in administrative and policy ideas. The main idea behind organizational learning—to improve agency work based on a considered assessment of performance—also lies at the heart of what we mean by both traditional and contemporary, results-oriented public administration. This case of successful and unsuccessful learning at NASA suggests some of the ways that we might encourage learning in public organizations.

This investigation of learning in NASA's shuttle program focuses on the events between the *Challenger* and *Columbia* accidents and what the agency did to address the organizational problems revealed by the first accident. Our study is presented in three parts, corresponding to a three-part operational definition of organizational learning that we develop in chapter 2: problem recognition, analysis, and institutionalization. Part One lays out the evidence that all organizations engaged in high-risk technologies must pay attention to opportunities for learning, and we use NASA as an example of an agency whose dramatic program failures highlight this critical need for awareness. Part Two presents four case studies of the NASA accidents, each investigating a particular organizational factor that has been identified as a contributing cause in both shuttle disasters. According to both of the commissions that probed the accidents, the organizational causes included deficiencies in the command structure and safety monitoring systems, an inability to cope with strong external political and budgetary pressures, and an obstructive organizational culture. To these we add a fourth possible cause: coordination difficulties between NASA and its many contractors and the disincentives for contractors to identify flaws in their work and seek out costly solutions. In each of the case studies, we use the operational definition of organizational learning to identify what was actually learned in the aftermath of the first accident and whether these lessons affected events leading up to the second accident. In Part Three, we have collated the evidence of NASA's learning patterns to develop a broadly applicable set of propositions about learning in public organizations and to offer lessons that could make learning more likely. In the end we argue that NASA did learn in some cases, at some times, about some things.

This book was first imagined over four years ago when both Julianne Mahler and Maureen Casamayou were members of the Department of Public and International Affairs at George Mason University. Early in the project Maureen's life took a different direction, and although she contributed to the case studies in many ways, her principal role became crafting chapter 5 on external forces.

This project is indebted to the contributions of many others. First, many thanks go to Beryl Radin, the editor of this series, who has been a supporter from the first, and to Don Jacobs at Georgetown University Press, the acquisitions editor. The gentleness with which he has delivered his suggestions and reminders has been much appreciated. In addition, thanks are due to the three anonymous outside readers whose insights into what had been written and what had been left out helped make this a much better book than it would have been otherwise. Finally, we both owe many thanks to our families. To Lou Casamayou, Maureen's "rock" and the love of her life, and the "girls," Gemma and Loki. To Julianne's sons, Seamus and Conor, who patiently put up with a more than usually distracted mother. And to her husband, Coilin, a Joyce scholar, who probably heard more than he really needed to about the inner workings of a government organization, even one so exciting as NASA. His wise advice and unwavering moral support made the work on this book possible.

PART ONE

Recognizing the Value of Organizational Learning

CHAPTER 1

Uncanny Similarities
The *Challenger* and *Columbia* Accidents

ON FEBRUARY 1, 2003, the space shuttle *Columbia* began its homeward journey, and at 8:44 a.m. it initiated re-entry into the Earth's atmosphere. During the ensuing sixteen minutes the orbiter would experience tremendous heat, with the leading-edge temperatures of the wings rising to more than an estimated 2,800 degrees Fahrenheit. At first all seemed to go well. Then, at 8:54, the flight director at mission control in Houston was informed by the maintenance, mechanical, and crew systems office, known as MMACS, that the temperature sensors on the left side of the vehicle were "lost." The following records the exchange:

> MMACS: "Flight—MMACS."
> Flight director: "Go ahead, MMACS."
> MMACS: "FYI, I've just lost four separate temperature transducers on the left side of the vehicle, hydraulic return temperatures. Two of them on system one and one in each of systems two and three."
> Flight: "Four hyd [hydraulic] return temps?"
> MMACS: "To the left outboard and left inboard elevon."
> Flight: "Okay, is there anything common to them? DSC [discrete signal conditioner] or MDM [multiplexer-demultiplexer] or anything? I mean, you're telling me you lost them all at exactly the same time?"
> MMACS: "No, not exactly. They were within probably four or five seconds of each other."
> Flight: "Okay, where are those? Where is the instrumentation located?"
> MMACS: "All four of them are located in the aft part of the left wing, right in front of the elevons, elevon actuators. And there is no commonality."
> Flight: "No commonality." [Columbia Accident Investigation Board 2003 (hereafter CAIB), 42]

3

In this context, *no commonality* meant that the temperature transducers were not on the same electrical circuit, and the implication was that a random malfunction in the electrical circuit produced the readings. Further developments did not augur well for the *Columbia*. An attempt by *Columbia's* commander, Rick Husband, to communicate with ground control resulted in a broken transmission: "And uh, Hou—." Immediately afterward, at 8:59, instrumentation at Mission Control indicated that there was no tire-pressure reading for the tires on the left side of the shuttle, both inboard and outboard. At the flight director's command, those in direct communication with the crew (CAPCOM) communicated the new developments:

> CAPCOM: "*Columbia*—Houston. We see your tire pressure messages, and we did not copy your last call."
>
> Flight: Is it instrumentation, MMACS? Gotta be . . ."
>
> MMACS: "Flight—MMACS. Those are also off-scale low." (CAIB, 43)

As the *Columbia* approached Dallas, Texas, at 8:59, a response of "Roger, [cut off mid-word]" came in from Commander Husband to Mission Control. At 9:00, while Mission Control was still trying to regain communication with *Columbia*, the orbiter was breaking up, a process that was recorded as bright flashes on the postflight videos and imagery. Clearly, NASA had a catastrophic event on its hands, one equal to the *Challenger* accident of 1986: a shuttle program failure that could have been avoided.

OVERVIEW OF THE *CHALLENGER* AND *COLUMBIA* ACCIDENTS

In both shuttle accidents, the safety issues that brought the NASA shuttle program to a standstill were "low-tech," had surfaced many times before, and were well-known to shuttle managers at key levels. With *Challenger*, the explosion in the first minutes of launch was caused by hot gasses escaping from the solid rocket booster at one of the joints between the segments of the rocket. Engineers began raising the red flag about the poor design of the joints and their seals as early as 1977. A steady stream of warning about the problem emerged from with the space shuttle organization up to the time in July 1985, just six months before the *Challenger* catastrophe, when managers determined that a new design for the joints was needed. But the shuttle continued to fly, even though the joint seal was classified as criticality 1, designating an essential component without a backup, so that any failure would lead to disaster. The fear was that any leakage of hot gases at one of the joints could quite easily rupture the fuel tanks. On January 28, 1986, this is exactly what happened. Shortly after liftoff, hot gases burned through the seals of one of the joints in the right solid rocket booster. In a matter of seconds the shuttle broke up, disappearing behind a cloud of vapor. As would happen with the *Columbia*, all crew members perished.

While it was a flawed O-ring in *Challenger*'s right solid rocket booster that had led to the destruction of that shuttle, the CAIB concluded in 2003 that the technical cause of the *Columbia* disaster was a large debris strike to the orbiter's wing from foam that had broken off the left bipod ramp that attached the shuttle to its large external liquid-fuel tank. Similar to the *Challenger* accident, numerous early warnings about the problem—in this case, the loss of foam and the dangers from debris striking the orbiter—had been sounded. In sixty-five of the seventy launches for which there was a photographic record, foam debris had been seen, and some of the largest pieces of foam striking the orbiter came from the left bipod ramp. Strikes from this ramp area were confirmed by imagery at least seven times, including the previous launch of the *Columbia* (CAIB, 123). In fact, the first known instance of foam loss took place during *Challenger*'s second mission (STS-7). The foam came from the left bipod ramp and was of a significant size, nineteen inches by twelve inches (CAIB, 123).

FAILURE TO LEARN

Although the technical flaws behind the *Challenger* and *Columbia* accidents differed, the accidents themselves were eerily similar in several ways. Of course, both were highly visible disasters, but both also involved a series of organizational and managerial failures. In researching the causes of the accidents, the 1986 Presidential Commission on the Space Shuttle *Challenger* Accident (often and hereafter called the Rogers Commission) and the CAIB looked at the contributing organization problems as well as the engineering and hardware flaws. In both accidents, early evidence of technical malfunctions had been noted and deemed undesirable but "acceptable." Decision makers were isolated, were under intense pressure to launch, did not listen to experienced engineers, and did not or could not openly acknowledge and discuss unresolved problems. In the words of Sally Ride, a member of the CAIB, former astronaut, and former member of the Rogers Commission, "there were 'echoes' of *Challenger* in *Columbia*" (CAIB, 195). The organization had received early warnings of safety problems in both cases, but it failed to take them seriously.

Pointing to these similarities, the *Columbia* Accident Investigation Board concluded that NASA was not a learning organization. Even after numerous instances of foam loss and a very serious debris strike just two flights before the launch of the *Columbia*, foam losses were still not considered dangerous enough to halt flights. In similar fashion, prior to the *Challenger* accident, instances of eroded seals between the segments of the solid rocket boosters were recognized but tolerated. The CAIB saw this pattern as evidence of "the lack of institutional memory in the Space Shuttle Program that supports the Board's claim . . . that NASA is not functioning as a learning organization" (CAIB, 127).

The charge that NASA did not learn is especially puzzling in light of the attention paid inside and outside the organization to improving just those organizational features that contributed to the accidents. The Rogers Commission laid down a series of nine major recommendations unanimously adopted "to help assure the return to safe flight" (Rogers Commission 1986, 198).[1] These recommendations were intended to prevent a problem like the one that destroyed the *Challenger*, an often seen and avoidable flaw, from ever happening again. [The commission pointed to several characteristics of the space shuttle program that contributed to this accident, including a "silent safety program" that did not assert itself or confront the managers who routinely downgraded the seriousness of the O-ring problems on the solid rocket boosters.] To remedy these flaws, the commission recommended a number of organizational changes as well as improved engineering designs. Greater authority was to be given to shuttle program managers to direct the project elements. NASA was to create a more robust safety organization of working engineers who would be independent of the shuttle project components they were to oversee and would only be accountable to the headquarters Office of Safety, Reliability, and Quality Assurance. Improvements in organization structure and reporting relationships and in tracking and resolving critical problems were recommended. NASA was to adopt a flight rate "consistent with its resources" to target the problems generated by pervasive launch-schedule pressures coupled with diminished resources (Rogers Commission 1986, 201). Other internal and external investigations reinforced these recommendations and are reported in the chapters that follow.

 In virtually all cases, the CAIB found little evidence of changes made in response to these recommendations at the time of the *Columbia* accident. It noted that "despite all the post-*Challenger* changes at NASA and the agency's notable achievements since, the causes of the institutional failure responsible for *Challenger* have not been fixed" (195). As later chapters will show, many of the factors contributing to the organizational failures behind the *Challenger* accident were equally important in shaping the organizational outcome that was the *Columbia* disaster. Our object is to understand how this could have happened.

QUESTIONS ABOUT LEARNING AT NASA

Two sets of questions are posed here. First, what does it mean to say that NASA did not learn? It seems surprising that such an accomplished organization would not be a learning organization. To make sense of the evidence supporting the claim that NASA did not in fact learn from the *Challenger* accident and did not become a learning organization, we must first establish what is meant by organizational learning and how we can recognize learning or failure to learn. This conceptual analysis leads in chapter 2 to a definition of the processes of learning. Using this definition, we will be able to closely examine case materials surrounding four commonly recognized causes of the accidents and the organizational and procedural changes adopted by NASA following the *Challenger* disaster to determine what led to the CAIB's characterization. In each of the four case studies, the accidents will be compared to determine whether they are essentially similar in their organizational and managerial flaws, thus justifying the CAIB's assessment, or whether there is evidence that learning, as defined here, occurred.

Second, after examining the evidence, we will ask *why* NASA failed to identify and act on the organizational danger signals. Did it ever effectively adopt the lessons from *Challenger*? If not, what blocked learning in an organization committed to acquiring knowledge? As an alternative to the hypothesis that NASA simply failed to learn, we will look at factors that might have intervened during the years between the *Challenger* and *Columbia* accidents, causing the agency to intentionally discard critical lessons in favor of new, apparently less useful, ones. In other words, we will look for evidence that NASA purposely "unlearned" the lessons from *Challenger*. As a third possibility, we will look for evidence that the agency did learn, but then somehow forgot, these lessons, and ask what could have led to the unintentional loss of administrative knowledge and a repeated pattern of error?

In answering these questions we have several aims. One is to uncover potentially hazardous public management practices at NASA and other large, complex organizations with technologically hazardous missions. We hope this analysis will help build the learning capacity of such organizations, especially advanced technology and national security institutions. Additionally, we hope to advance our understanding of how all organizations, but especially public organizations, learn or fail to learn. Thus our analysis of NASA's response to the space shuttle accidents offers an opportunity to develop a specialized theory of organizational learning and its contributing processes in public agencies and provides a basis for moving beyond assessing the *potential* for learning in public organizations to explaining the *process* of learning and its limitations (Brown and Brudney 2003).

Several books have examined particular lessons about management that the NASA case offers, and we review a number of these below. Our investigation, however, differs from these. It looks at the underlying processes of organizational learning and the factors that limited NASA's learning capacity. We also suggest the NASA case offers an unusually good laboratory within which to study organizational learning because of the intensity of the investigations into the events surrounding the accidents and into the actions, motives, and perceptions of key actors before and after the accidents. There has been an almost continuous stream of internal and external inquiries into NASA's administration, offering a unique opportunity to study just those elements of learning that have been most elusive.

WHY STUDY ORGANIZATIONAL LEARNING?

Much is hoped for from learning in government agencies. In principle at least, organizational learning is claimed to be a model for self-correcting, self-designing organizations that can address many of the concerns of reform-minded public administration practitioners and theorists who want to decentralize and deregulate organizations without detaching them from their authorized missions. From this perspective, organizational learning is an especially valuable method of agency change and continual self-improvement.

Learning engages agency professionals themselves in an ongoing internal and external search for effective program technologies and management developments, and makes use of their own contextual interpretations of why a program is failing and how it could do better, even in the face of environmental and budgetary constraints. Unlike other recent public management change models such as TQM or re-engineering, learning is not a sweeping, generic, consultant-driven technique. Rather, as the idea is developed here, it is an indigenous organizational process: Agencies naturally tend to learn. Grandori (1984), in discussing the possibility of a contingency theory of decision making, considers that satisficing is heuristic decision making, adding to organizational knowledge with each choice. Similarly, learning may be reasonably common in analyzing and making decisions about programs and management. It may lead to a major change in the face of undeniable failure, but it may also occur less dramatically, almost routinely, as agency actors, motivated by professional norms, political values, the public interest, personal ambition, or agency growth and survival seek to elaborate and improve their programs based on a consideration of past results. Yet many circumstances thwart the learning process, as we show in succeeding chapters. Thus to foster learning may be to enhance or unblock an indigenous process rather than impose a designed, generic one.

Learning theories highlight the role that administrative ideas play in the design of new programs, procedures, structures, or management techniques. These ideas may be bred from the unique experience of the agency or from views imported from outside professionals, policy elites, and management gurus. Learning in agencies, as developed here, examines the evolution of new ideas about administration as the basis for changes in policy and management. It considers the ways new ideas and beliefs are discovered and evolve to prominence within the agency. The adoption of the learning perspective also represents a shift in understanding change in government agencies from sole reliance on analyzing power, resource acquisition, the self-interest of actors, or legal mandates as the sources of change to an appreciation of the role of program and management ideas. To be sure, change occurs against a background of shifting resources, political conditions, and policy requirements, but it may also reflect the considered experiences, professional analyses, and scholarly developments in the field.

WHY STUDY NASA?

This study focuses on NASA for several reasons. First, NASA's mission fascinates countless Americans and space buffs around the world. One indication of the widespread interest in the organization is the sheer number of books published about it. Amazon.com lists over sixteen thousand titles by or about the agency and its programs. A small sample of these books, and the approaches they take to the study of NASA, are described below. We are also among those who think the agency's work is important to understand our place in the cosmos, and we would like to make a contribution to its success as an organization.

In addition, NASA is an important *type* of public organization, fitting the model of a highly complex organization with a hazardous mission. It is the kind of organization that Charles Perrow (1999) has characterized as subject to "normal accidents." That is, its core processes are tightly coupled, their interactions are not wholly predictable, and failure is enormously costly in lives, resources, and national stature. In addition, the CAIB was critical of NASA's failure to operate as a "high reliability organization" (LaPorte and Consolini 1991), capable of recognizing crises and shifting from a tightly programmed mode of operations to a self-organizing mode in response. We will have more to say about these models in the next chapter. Here we simply note that examining the successes and failures at NASA can help us understand the wide range of organizational processes that are critical to the safe management of increasingly complex and dangerous organizational technologies in public health, energy production, and national security.

Finally, because of the care and intensity with which NASA itself, external scholars, journalists, and government investigators including Congress and the GAO have studied the agency, we have a wealth of information about NASA. Published studies of its leaders, organizational structures, culture, history, and procedures—and how they changed over time—have been conducted by scholars, government panels, and journalists. Exhaustive accounts of testimony by NASA and contractor personnel before Congress, the Rogers Commission, and the CAIB have been published. NASA's own extensive internal and external panel findings and reviews at many critical stages between the two accidents are also easily accessible. It is this period, from 1986 to 2003, that is of greatest interest, for it was in this time span that learning, if it occurred, would appear. It is also the time during which unlearning or forgetting might have taken place. These documents provide a record of the participants' own words and interpretations at the time of the events in question, unclouded by later tragic events and the natural effects of the passage of time. Such contemporary insider accounts from interviews and testimony are precisely the kinds of information needed to investigate learning in large public organizations, and it is for this reason that these sources, rather than present-day interviews, form the basis of the case studies of commonly acknowledged causes of the accidents in chapters 3 through 6. The core process of organizational learning (i.e., change in the understanding of causes and effects) has been the most difficult to identify. In consequence, most scholarly efforts to investigate organizational learning focus instead on determining the availability of information that *could* lead to learning. Rarely do we have the documentation for a case that allows us to track the learning process itself over time. NASA is such a case.

LITERATURE ABOUT NASA

In addition to the investigative reports mentioned above, NASA and its space science programs have generated an enormous amount of literature that runs from the scholarly to the popular. Examples of the latter are histories of the agency, such as *The Right Stuff* by Tom Wolfe (1979), who chronicles the exhilarating, though sometimes grim, experiences of the courageous astronauts in the Apollo program.[2] Many of these astronauts were formerly test pilots for the U.S. Navy and Air Force and were survivors of an extremely high-risk occupation, testing jet prototypes. In a similar vein, over thirty years later, Cooper (1987) describes the selection and training of the space shuttle crew for mission 41-G that was launched in 1984. The political history of the space age is chronicled in *The Heavens and the Earth* (McDougall 1985), including the contributions of the great pioneers of modern rocketry and NASA's role in space exploration.

Other popular works on NASA were generated by the *Challenger* accident in January 1986. Malcolm McConnell's work, *Challenger: A Major Malfunction* (1987), covers the early years of NASA as well as the accident and its causes. Joseph J. Trento's *Prescription for Disaster* (1987) is another excellent example of popular literature and has the advantage of drawing almost exclusively from contemporary interviews with NASA's administrators and other key officials at the agency and in the space-policy arena. Ten years after the accident, another popular work, *No Downlink: A Dramatic Narrative about the Challenger Accident and Our Time* by Danish author Claus Jensen (1996), offers a detailed overview of the accident and its causes.

More recent works followed the *Columbia* accident in February 2003. In *New Moon Rising*, by Frank Sietzen Jr. and Keith L. Cowling (2004), the authors do not dwell on the causes of the accident but rather on its political consequences with regard to the Bush administration's formulation of a new national space policy and vision. Other works focus on the *Columbia* accident itself and, similar to works on the *Challenger* accident, analyze the reasons for the shuttle tragedy. *Comm Check . . . The Final Flight of Shuttle Columbia*, by Michael Cabbage and William Harwood (2004), draws from interviews with NASA personnel and materials to document key meetings on flight readiness. The authors demonstrate that officials failed to recognize the seriousness of the safety problems posed by foam debris, and they show how launch-schedule pressures accompanied by tight budgets contributed to the accident. Greg Klerkx (2004) argues that NASA's political and budgetary strategies distracted it from its mission and contributed to the *Columbia* accident by embroiling the agency in complex relations with aerospace firms.

Scholarly research on NASA and space policy is also plentiful. McCurdy's policy-oriented historical work, *The Space Station Decision: Incremental Politics and Technological Choice* (1990), focuses on the incremental nature of U.S. space policy with its associated strengths, such as flexibility for politicians, and weaknesses, such as the absence of a long-range space policy. McCurdy's starting point is spring 1961—when President John F. Kennedy committed the nation to a moon landing by the end of the decade—and he concludes in the early 1980s during the Reagan administration. Paula Berinstein (2002) offers an analysis of the feasibility of developing space exploration through private entrepreneurship and provides a remarkable account of the privately funded projects geared to opening space to tourism and settlement.

The space shuttle program in particular is the subject of Roger Handberg's *Reinventing NASA: Human Spaceflight, Bureaucracy, and Politics.* Handberg traces the agency's dogged determination to pursue its dream of establishing a permanent presence for humans "in all their diversity, in outer space including eventual permanent residence on other celestial bodies" (2003, 6). NASA pursued this objective despite an external environment that has been, at best, lukewarm in its support. Even during the Apollo days, President Kennedy soon lost interest when it became patently obvious that the United States had achieved "technological superiority compared to the Soviets" (46, 218). Nevertheless NASA tenaciously clung to its vision, but compromised in the process by accepting international cooperation in building the space station, reducing the organization's size through privatization, and reorganizing or consolidating programs (188–91). Handberg's book demonstrates the critical role the external environment played in affecting the agency's ability to achieve its goals. Drawing from principal–agent theory, Handberg illustrates the tensions between NASA, in its drive for relative autonomy, and both Congress and the White House, which attempted to control the agency using their authority to appoint administrators and control the agency's budget.

NASA's organization and culture are also the subject of a number of scholarly works. McCurdy (1993) explores the beliefs, norms, and practices that shaped its management of risk. In *Bureaucracy in Crisis* (1993), Maureen Casamayou examines the importance of perceptions of risk in accounting for both the *Challenger* disaster and the accident at Three Mile Island. Diane Vaughan's work, *The* Challenger *Launch Decision: Rising Technology, Culture, and Deviance at NASA* (1996), builds on this theme. Published ten years after the *Challenger* accident, the book argues that the agency and solid rocket booster contractor alike downgraded the seriousness of early warnings about the O-ring seals through a process she identifies as "normalization of deviance." Adams and Balfour's *Unmasking Administrative Evil* (2004) examines ethics and culture at NASA by investigating the early years of the agency and the German rocket scientists who led its research teams.

The organizational lessons to be drawn from the *Columbia* accident and the investigations that followed are the subjects of a compendium edited by William H. Starbuck and Moshe Farjoun (2005). As a whole, the anthology provides a comprehensive analysis of the factors that contributed to the *Columbia* accident and attests to a lack of learning at NASA. Equally important, the authors make important recommendations to help NASA address what they see as the agency's serious inability to learn from the *Challenger* accident. The concluding chapter lays out the difficulties that NASA continues to face in learning from the *Columbia* accident.

This book differs from these others in several ways. While we are interested in the events that led up to the two shuttle accidents, the subject here is not the history of NASA or space policy. The focus is on NASA and the shuttle program as a public sector organization and on evidence of organizational learning during the critical time between the two accidents. Others have looked at lessons about shuttle design and NASA management that can be drawn from the two tragedies. In contrast, this book is concerned with the *process* of learning at NASA and, by implication, with how large, complex public organizations learn or fail to learn. The purpose here is to investigate the conditions that foster the learning process and those that thwart it in difficult governmental settings. Understanding these hazards can improve the capacity for knowledge-based change in the public sector.

OVERVIEW OF THE CHAPTERS

In chapter 2, an analysis of the considerable literature on organizational learning yields a working definition of the concept. This definition guides the examination of the evidence for organizational learning in the period between the shuttle accidents. In chapters 3–6, we present four case studies of organizational failure at NASA, each investigating an explanation for the accidents. Three of these explanations, the structure of the shuttle program, outside political forces, and the culture at NASA, appear explicitly in the Rogers Commission and CAIB reports (CAIB, 97) and so are good places to begin to look for evidence of learning or its absence. To these we add a fourth factor: contracting in the shuttle program. The possibility that contracting played a role in the accidents emerges from NASA's very heavy reliance on contractors (CAIB, chapters 5 and 6; Bromberg 1999), the suggestion in the Rogers Commission report that perverse incentives for contractors may have played a role in the *Challenger* accident, and public administration analyses of the effects of contracting on learning (Kettl 1994).

Evidence of NASA's efforts to remedy organizational weaknesses and to institutionalize improvements in the period following *Challenger* is examined in chapters 3–6. Chapter 3 focuses on questions related to the command structure, the communication system, and the safety monitoring program at NASA. For example, we ask what part the complex, decentralized organizational structure that characterized the agency at the time of the *Challenger* and *Columbia* accidents played in each accident. There is some evidence that problem-tracking systems and safety organizations did not function as they were supposed to and that information needed to identify hazards was not always available. We explore what factors may have blocked communication about safety and why the changes put in place after the *Challenger* were not evident at the time of *Columbia*.

A related set of issues is taken up in chapter 4. How well did NASA manage its large numbers of contracts, both in the pre-*Challenger* era and in the 1990s before *Columbia*? We explore whether these contracts may have interfered with NASA managers' ability to acquire information about potential technical or safety problems. To determine what shuttle managers may have learned about managing contractor work, we look at how they addressed known contractor-related problems after *Challenger* and whether remedies were in place at the time of the *Columbia* accident.

Chapter 5 looks at the effects of external political pressures on shuttle program management. Congressional and administration pressures to maintain the optimistic launch rate NASA had promised as part of the political bargain to fund the space shuttle and the space station, especially in the post–cold war period, have been implicated as factors driving launch decisions before each of the accidents. Did these launch pressures and the cost-cutting that was a part of the Clinton–Goldin era of NASA management limit the capacity of the agency to investigate potential hazards and restrict the exploration of organizational and engineering solutions? Some evidence suggests this was the case. The CAIB concluded as much when it said both Congress and the White House "must recognize the role of their decisions in [the *Challenger*] accident and take responsibility for safety in the future" (196). Our analysis looks for indications that NASA recognized the effects of outside pressures and took steps to cope with their consequences.

Part Two concludes with chapter 6, in which we examine the influence of NASA's culture on the events leading to the accidents, especially as it shaped communication about unresolved technical and safety problems. Studies of organizational culture and attitudes conducted at different times by NASA, GAO, and outside scholars make it possible to characterize some of the cultural attributes of the agency, especially the critical years between the shuttle accidents. We explore the relatively low status of safety work, the use of qualitative risk analysis within the laboratory culture, and the management style at Marshall to determine the parts they may have played in the accidents. We also examine evidence that NASA tried to mitigate the effects of certain cultural beliefs and assumptions on shuttle program management.

The last two chapters of the book comprise Part Three and are devoted to refining the general theory of organizational learning developed in chapter 2 by incorporating findings from the case studies. Chapter 7 addresses the effects that the interaction of the four kinds of organizational failings described in the case studies had on NASA's capacity to learn. We suggest that these failures in information-processing, contractor relations, external pressures, and culture combined in a particularly unfortunate way to intensify the difficulty of learning from the *Challenger* accident. Based on NASA's experience, we offer hypotheses about the conditions that encourage or thwart the processes that define the learning cycle, and we conclude that the public sector is a particularly harsh learning environment, but that learning does occur. Finally, in chapter 8, we consider lessons that can be drawn from the NASA case about how to foster learning. Among the findings are that accountability, the first requirement of public organizations, is double-edged with regard to learning and that self-consciousness about the learning process and its barriers can lead to more successful learning.

As this is written, NASA is about to launch the *Discovery* amid some controversy. Foam shedding still poses a problem. The launch video from the first flight since *Columbia* showed foam falling from the external tank. This event set off a close examination of the damage and a spacewalk for repairs, both reflecting a change since *Columbia*. After initially voting to halt the flight, NASA's chief safety officer has agreed that the condition does not "pose an unacceptable risk to the crew" (Gugliotta 2006a, A01). In addition, the new NASA administrator, Michael Griffin, recently asserted to his political overseers that programs must be curtailed under current funding restrictions to maintain the space station launch schedule, a key lesson that the Rogers Commission brought home to NASA in 1987 (Gugliotta 2006b, A3).

While much of what has been written about NASA, especially since the *Columbia* disaster, has been critical, our objective is not to criticize agency personnel or the decisions that they made. These judgments are well made elsewhere (Casamayou 1993; Vaughan 1996; Klerkx 2004; Starbuck and Farjoun 2005, among many others). Our focus is on the effects of agency administration, cultural history, and political circumstances on NASA's capacity for organizational learning.

And while this is a study of NASA, it is also a broader exploration of the conditions in which complex public organization can learn, unlearn, and forget. With its wealth of available information, the NASA case provides a unique opportunity to study learning. This study is a journey to reach a detailed understanding of just what sets of events, circumstances, and actions help public organizations learn from their failures.

CHAPTER 2

Identifying Organizational Learning

WHAT COULD THE Columbia Accident Investigation Board have meant when it said that NASA was not a learning organization? To answer that question we must consider what is implied by the term organizational learning and what kind of explanation it offers. In this chapter we present an extended definition of organizational learning that will be used over the next four case-study chapters to identify instances of learning at NASA. This definition is extracted from an analysis of a number of social science theories of the organizational learning process, its origins and its effects, and it makes explicit the processes that comprise a general theory of organizational learning. Chapter 7 offers a refinement of this general theory for learning in public organizations based on the four case studies.

Creating a working definition of organizational learning is challenging because the literature offers such an untidy range of descriptions to work with (Lipshitz, Popper, and Friedman 2002). Levitt and March tell us that organizations learn "by encoding inferences from history into routines that guide behavior" (1988, 318). Lebovic, studying foreign policy decisions, says that learning is "found whenever beliefs change through feedback, information acquisition, and/ or modeling the behavior of others" (1995, 837). A broad and inclusive definition of learning that incorporates subtle forms of cognitive change and proactive learning is offered by Huber (1991), who suggests that organizational learning results when new options for action are recognized as a result of analyzing organization information. Thus, according to this set of definitions, the charge that NASA did not learn means most simply that the agency did not engage in self-conscious examination of results to uncover new and improved ways of managing the complex shuttle project.

The term organizational learning, however, implies more than just the acquisition of new knowledge by individuals. Just as social learning means that lessons

17

are passed on from one person to another rather than being acquired anew through direct, personal experience, organizational learning means that knowledge is conveyed over time from one person to another through institutionalized routines, rules, and procedures, both formal and informal. The institutional character of organizational learning is represented by Argyris and Schön, who note, "There are too many cases in which organizations know less than their members. There are even cases in which the organization cannot seem to learn what every member knows" (1978, 9). It is not, therefore, that organizations as disembodied entities learn, but rather that when people in an organization figure out how to improve their results by drawing new inferences about cause and effect, this knowledge is stored in programs, procedures, policies, and even the stories or cultural values and assumptions of the organization (Brown and Duguid 1996; Schein 1992). In this way the lessons learned become a resource that all members of an organization can tap.

As the concept is developed here, organizational learning is a collection of processes by which organizations improve their ability to accomplish their objectives by analyzing their past efforts. Learning organizations scrutinize unsatisfactory results to discover the reasons behind them and make cause–effect inferences about how to alter their outcomes. Agency officials as a whole or in part come to a new understanding about how to accomplish their mission. Based on some kind of intentional, systematic analysis or sudden spontaneous insight, they see that what they have been doing does not have the desired results. As Korten says, they "embrace error" (1980, 498). They take stock of what they know about the effects of their current work and make judgments about likely replacements from internally developed ideas or attractive lessons learned elsewhere.

In a learning organization, problems are openly acknowledged, causes are intensively investigated, and procedures are corrected. New techniques are searched out, all in order to bring results more closely in line with agency expectations, external mandates, and professional or personal values. As these new ways of thinking about how to be effective are absorbed into formal procedures and informal practice, the new ideas are learned by the organization and become part of the evolving institution. It is this last step that establishes the learning as organizational rather than personal or professional. Thus the organizational learning model invites us to consider agencies in institutional terms, interpreting new information against established memories, values, regulations, and procedures to make sense of the work and its results.

However, organizational learning is clearly not inevitable. The information needed to recognize problems or search out solutions may not be available

(Brown and Brudney 2003). Many organizational actors ignore internal or external warning signals of unsatisfactory results because they do not think changes are possible, they do not want to admit that their performance is unsatisfactory, or they do not want to undertake an unpopular or troublesome change. In some cases, the most common program technologies used in an agency are products of tradition, professional ideology or cultural loyalty and have not been demonstrated. As a result, officials may not know how to use experience or information about negative results to "fix" programs.

The NASA case offers a particularly well-documented example of many of these issues. The Columbia Accident Investigation Board analysis identified lapses in communication and information dissemination about earlier problems and instances of inadequate resources for testing and experimentation. It also highlighted substantial downsizing of staff and outsourcing that could account for a loss of institutional memory. Employees' fears of being labeled timid or uncooperative for raising alarms were deeply embedded in NASA culture, and efforts to change this pattern became the focus of a concerted program in the years between the accidents, as we will see in later chapters. Further, external pressures for maintaining a rapid launch schedule to complete a particular segment of the International Space Station sharply limited the willingness of NASA managers to wait for the results of investigations into the causes of past problems. All these are examples of the kinds of factors that can block learning, and they suggest the relevance and usefulness of an in-depth analysis of NASA from a learning perspective. Thus to investigate the agency as a learning organization is to inquire into the capacity of NASA's shuttle program to "embrace error," to undertake the organizational scrutiny needed to uncover faulty program structures and practices, and to make lasting, effective changes.

THEORIES OF LEARNING

The organizational learning literature identifies a number of key variables and concepts and accommodates a variety of theories and prescriptive accounts of the learning process. Four questions address controversies about these ideas: How does learning occur? How deep do the learned changes go? How does learning differ from other forms of organizational change? And who or what can be said to learn? Answers to these questions provide the basis for proposing an operational definition of learning that can be used to help recognize learning episodes as well as lost opportunities for learning.

How Does Learning Occur?

In recent years a number of accounts have appeared suggesting that organizational learning is actually a collection of related forms of institutional knowledge acquisition with core similarities: Actors adopt new organizational practices based on considered assessment of past events. Researchers have identified many forms of this process, including improvisational, experimental, and trial-and-error learning (Miner, Bassoff, and Moorman 2001); learning from the lessons others have drawn from their experience, usually called vicarious learning (Levitt and March 1988); and, when experience is scarce, learning from speculation about likely outcomes (March, Sproull, and Tamuz 1996).[1] Miner, Bassoff, and Moorman distinguish between behavior models, which focus on the direct effects of learning on organizational routines, and cognitive models, which emphasize the adoption of new mental theories about causes that may not immediately change behaviors (Miner, Bassoff, and Moorman 2001). However, these authors include both models in a working account of learning, as do we. Others have explored the effects of counterfactual thinking (Morris and Moore 2000) and the variety of failures encountered (Haunschild and Sullivan 2002) on learning. These close views of learning and cognition will be used in later chapters to show how features of the shuttle program's information-tracking systems and culture, in particular, limited the capacity of the organization to learn from past results.

One key issue underlying these characterizations of learning concerns the core of the learning process—how new inferences about cause and effect are made. Though there are many descriptions of this process, much of the literature adopts one of two versions: learning as the working of a more or less rational information-based system (Brown and Brudney 2003; Lebovic 1995; Levitt and March 1988) or learning as a socially constructed process (Daft and Huber 1987; Dixon 1992).[2] The former version is an elaboration of the information-processing theory of organizations, while the latter is indebted to interpretive theories in the social sciences (Rabinow and Sullivan 1987; Burrell and Morgan 1979).

Most writers characterize the learning process as a more or less analytic activity in which members assemble information about past efforts, search out problems and solutions, and change operations, routines, or standards in an effort to improve an organization's responses. This view of learning is closely linked to information-processing theories of decision making, such as rational choice and bounded rational choice. But within this approach to learning, the key element is information processing: the acquisition, distribution, storage, retrieval, and interpretation of information for decision making (Huber 1991; Walsh and Ungson 1991). Knowledge acquisition includes both intentional monitoring and data collection strategies such as experiments and self-appraisal, vicarious or indirect observation, and the collection of information serendipitously through direct experience. The interpretation of information is influenced by the detail and richness of the forms of information exchanges, the compatibility of the cognitive maps of senders and receivers, and the reactions and distortions that result from information overload (Graber 2003). Organizational culture may also shape the interpretation of ambiguous information (Mahler 1997). Finally, information must be stored somehow in ways that allow it to be retrieved and used by appropriate actors when it is needed. Expert systems and various computer-assisted decision-making systems are formal tools for preserving data about results and cause–effect experiments (Brown and Brudney 2003). Information may also be stored informally in the memories of long-time members and in stories, myths, and rituals. It is important to note that all of these systems can break down, short-circuiting learning. The collapse of information processing when technologies are poorly understood or goals are not agreed upon leads to organizational anarchy and incomplete, interrupted learning (March and Olsen 1976; Wilson 1989).

Thus the general theory of organizational learning based on information processing tells us that organizational performance and capacity are improved when members collect and analyze information about unsatisfactory results to find causes and solutions to problems and then find ways to share the solutions with others in the organization.

Other theorists emphasize the intersubjective character of organizational knowledge and the interpretive character of the learning process itself: Learning proceeds through sharing interpretations of events and through reflecting on these interpretations, leading to changed assumptions (Walsh and Ungson 1991; Daft and Huber 1987; Argyris and Schön 1978). Learning is characterized by dialogue in which the richer the medium of communication (e.g., face-to-face rather than electronic) the deeper the sharing and the greater the potential for learning (Daft and Huber 1987). Within this model, organizational practices are built from members' myriad separate interpretations and beliefs over the history of the organization (Brown and Duguid 1996; Weick 1979). Dialogue about alternative policy goals and technologies, and reflection on the interpretation of evidence and beliefs, can motivate the actors to change their positions and find a mutually understood and supportable position.

Interpretive theories of learning argue that tensions resulting from the equivocality of much organizational information (Weick 1979) and from the contrast between the new logic of an innovation and the existing dominant logic can lead to the capacity for long-term learning and fundamental change in organizations.

Such can occur when actors are able to confront each other and debate their views. In a series of cases studies of learning in industrial organizations, the greatest innovations were seen when members met head-on, repeatedly, while attempting to make basic changes in the work organization but were also made aware of how their conflict was affecting their search for solutions and what progress they were making (Bouwen and Fry 1991). In this view, tension leads to struggle and confrontation and is resolved through the negotiated reconstruction of the organization. Learning is preserved in shared interpretations stored in organizational memory and in the enacted organizing process (Weick 1979).

Both of these theories, information-processing and interpretive, are useful in accounting for learning, but the former approach forms the basis of the analysis here because it addresses more effectively the available evidence in the NASA case and it accounts more directly and in more detail for the events. It lends itself both to examining the routing and interpretation of safety data from past flights and to probing the effects of problems with collating and comparing mission results in the context of shifting political priorities, budget constraints, and program interpretations. The three-part definition of learning described below rests principally on the general information-processing theory of organizational learning that identifies the collection and analysis of information as the basis for learning and organizational improvement.

How Deep Do Learned Changes Go?

The depth of change associated with organizational learning may also vary. Learning may be incremental and adaptive or it may lead to radical change such that even basic assumptions about organizational technologies, what counts as a crisis, and how performance should be evaluated are all overturned. In incremental or "single-loop" learning, actors make corrections to existing programs and practices according to current doctrines about cause and effect in program technologies and management procedures (Argyris and Schön 1978; Schön 1975). This type of learning is based on the assumption that the problems and solutions are well understood, even codifiable, and feedback about performance offers cues for corrective action based on widely shared technological knowledge or established procedures. Lebovic (1995) offers an example of incremental learning when he describes how estimates of foreign military spending by the United States Arms Control and Disarmament Agency improve gradually over time.

Alternatively, organizations may undergo deeper or more fundamental changes in beliefs, termed turnover or turnaround learning (Hedberg 1981, 10) or "double-loop" learning (Argyris and Schön 1978) in which not only are routines altered but the doctrines and paradigms behind existing routines that guide problem identification, data interpretation, and problem solving change. In other words, the standards and methods that guide the definition of a problem or a performance gap, as well as the search for solutions, are recreated in response to a new understanding of the situation the agency faces. This more fundamental form of learning is uncommon but can lead to organizational transformations and, sometimes, breakthroughs in organizational success. As the case studies below show, the space shuttle program presented opportunities for both kinds of learning. We will look particularly for evidence of single-loop learning over the short term in the months before the accidents as evidence of seal erosion accumulated and for instances of double-loop learning in the longer term over the years between the accidents.

How Does Learning Differ from Other Forms of Organizational Change?

The relationship between learning and organizational change is not simple. Of course it is possible, even likely, that an agency can change but that forces not related to learning would propel that change. Changes in policy made by executives, courts, or legislatures typically alter programs and procedures: Major modifications in agency programs may be imposed by powerful internal and external actors; professionally repugnant changes may be undertaken in response to legislative mandates tied to budgets. Alternatively, changes may result from a change in administration, new political appointees, or an influx of personnel with different political interests, values, or constituencies (Jenkins-Smith and Sabatier 1993), as occurred in the shuttle program in the 1990s. Program change may also be undertaken as a strategic adaptation to conflict, but as Argyris and Schön note about such cases, conflicts may be "settled for the time being, but not by a process that could appropriately be defined as learning" (1978, 23). Ideas about goals, norms, routines, and technologies have not changed; they have simply been defended and, if necessary, compromised.

It is also possible, however, that political pressures may make it imperative for an agency to undertake some kind of change yet not determine its direction or content. That is, an agency may be driven to change, and under those circumstances it begins to learn. External forces may require change, but it is the agency actors themselves who decide whether to undertake learning, with its analysis of results and their causes, or to pursue some other kind of change. Officials may also make changes out of a concern for preserving agency resources, or they may respond to threats to agency authority or autonomy. They may redesign programs to maintain good constituency ties.

Thus a distinction may be made between the process of change, in which organizational learning is distinguished by its emphasis on ideas, and the motivations for the change, which arise from any number of sources: public interest values, commitment to professional standards, personal advancement, or agency preservation. Officials may be encouraged or even forced by external circumstance to undertake the kind of self-examination that leads to learning. But there is an important difference between being motivated by outside conditions to seek alternatives and being forced by outsiders or circumstances to adopt specific changes. The former is learning; the latter is strategic adaptation. The distinction, while not easily made in practice, guides the identification of genuine learning episodes in the chapters that follow.

Who (or What) Learns?

There are also contending views on "who" learns. Some emphasize that learning is a cognitive process that only individuals can undertake. In this view, organizational learning is simply a metaphor. It refers to individual learning within organizations that affects overall organizational performance (Epple, Argote, and Devadas 1991, 83). The opposite viewpoint is also represented in the literature: Organizational learning means that organizations themselves learn, in ways that are independent of what individual members learn. Cook and Yanow (1996) perhaps put this view best when they suggest that, just as an individual cannot be said to perform a symphonic work, organizational learning is a result of organizational, not individual, processes. Weick and Roberts (1993), examining learning in the "heedful interrelating" that occurs on aircraft carriers, argue also for a concept of collective mental processes, that is, the integration of memories among organizational members.

A third approach, the one taken here, moderates these views to argue that learning is undertaken by individuals but that the lessons they learn are institutionalized so their impact survives over time and can be integrated into organizational activities. Berends, Boersma, and Weggeman (2003, 1041), offering a related view, describe organizational learning as a process of structuration, in which individuals learn and enact structures that in turn constrain and shape opportunities for further learning in an ongoing process of knowledge development. Thus organizational learning really means that individual members make inferences from information about results that have implications for management practices or program administration, and these insights are put into widespread practice or are kept in reserve as mental models (Senge 1990), stories, or culture-bearing artifacts. Again, this process may not succeed. New inferences about cause may not be institutionalized for countless reasons, many of which are explored in the case of the shuttle program.

Despite differences in the conceptualization of organizational learning in the literature, the core idea remains intriguing to a large number of organization theorists and practitioners because it identifies a central feature of organizations: their intelligence function. In essence, organizational learning is about the astuteness of the organization, and the honesty and curiosity of its members in uncovering problems. It focuses on the capacity of organization members to assess causes and effects in program and management operations and to search out and reflect on possible solutions, to make choices, and to incorporate them into the organizational establishment. This potential for intelligence is the promise of public organizational learning and an implicit hope behind many of the current reforms and improvement efforts being adopted by public agencies.

ORGANIZATIONAL LEARNING PROCESSES

The above analysis of core controversies in the literature suggests several key characteristics of organizational learning. First, it implies that learning is not so much a single event as a collection of processes. Second, it suggests a minimum set of processes necessary to distinguish organizational learning from other kinds of administrative change and program development: problem awareness, analysis to arrive at inferences about cause and effect, and the institutionalization of these inferences. These three processes reflect key elements of the general information-processing theory of learning and highlight the importance of the organizational context.

Over the next four chapters a variety of evidence will be examined to determine if NASA's actions before the *Challenger* accident, in the wake of the accident, and in the run-up to the loss of the *Columbia* reflect these processes and whether or not NASA as an organization can be said to have learned. The three processes thus serve in chapters 3–6 as an operational definition of learning, and in chapter 7 as a basis for refining the general information-processing theory of learning for the public organizational context.

Problem Awareness

Problem awareness means that agency actors are able to admit that results are unsatisfactory or to acknowledge the potential for improvement. This recognition may result from systematic data collection, cumulative frustrations, or a dramatic failure (Birkland 1997). What is essential for a first step in learning is some sign of recognition by agency officials that performance is not acceptable, that it falls short of desires or expectations, and that it is a problem to be acted upon rather than an unalterable condition to be accepted. Without this, organization actors would not be motivated to seek out improvements, and it would be difficult if not impossible to distinguish learning from other sources of agency change.

But important information about results, especially failures, may not be available to the decision makers who count. Faulty design of communication systems and unintentional or intentional distortion of information are common organizational pathologies (Halperin, Clapp, and Kanter 2006; Graber 2003) that could obstruct the recognition of performance gaps. Negative feedback about programs may be blocked or ignored because actors do not want to or do not know how to redesign program offerings (Kaufman 1973). Actors may also track some indicators but not others, shaping and biasing their view of results (Argyris 1991; Wilson 1989, chapter 9). Moreover, the common tendency to discredit negative feedback can affect judgments about whether a problem exists and what kind of problem it is (Barzelay 1992). In Part Two, the case-study chapters, the design of NASA's information-processing structures, the inordinate complexity of its safety-tracking programs, the increase in contracting for shuttle program operations during the 1990s, strong external pressures to maintain launch schedules, and well-embedded assumptions about the character of space-science work are all examined for their potential to blunt problem awareness.

External accountability and the need to court a public image of success and expertise can also be expected to make acknowledging errors costly and painful. Current research on near misses in airline accidents demonstrates that higher levels of accountability and the potential for punitive action are clearly associated with lower levels of lesson-drawing and performance improvement over time by air crews (Morris and Moore 2000). Government organizations operating in the public eye may be loath to admit failure that can limit hoped-for growth in program authority or budgets. NASA's long tradition of science and engineering achievements, astronauts with the "right stuff," and a reputation as the "best place" make organizational culture another potential influence on the agency's ability to "embrace error" (Korten 1980).

Analysis and Inference

A second defining process of organizational learning is the analysis of the gap between performance and expectations to draw inferences about cause and effect. This is the core of what is meant by any kind of learning: to search out "what goes with what." This step also requires organizational information and norms that permit the exploration of alternative interpretations of events and information about results. Such exchanges promote the creation of new inferences (Brown and Duguid 1996; Hutchins 1996). Agency culture can also affect the credibility and meaning of information gathered about results and can shape the inference process directly (Mahler 1997). The ability of NASA managers to investigate different interpretations and draw conclusions about needed changes may have been inhibited in several ways. The CAIB noted the reluctance of NASA managers to communicate with each other between levels of hierarchy and across multiple shuttle program centers. The culture surrounding risk may also have influenced the credibility of information about dangers and limited the exploration of alternative points of view (Casamayou 1993; Vaughan 1996).

Analysis of cause and effect may also be thwarted if an organization lacks requisite variety, experiencing too few chances to observe different procedures and their outcomes to gauge which procedures bring about which results. If we can only observe one kind of outcome, we cannot judge which changes will alter or improve the outcome. Research on close calls in the airline industry, for example, demonstrates that the more diverse the range of incidents reported, the more likely it is that learning and improvement will occur (Haunschild and Sullivan 2002).

The chance to observe the effects of a diversity of procedures may also be limited in several ways. A rush to codify program regulations to satisfy clients or legislators can lead to premature closure and a lack of experimentation (Landau and Stout 1979). Others have noted that history is often stingy with its lessons (March, Sproull, and Tamuz 1996). Once again, we see examples of such barriers to learning at NASA. Congressional budget pressures led the agency to adopt quick fixes in order to maintain a rigorous launch schedule. In the aftermath of the *Challenger*, NASA tried to find immediate solutions to the problems outlined by the Rogers Commission and return to flight. Restricted funding and the administration's push to make the shuttle program more efficient through downsizing and outsourcing all but eliminated the experimentation and redundancy that might have fostered learning.

Institutionalizing Lessons Learned

Finally, learning by agency actors becomes organizational when insight gained from problem awareness and analysis is incorporated into the organization's current formal or informal body of knowledge and becomes available to everyone. Examples of how lessons might be formally embedded include official changes in program rules, guidelines, and regulations; in standard operating procedures and routines; and in program technologies or policies. Lessons may be stored in decisions about what information to collect or how it is to be done. These policies affect the organization's ability to detect performance gaps and determine which gaps it notices in the future.

Informal means of institutionalizing new lessons include changes in tacit expectations, unofficial communications networks, professional standards, culture-bearing stories and rituals, and the unarticulated norms of communities of practice that develop over time about how to do the work in the agency (Brown and Duguid 1996). These lessons surface in mental models that reflect deeply held assumptions about the way programs work and that guide interpretation of later events (Perrow 1999; Senge 1990). In the NASA case, we will investigate the overt changes made after the *Challenger* accident, especially the changes in structure, reporting relationships, problem-tracking systems, contractor arrangements, and culture. We will also look at the effects of new leadership and downsizing on these changes to help explain why so many of them were not in evidence at the time of the *Columbia* accident.

Lessons may not be permanent even if they are institutionalized. Wholesale reduction of personnel may lead to loss of institutional memory and unintentional forgetting of lessons learned (Epple, Argote, and Devadas 1991). Time and culture change may also erode institutionalized knowledge. Alternatively, organizations may question and ultimately jettison old lessons under pressure from the political environment to bow to political necessity in acts of strategic adaptation. Or established lessons may be superseded by new ideas about programs and procedures in an intentional act of "unlearning" (Hedberg 1981; Starbuck 1996). But such changes may well be difficult because established methods and policies may be deeply entrenched (Levitt and March 1988) or politically favored. Unlearning, as the term has been used, is a necessary step in successful, continual organizational learning, but it may also mean the elimination of useful knowledge in favor of ill-considered lessons from less profitable inferences. In the shuttle program we see examples of all these variations in the end point of NASA's learning cycles.

Before applying our extended operational definition to the task of determining the extent of organizational learning at NASA, several alternative formulations of the organizational failures in the shuttle program should be considered. Theories of reliability and risk also offer insights into the case and can, in turn, be linked to learning.

Normal Accidents, High Reliability, and Learning

Two prominent accounts of the organizational and technological challenges of complex, hazardous systems that bear on the problem of learning, particularly in organizations like NASA, are normal accident theory and high reliability theory. Each of these can be and has been applied to NASA operations. However, it is argued here, reliability is also a learned organizational characteristic. In the end reliability is based on learning from warnings and near misses, not only from system failures. These accounts of the accidents do not so much offer alternative explanations as pose further questions about puzzling absence of learning at NASA. As we will see in later chapters, shuttle program officials responded at some points in ways that were diametrically opposed to high-reliability practices.

Charles Perrow (1999) coined the term "normal accident" to explain the relatively rare but disastrous outcomes that arise from systems that are both complexly interactive and tightly coupled. That is, they are composed of elements that interact in complex and hidden ways that confound the expectations and designs of designers. In tightly coupled systems, automatic responses link the parts. Reactions are not buffered, so that one event triggers others rapidly, allowing little or no opportunity to intervene or stop the process. In time, technology systems that are both complexly interactive and tightly coupled will experience unlikely, multiple failures of components, and then unpredictable and virtually unstoppable system interactions will result in catastrophic accidents. Mental models of what is occurring shape efforts to contain the disaster, but often the model chosen is the wrong one, or partial, or overly simple.

Redundant backup parts or procedures may actually make matters worse by increasing the complexity of the systems, dispersing responsibility, or allowing organizational leaders to try to run the system faster, further, or cheaper, defeating the improvements in system stability (Sagan 2004; Perrow 1999, 275, 339). Heimann (1993) takes the analysis of redundancy further by distinguishing between serial and parallel forms of structural redundancy. He demonstrates that over time, errors are more likely to be caught with serial or hierarchical structures, a counterintuitive finding described in more detail below.

There is much to suggest that the losses of the *Challenger* and *Columbia* can be classed as normal accidents.[3] They were both cases in which small errors cascaded into system collapse because of the tight coupling of the launch processes and the unexpected, complex interactions of the shuttle design and its organizational environment (Perrow 1999, 45, 70–71). As we will see, questionable design features in the system were tolerated because of production pressures, a common accompaniment to normal accidents (125). These designs were also the unintended consequences of decisions about the original shuttle program and the International Space Station made elsewhere by other government actors (39). Minor abnormalities in the system were ignored by management, and their implications for destroying the system were not understood (57). The piece that does not fit the normal accident pattern, however, is that at least some of the actors, in some parts of the organization, did know about the potential for disaster but were not heard or did not act. While this is not unknown among the cases Perrow surveys, it is rare. The standard case shows operators at all levels being surprised by unsuspected interactions and confounded by their loss of control. One other characteristic of normal accidents found by Perrow and colleagues does mirrors the shuttle case, however, surprisingly often, learning does not follow near misses (46–48, 370).

Perrow uses his analysis to suggest optimal organizational designs for systems with combinations of tight and loose coupling and complex interactions. In those characterized by loose coupling and complex interactions, front-line operators need discretion "to cope with unplanned interactions of failures" (332) and to creatively adjust their routines to new problems. These adjustments may fail if the operator's mental model is incorrect, but without discretion and decentralized authority, operators cannot respond. Tightly coupled systems, on the other hand, need highly centralized structures to ensure high-level, rapid coordination and a panoramic perspective on the uninterpretable signals that operators receive in the midst of rapidly deteriorating situations. This is why, Perrow argues, military organizations have been relatively successful in managing tightly coupled systems such as those found on aircraft carriers.

For systems that are both tightly coupled *and* complexly interactive—those most vulnerable to normal accidents—Perrow offers surprising and generally unpopular advice: Abandon the most extreme and catastrophic technologies such as nuclear weapons and nuclear power, restrict those technologies that have only limited capacity to inflict harm, and try to improve those systems for which there are not feasible alternatives. In this last category, Perrow includes the space exploration program generally. The reason for his prescription is that he believes the organizational and managerial requirements for safely managing such systems are incompatible. Decentralized authority is required to allow operators to find creative solutions to unexpected interactions; centralized authority is required to direct a coordinated response when tightly coupled systems begin to collapse. Perrow argues that no organization can support both. The most we can expect from organizational and managerial remedies is to find ways to loosen the coupling and alter the characteristics of such systems.

It is on this prescription that normal accident theory and high reliability theory disagree. LaPorte and Consolini (1991) argue that society requires that some hazardous and complex, tightly coupled systems remain error-free, and with extraordinary effort some are able to do so. They become high-reliability organizations. In this period of unease about institutional capacities of national security and disaster preparedness organizations, the promise of high reliability is extremely attractive. Based on research on such hazardous systems as nuclear-powered aircraft carriers, the air-traffic-control system, and Pacific Gas and Electric's power grid, including its nuclear power station, LaPorte, Consolini, and others in their team found that the theoretically contradictory qualities needed to manage organizations that are vulnerable to normal accidents do, in practice, coexist.

Under normal operations, the high-reliability organization is intensely hierarchical and centralized, governed by strongly entrenched standard operating procedures, buffered from environmental disturbances, and characterized by routine decision making. Negotiation and feedback from subordinates is not acceptable. But within these high-reliability organizations are nested two other modes of authority and practice. When the systems are stressed by environmental pressures or peak demands, a contingent "high tempo" authority structure takes over. Collegial, cooperative relations emerge between experienced front-line practitioners and high-ranking officials. Technical expertise is respected and acceded to. Units become self-organizing, relying on substantial feedback and accommodation to solve the problems at hand. Superiors and subordinates may even exchange roles as all contribute knowledgeably to coping with the situation. A third, even more intense, response mode is reserved for well-defined emergency situations in which problems threaten to cascade into major system failures. Typically, actors have extensive practice with preprogrammed responses for these emergencies (e.g., fire-fighting on a flight deck or the failure of air-traffic-control computers), though there is some reliance on expert adaptive responses in these situations as well. In LaPorte and Consolini's experience, these three modes of authority and operation coexist successfully within high-reliability organizations and are called into play based on well-socialized rules.

McCurdy (2001) found adherence to some of these prescriptions in theory but not in practice at NASA in the 1980s under agency administrator Daniel Goldin and his "faster, better, cheaper" approach to project management. The idea was to reduce cost but maintain reliability by creating smaller, less-complex projects, including unmanned vehicles and microminiaturized components, for example, and then establishing correspondingly small, highly coordinated, self-organizing teams to solve long-term reliability problems even while adopting innovative and risky designs. McCurdy found, however, that after initial successes the failure rate rose with the loss of several Mars crafts. McCurdy accounts for this trend by arguing that the problem lay "in the relationship among cost, schedule, and complexity. In short, proponents of the approach created failure when they reduced cost and schedule faster than they lessened complexity" and were not able to generate the level of fine-tuned teamwork the approach required (McCurdy 2001, 25).

The CAIB contrasted NASA's performance with that of high-reliability organizations in particular. Though they noted that "neither High Reliability Theory nor Normal Accident Theory is entirely appropriate" (CAIB 180), they recommended that NASA adopt elements of the former model. They did not account for why NASA, with technologies similar in some respects to those addressed by the theories, had not devised its own version of high-reliability practice during the decades of its existence, or if it had, how it was lost. Here we hypothesize that the same features that blocked learning in other respects may have contributed to NASA's inability to adopt or maintain a high-reliability culture. Highly reliable organizations, according to researchers working on this model, are typically self-conscious about learning. The standard operating procedures that direct normal operations and the emergency routines that take over when the system threatens to collapse are both the product of formal pre- and postaction analysis (LaPorte and Consolini 1991, 29) until the organization is confident that it can achieve "trials without errors" (28). Learning from experience about how some apparently "minor error can cascade into major, system-wide problems and failures" (27) leads to determined efforts to find ways to recognize, avoid, or halt impending accidents. Though incremental trial-and-error learning is not acceptable during a crisis, later analysis of crisis events does contribute to enhancing effective responses under all modes of operation. Thus highly reliable organizations encourage members to report errors and monitor each other without creating either mutual distrust or "a lax attitude toward the commission of errors" (29).

Why do we not see these characteristics in the shuttle program, given its long experience with hazardous, often tightly coupled and complex technologies? Or why did they not emerge when needed? High-reliability theory, normal accident theory, and related research on the design of dependable systems suggest a closer examination of a number of features of NASA's organization just before the accidents. Did NASA alter its authority structure and decision-making procedures in response to signals of possible problems with the launch? We will seek out evidence that alternative emergency procedures did, in fact, take over when managers were operating in a crisis or high-tempo mode or in the face of unexplained anomalies. We will also look for indications of trial-and-error learning in the more error-tolerant periods between launches when anomalies were uncovered, or for efforts to reduce the complexity of interactions or the tightness of coupling of the shuttle system elements following Perrow's advice. Perrow's analysis suggests that, despite the seriousness of hazards from the technologies he examines, ignoring potentially serious problems is not so unusual (1999, 10), and learning is therefore often absent. In such cases, there is often little time to puzzle out possible causes, or it is not in the interests of those most able to foster learning to press for embarrassing and expensive examination of errors. We investigate all of these possibilities to improve our understanding of the role of learning in creating and maintaining reliability.

NASA AND RISK REDUCTION

Many of the post-accident criticisms leveled at NASA's decisions about the shuttle program concern the organization's treatment of risk, and risk analysis offers yet another perspective from which to analyze the uneven history of organizational and managerial improvements in the shuttle program. The CAIB criticized NASA decisions regarding what constituted "acceptable risk," and a key GAO study conducted between the two shuttle accidents criticized the absence of quantitative risk analysis based on the probabilities of component failures (GAO 1996). Instead, NASA maintained a partially qualitative approach to risk assessment that charted the criticality and redundancy of components. The ways this qualitative approach may have factored into the shuttle program's inability to spot dangerous trends in bench tests and launch results is described in chapters 3 and 6.

The issues raised by critics of NASA's approach to risk echo controversies in the risk literature itself. In very broad terms, risk is approached in the literature prescriptively as a quantitative problem or descriptively as a social or psychological phenomenon. Quantitative, prescriptive approaches are based on probabilistic risk assessment (Freudenberg 1992). Estimating risk from incomplete data, overconfidence in the ability to calculate all possible failure modes, and unforeseen errors from system interactions and interdependencies are just three from an impressive list of potential miscalculations (Freudenberg 1992, 231–49; Tversky and Kahneman 1988; Keeney 1983; Lowrance 1976).

Cultural theories of risk argue that the meaning of risk, its perception, and management are influenced by factors rooted in our social organizations (Raynor 1992, 84; Douglas and Wildavsky 1982). This research indicates that individuals perceive and respond to risk from a subjective perspective rather than from "an objective risk level or the scientific assessment of risk" (Golding 1992, 66). Two related difficulties in assessing responses to technological hazards are the seemingly intractable problem of ascertaining "how safe is safe enough" (Slovic 1992; Starr 1969; Wildavsky 1988) and the serious limits to weighing or balancing social and technical considerations (Slovic 1992, 150). Mirroring NASA's approach to risk, another school of risk perception maintains that regardless of how accurate the experts' estimation of acceptable risk, it is actually the redundancy built into the organization that can minimize failures (Landau 1969). Other approaches to minimizing organizational failure focus on the need for well-designed and managed procedures for operators of high-risk technology (La Porte 1987, 1988).

One particular stream of research on risk and reliability is especially concerned with NASA's safety organization and the critical role of political overseers in shaping the management of risk. After categorizing organizational miscalculations into either errors of commission or errors of omission, Heimann (1993) notes the tension between these two types of errors: type I errors, in which an agency acts when it is improper to do so (in NASA's case, launching the *Challenger* when it should not), and type II errors, in which an agency fails to act when action should be taken (in NASA's case, the decision to delay a launch when there is no real safety issue). Type I errors are minimized and type II errors are maximized in organizations in which decision-making components or units are sequential or serial because it takes only one component to refuse to take action. Similarly, type I errors are maximized and type II errors are minimized in organizations in which decision-making components are parallel. When political overseers dispense resources unevenly and the agency attempts to preserve its workforce by increasing the number of program offices, parallel decision making predominates, and the likelihood of type I error increases. Serial structures, which had effectively preserved the safety of the early human space-flight projects, were replaced at the NASA's Marshall Space Flight Center by parallel structures to reduce costs and prevent launch delays (432). Heimann's solution to this dilemma is the even distribution of agency resources to increase the redundancy for both serial and parallel structural forms. His work offers useful conceptual tools for understanding how political decisions affect organizational structure and either increase or decrease the level of risk and probability of failure at NASA. These and other effects of political pressures and resource constraints on decision making are considered in chapter 5 and in the analysis of organizational learning in chapter 7.

We can now turn to the events of the shuttle disasters, organized in four case studies around the likely organizational causes, to determine whether there is evidence that learning, defined as a three-part process, emerged in the period between the accidents. The four organizational causes for the accidents are NASA's information-processing structures and safety systems, its heavy reliance on contractors, its external political and budgetary pressures, and its culture. In each case study we will investigate whether learning, as we define it, has emerged and if not, why not. We collect these instances of learning and failing to learn in chapter 7 to refine the general theory of organizational learning to reveal the effects of the political context on learning in specifically public organizations. We conclude that while it is clear that NASA did learn, it is also clear that it did not learn all the lessons it might have from the loss of the *Challenger.* In the end, we argue that public organizations can, but often do not, learn because of a relatively small set of key organizational and political factors that block or divert the processes that constitute learning.

PART TWO

Analyzing the Causes of the Shuttle Accidents

CHAPTER 3

Structures for Processing Information

WE BEGIN OUR INVESTIGATION of learning at NASA by looking at the agency's command structure and its capacity to process and integrate information, especially information about safety. The critical question in this chapter is why many of the failings of the organization's structure and safety systems cited by investigators after the *Challenger* accident were seen again in the case of the *Columbia*. The two accidents appear unfortunately similar in so far as evidence of the technical problems that led to the loss of the shuttle in each case had been available for years yet did not prevent the approval of each launch, despite elaborate preflight safety reviews. In each case, weaknesses in NASA's management structure, its capacity to integrate information, and its enforcement of safety-review procedures were identified by investigators as contributors to the accidents. For NASA to learn lessons about the design of reliable safety systems would require the agency to recognize problems with the review procedures, analyze the sources of these problems, and institutionalize knowledge-based solutions.

Did this learning process occur at NASA? To answer the question, we first look closely at the events leading up to the *Challenger* accident with special attention to problems of the management structure and safety systems. We then describe the many rounds of reorganization and the changes in the safety systems adopted after the accident. Finally, we examine the systems in place at the time of the *Columbia* accident to determine whether the lessons about information processing from *Challenger* were still in place at the time of this second disaster.

THE *CHALLENGER*

In the aftermath of the loss of the *Challenger*, two official investigations were initiated, the Presidential Commission on the Space Shuttle *Challenger* Accident (the Rogers Commission) in 1986 and the hearings of the U.S. House Committee on Science and Technology (also in 1986). Both investigations concluded that NASA had serious problems with its communication channels and safety information systems. The Rogers Commission found that

> the decision to launch the *Challenger* was flawed. Those who made that decision were unaware of the recent history of problems concerning the O-rings and the joint and were unaware of the initial written recommendation of the contractor advising against the launch at temperatures below 53 degrees Fahrenheit and the continuing opposition of the engineers at Thiokol after the management reversed its position.[2] . . . If the decision makers had known all of the facts, it is highly unlikely that they would have decided to launch 51-L on January 28, 1986. (Rogers Commission 1986, 82)

Of the commission's twelve specific final recommendations, eight were concerned with these issues, including recommendations to establish independent safety- and design-oversight panels and to improve management structures and communications systems in order to prevent the isolation of decision making within shuttle program centers . The Rogers Commission noted that the "project managers for the various elements of the shuttle program felt more accountable to their Center management than to the shuttle program organization" (199).

In particular, the commission recommended redefining the role of the program manager to include "the requisite authority for all ongoing STS [shuttle] operations" because under the present organizational structure shuttle-funding decisions and "vital program information frequently bypass the National STS Program Manager" (199). In a pointed criticism of the Marshall Space Flight Center in Huntsville, Alabama, the commission noted a "tendency at Marshall to management isolation" that led to a failure to "provide full and timely information bearing on the safety of flight 51-L [*Challenger*] to other vital elements of shuttle program management" (200). It also recommended creating a new Office of Safety, Reliability and Quality Assurance to be headed by an associate administrator, reporting directly to the NASA administrator, with significant new resources and organizational independence from the program offices they were to monitor. Finally, the commission recommended that shuttle crew participate in preflight reviews to ensure a full hearing of safety issues (199).

The U.S. House Committee on Science and Technology went further in their criticisms and disagreed with the Rogers Commission on several points. In particular, while concurring with the commission that NASA's management structure and communications were flawed, the House committee reached different conclusions about the nature of NASA's communication problems. As the House report reads:

House Comm

The Rogers Commission concluded that NASA's decision-making process was flawed. The Committee does agree that the Marshall Space Flight Center should have passed along to higher management levels the temperature concerns that Thiokol engineers raised the night before the launch of mission 51-L. However, the Committee feels that the underlying problem which led to the Challenger accident was not poor communication or inadequate procedures as implied by the Rogers Commission conclusion. Rather the fundamental problem was poor technical decision-making over a period of several years by top NASA and contractor personnel, who failed to act decisively to solve the increasingly serious anomalies in the Solid Rocket Booster joints.

Information on the flaws in the joint design and on the problems encountered in missions prior to 51-L was widely available and had been presented to *all levels of shuttle management.* Despite the presence of significant amounts of information and the occurrence of at least one detailed briefing at Headquarters on the difficulties with the O-rings, the NASA and Thiokol technical managers failed to understand or fully accept the seriousness of the problem. (U.S. Congress, House Committee on Science and Technology 1986, 5; emphasis added)

nasa!

Thus, the House report found that the chief flaw in NASA's information-processing system was the inability of space shuttle officials to recognize the gravity of the safety information they received and to resolve the problems, rather than the failure to obtain the information itself. The two investigations agreed, however, in indicting existing safety-tracking systems and management procedures that failed to prevent launch in the presence of unresolved findings with catastrophic implications for mission safety. We examine the problems with communication, decision making, and the safety organization closely later in this chapter to see how they contributed to the loss of the *Challenger* and how NASA tried to remedy them.

Questions about organizational structure, information processing, interpretation, and safety systems at the time of the *Challenger* accident arise in two ways. On the day preceding the launch, information about Thiokol engineers' serious reservations about launching in the predicted cold weather were minimized and finally disregarded by NASA managers at Marshall who oversaw the solid rocket booster program. These managers also decided not to communicate the engineers' reservations to higher level decision makers. Both of these decisions were criticized after the accident. However, the case also raises larger questions about safety and reliability in the shuttle program as a whole. Concerns about the seals and O-rings had appeared years earlier, at least since 1980. But the seals were not redesigned. Instead, "NASA and contractor management first failed to recognize [the issue] as a problem, then failed to fix it and finally treated it as an acceptable flight risk"(Rogers Commission 1986, 120). We begin with the larger setting of the safety system's treatment of the seal problems and the decentralized management structure in place prior to the accident, and we then focus on the communication events on the day before the launch.

Pre-Challenger *Management Structure* Fragmented autonomous centers

At the time of the *Challenger* accident, the management structure of the shuttle program was relatively decentralized. The agency overall was operating under the "lead center" management approach in which core elements of the shuttle projects were each put under the command of a NASA center. The principal centers for the shuttle project were as follows: the Johnson Space Center in Houston, for the orbiter itself; the Marshall Space Flight Center in Huntsville, Alabama, for the propulsion systems, the solid rocket boosters, the external tanks, and the shuttle main engines; and the Kennedy Space Center in Florida for launch operations. The project directors for the various elements of the shuttle reported to the director of the center that had the lead role in the project. But under this management design, it was the responsibility of the project director to achieve coordination with project elements in other centers. According to respondents interviewed by McCurdy (1993), this lead-center structure was designed to justify a key role for each of the centers and protect them in the tough congressional funding environment NASA faced in the 1960s. It represented a change from the relatively centralized structure of earlier projects, such as Apollo, in which the project director had headquarters status and directed elements across the centers (McCurdy 1993, 131). But as the centers became engaged in increasingly bitter contests for scarce funds and project authority, NASA headquarters intervened to negotiate the lead-center concept (Dunar and Waring 1999, 183). As we will see, this decentralized structure interacted with lapses in the safety systems to contribute to the *Challenger* accident.

The relative autonomy of the centers under this design also reflected the institutional history of NASA. The agency was created in 1958 principally from three separate agencies: the National Advisory Committee for Aeronautics, parts of the Naval Research Laboratories, and the Army Ballistic Missile Agency in Huntsville. The Johnson Space Center, in Houston, was added in 1961 as the Manned Spacecraft Center, and the Kennedy Space Center began as the Cape Canaveral Spaceport in 1962. The Huntsville establishment became the Marshall Space Flight Center. It evolved from the even earlier Redstone Arsenal and was at the center of efforts to create a military missile program in the immediate postwar period. Early on, this program was headed by Wernher von Braun, a chief architect of the German rocket program, now working in the United States. He practiced a distinctive management style founded on an informal, organic, team-based strategy rather than "formalized, standardized document-intensive techniques" of systems engineering (Sato 2005, 563). The piecemeal design of NASA and the distinctive histories of the centers and their founders help account for the lapses in problem tracking and problem resolution and what will be described in more detail in chapter 6 as the rivalries among the centers. In an assessment of NASA management structure, Levine argues that the structure was less decentralized than fragmented (Levine 1992, 199). History, political necessity, and intercenter competition all contributed to fragmenting the shuttle program design.

Safety Systems: Problem Assessment and Tracking for the Shuttle — no integration

The pre-*Challenger* safety-tracking system included four elements: the flight readiness reviews, the critical items list, the quality assurance program, and in-flight anomaly reporting procedures. An examination of each of these, and the problems each posed for tracking results as they existed prior to the *Challenger* accident, demonstrates that their combined effect was to reduce the reliability of the safety reviews and make it difficult to achieve a comprehensive understanding of the shuttle's status. Information about shuttle performance gaps was available in some offices but not in others, and communication among the offices was compromised by a number of structural and cultural factors. Without an integrated information base and a reliable review process, it was possible to avoid acknowledging the severity of the problem, keep the program on schedule, and resist undertaking the kind of problem assessment and analysis that leads to short-term corrections and learning.

FLIGHT READINESS REVIEWS

A key part of the safety program is the shuttle flight-readiness-review process before each flight. This four-tiered certification process reviews problems that could affect the flight, including fixes made to problems in past launches. At the time of the *Challenger* accidents, these four tiers corresponded to the program chain of command and thus placed the Johnson Space Center (Level II) above the Marshall Space Flight Center (Level III) in the program review hierarchy illustrated in figure 3.1. This design feature had the unintended effect of exacerbating intercenter rivalry and motivating Level III to withhold information

FIGURE 3.1   Shuttle Program Management Structure

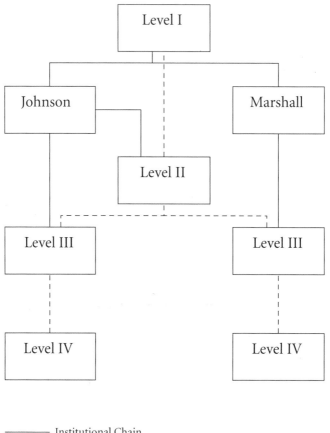

———— Institutional Chain

– – – – – – Program Chain

Level I: Associate administrator for space flight. Oversees budgets for Johnson, Marshall, and Kennedy centers; responsible for policy, budgetary, and top-level technical matters of shuttle program.

Level II: Manager, National Space Transportation Program. Responsible for shuttle baseline and requirements; provides technical oversight on behalf of level I.

Level III: Program managers for orbiter, solid rocket booster, external tank and space shuttle main engine; responsible for development, testing, and delivery of hardware to launch site.

Level IV: Contractors for shuttle elements. Responsible for design and production of hardware.

Rogers Commission 1986, 102.

from Level II. These review processes began about six weeks before a launch date at Level IV with certification by contractors that their components were ready. "Open" problems, flaws uncovered on past flights, were to be "closed" (i.e., resolved) or "waived" if they were not applicable to the launch under review. Next, reviews of any open problems were carried out at Level III, which included certifications of readiness by NASA project managers at the Johnson Space Center for the shuttle orbiter, and at the Marshall Space Flight Center for the elements of the rocket propulsion system, including the solid rocket booster designed and manufactured by Morton Thiokol in Utah, and at Kennedy Space Center for launch support. Detailed certifications of readiness and reports of any open problems for each program element were communicated to Level II for review by the top shuttle program manager, who was then located at the Johnson Space Center. The final Level I conference, held about two weeks before the launch, was chaired by NASA's associate administrator for space flight, who was also the director of the Johnson center. This post embodied the final crossover authority between the shuttle program components and center management.

As the *Challenger* case unfolded, it became clear that it was the key reporting link between Levels III and II that failed. As noted repeatedly in the Rogers report, information about the long- and short-term problems with seals and O-rings were not consistently communicated up to Levels I and II (Rogers Commission 1986, 82). Competition among the centers for primacy in program leadership seems to have led to isolated decision making within the Marshall center. In order to avoid admitting to having unresolved problems, Marshall managers did not pass on all of the information they had about the emerging issues with the seals. Some of this information was known at all levels but was not deemed of critical importance. The conduct of the preflight reviews at the time of the *Challenger* accident was also lax. An astronaut in training at the time of the accident recounted in an interview that the reviews were "informally attended" and conducted by teleconference. This format changed after *Challenger* (Cowling 2003).

SAFETY, RELIABILITY AND QUALITY ASSURANCE PROGRAM

At the time of the *Challenger* accident, the flight readiness reviews took place within the ongoing safety-tracking system of the Safety, Reliability and Quality Assurance Program overseen by the chief engineer at NASA headquarters.[3] This office was charged with monitoring the program for potential hazards but had only a very small staff of twenty, of whom only two were assigned, part-time, to "shuttle maintainability, reliability and quality assurance" (Rogers Commission

1986, 153). After the shuttle was declared to have moved from the test phase to operational status in late 1982, the safety organizations were downsized and reorganized. Marshall, where the solid rocket booster program was managed, lost safety staff (160), and there were additional problems with the design of the safety program. Marshall's director of reliability and quality assurance reported to the director of science and engineering, who managed the shuttle hardware projects and so cannot have been an independent voice for safety (153). In fact, the safety program was largely silent about the problems with the seals in the years leading up to the *Challenger* accident (152). The Rogers Commission also noted that there was no one from the safety or quality assurance organizations at the meetings on the day before the launch where the seriousness of the threat posed by the forecasted cold weather and the reliability of the seals were the main topic (152). Both the assiduousness and independence of the safety organizations were questioned in the Rogers Commission Report.

CRITICAL ITEMS LIST

Another part of the safety program implicated in the *Challenger* accident was the failure-modes-and-effects analysis, a bottom-up, partly qualitative risk-analysis methodology that generated the "critical items list" (GAO 1996). This list identified the seriousness or "criticality" of the failure of a part and determined whether problems with it would ground the project or, less seriously, trigger further research. Components determined to be criticality 1 are those whose failure would lead to the loss of the vehicle. Those designated criticality 1R are those for which there is a redundant mechanism, but the failure of both parts would result in the loss of the shuttle. As we will see, evidence of erosion in the second or redundant O-ring in some of the solid rocket booster joints should have led to reclassifying the seals as parts without redundancy (Rogers Commission 1986, 159). But this designation was either not consistently applied or was not widely communicated. Considerable confusion and evasion followed. Even in testimony before the Rogers Commission, Jesse Moore, who was both the Level I administrator at NASA headquarters and director of the Johnson Space Flight Center, denied being aware that the seals, about which so much had been said, had been designated as having lost their classification as redundant (Rogers Commission 1986, 159).

Furthermore, flaws in the tracking system for critical items called into question the real capacity of the personnel at Johnson to perform the Level II flight readiness reviews. A tracking system to link critical components to "requirements and specifications," and so make engineering judgments about their adequacy, was not available at Johnson for the shuttle program components managed at Marshall. Further, launch procedures at Kennedy did not identify the criticality of components, limiting their ability to monitor these sensitive items (Rogers Commission 1986, 153). Even two years after the *Challenger* accident, a NASA risk analysis found that the "NASA critical items list['s] . . . waiver decision-making process [is] subjective, with little in the way of formal and consistent criteria for approval or rejection of waivers" (quoted in CAIB, 188). The complexity of the shuttle engineering and sheer size of the critical items list must also have contributed to the confusion. After the *Columbia* disaster, the CAIB observed that there were 4,222 components designated criticality 1 or criticality 1R (CAIB, 189). While this number is large, according to an often-quoted statistic, a successful shuttle launch requires more than 1.2 million procedures to be completed as planned (GAO 1996, 1.1).

IN-FLIGHT ANOMALY REPORTING CHANNEL

NASA had also created ongoing problem-reporting systems to identify and track possible malfunctions as they arose. However, the Level II review at Johnson was "streamlined" in 1983 as part of the move of the shuttle from the test phase to operational status, eliminating the examination of some flight-safety problems and trends (Rogers Commission 1986, 153). The Rogers Commission reported, "With this action, Level II lost all insight into safety, operational and flight schedule issues resulting from Level III problems" (154). Under the streamlined process, monthly Level III problem reports from Marshall were no longer forwarded to Level II at Johnson, and only a statistical summary of the number of problems, but not the problem descriptions themselves, went up the hierarchy.

The result of all this was a safety system that was fragmented and unable to integrate available information. The Rogers Commission notes, "Unfortunately, NASA does not have a concise set of problem reporting requirements. Those in effect are found in numerous individual documents, and there is little agreement about which document applies to a given level of management under a given set of circumstances for a given anomaly" (Rogers Commission 1986, 154). The lack of clear reporting requirements meant that the anomalies were not consistently reported up the chain of command. Worse, decisions based on these reports did not consistently follow the procedures that did exist. For example, waivers to permit a 1983 launch were processed outside the official channels and were approved by officials at Levels I and II, principally to make it possible to launch the next shuttle flight on time (Rogers Commission 1986, 128).

The content of the rules for collecting and acting on information is an important issue in organizational learning. Decisions about which data to collect, preserve, and disseminate have an immediate effect on the ability of organization actors to recognize and analyze problems. In the NASA case, we clearly see inconsistencies in rules and actions about core feedback processes.

The Ominous Trend in Seal Performance

The Rogers Commission identified problems with the O-ring seals between the joints of the solid rocket booster as the material cause of the loss of the *Challenger*. These problems had been seen from the earliest days of the shuttle program, but for reasons explored here, this information was not reliably conveyed up the hierarchy to upper-level safety reviews or, when it was conveyed, it was not acted upon.

At the time of the *Challenger* accident, the seals between segments of the rocket included two O-rings to block the escape of superheated gasses as the rocket was launched and pressure increased inside the rocket. Originally, the secondary O-ring was designed as a backup, giving the seal a measure of redundancy. But very early on, even before the first launch (Rogers Commission 1986, 123), bench research revealed that under launch pressures, "joint rotation," or bending at the joints of the rocket, occurred that could prevent the secondary O-ring from sealing. This should have meant that the redundancy designation of the seals was changed. Yet this change did not occur. Even after the second launch in November 1981, when postflight inspection discovered evidence of erosion in the O-rings from hot gasses, the "anomaly" was not reported in the Marshall problem-tracking system. Nor was it considered in the flight readiness review undertaken before the third launch (125).

Only at the end of 1982 was the seal formally redesignated C1, indicating a nonredundant element. The "rationale" (126) for continuing to use the design was the expectation that the primary O-ring itself would provide the seal, though the significant reservations of Marshall engineers about this were not conveyed to Level I and II administrators (127). In explaining why he signed a waiver for this problem, allowing flights to continue, a Level I administrator explained: "We felt at the time—all of the people in the program I think felt that this Solid Rocket Motor in particular or the Solid Rocket Booster was probably one of the least worrisome things we had in the program" (128). Of much greater concern to managers were the complex shuttle main engines (Dunar and Waring 1999, 349). Marshall engineers had less confidence in the joint structure, however. Leon Ray argued to supervisors in the lab responsible for the solid rocket booster motors that the joint did not meet the contract specifications, but he was not able to convince senior managers. He and others "stopped short of recommending that the solid rocket booster motors not be flown" (Dunar and Waring 1999, 349) because they did not feel they could push any harder in their positions (350).

Then, early in 1985, one year before the *Challenger* accident, in the coldest launch temperatures to date, hot gases burned through a segment of the *primary* O-ring. The Marshall mission closeout report described "O-ring burns as bad or worse than previously experienced" (Rogers Commission 1986, 136) and called for design changes and a review of O-ring erosion in the next flight readiness review. Thiokol's subsequent analyses of erosion for its Level IV review noted temperature as an issue for the first time—"'Low temperatures enhanced the probability of blow-by'" (Rogers Commission 1986, 136)—and later tests demonstrated a lack of resiliency in the seals in temperatures under 50 degrees Fahrenheit. Thiokol concluded that "the condition is not desirable but is acceptable" (136).

The rationale for acceptance was again said to be the redundancy of the seal (136), even though the classification of the secondary seal as redundant had been retracted. The ambiguities of the tracking system seem to have obscured the loss of the redundancy designation, but decisions at Marshall also reflect pressure on the centers and the agency as a whole to meet accelerated launch schedules. On February 21, 1985, at the Level I conference for the flight readiness review for the next launch, the seal problem was deemed "acceptable" because of "limited exposure time and redundancy," and there was no mention of temperature issues (136). Managers had come to accept the erosion as an acceptable condition and did not press for immediate redesign (Dunar and Waring 1999, 370). In any case, Level I reviews had at this point become increasingly "ritualistic" (Dunar and Waring 1999, 360).

In June 1985, after shuttle flight 51B, erosion was found in *both* the primary and secondary seals of the joint at the motor nozzle to a degree not previously thought possible. This finding did have an immediate impact. Lawrence Mulloy, the solid rocket booster project director at Marshall, put a formal "launch constraint" on the joint seal that had failed (but not on the one that downed the *Challenger*), halting further launches until the problem could be resolved or it could be shown not to reoccur. In August 1985 the problems with the seals were presented at a meeting of Level I and Level III managers by NASA officials from the solid rocket booster program and by Thiokol seal experts. Both the Rogers Commission and Marshall historians argue that the evidence presented at this meeting should have led to correction of the problems before the next launch (Rogers Commission 1986, 148; Dunar and Waring 1999, 349). But the information did not, in fact, trigger a halt to further launches.

For the next six consecutive launches, including *Challenger*, this "launch constraint" was waived by Mulloy (Rogers Commission 1986, 137). The effect of the waiver was that the seal problem was not considered at the flight readiness reviews. Mulloy had the authority to approve waivers as the solid rocket booster project manager who certified the readiness of the rocket for launch in the Level III reviews. His rationale for doing so was that his staff was monitoring the situation. In addition, at NASA's request, Thiokol set up an O-ring task force to recommend short- and long-term solutions (140). Thiokol and NASA program managers reported to NASA headquarters that the shuttle was "safe to fly," as long as they continued to use the new high-pressure leak-check procedure. Ironically, this test was later found to increase the chances of blowing holes in the insulating putty, allowing hot gasses to escape and burn the O-rings, a finding then not widely known (Rogers Commission 1986, 133). Meanwhile, launches in October and November 1985 exhibited more seal erosion and blow-by, but these anomalies were not mentioned in the subsequent Level I flight readiness reviews (141). Finally, Thiokol recommended closing out the O-ring problem status after filing the same set of "open problem" reports month after month as the efforts of an O-ring task force slowly proceeded. The engineers on the task force later testified that the director of science and engineering at Marshall, in charge of safety and quality assurance programs, had requested that the problems be closed out (Rogers Commission 1986, 143).

In testimony before the commission, the solid rocket booster project manager at Marshall, Lawrence Mulloy, stated that the acceptance of these letters closing out the seal problems was in error (Rogers Commission 1986, 144). Nevertheless, letters from Thiokol declaring the problem closed were sent in December 1985 and January 1986, and entered into the problem-assessment system. Because of this, the seal issues were not addressed at any level in the flight readiness review in progress for the *Challenger* launch in January. Lawrence Wear, from the solid rocket motor project office at Marshall, commented on this omission: "On this particular occasion, there was no heads up given because their Problem Assessment System considered that action closed" (Rogers Commission 1986, 144). According to testimony before the Rogers Commission, the seal erosion problem was either not reported or "winnowed down to one bullet entry" (Casamayou 1993, 33). There was no mention of the O-ring problems in the Level IV certification of flight readiness signed by Joseph Kilminster, who was the program manager for the booster program at Thiokol, on January 9, 1986, and there was nothing about it in the Level III certification, signed on January 15, 1986, by Lawrence Mulloy. As the Rogers Commission summarized: "No mention appears in several inches of paper comprising the entire chain of readiness reviews for 51-L" (1986, 85).

All of these lapses impaired the ability of shuttle program actors to process information about safety and learn from results, but they also appear to indicate that existing review procedures could be evaded and that the managers' technical decisions were flawed, as both accident investigations determined. Research on the seals was moving ahead, slowly, under a task force of Thiokol engineers, but O-ring erosion had been deliberately dropped from consideration by Level III reviewers at Marshall, so was not being fully disseminated to Level II or Level I decision makers. The complexity of the review procedures, the autonomy of center actors, their desire to avoid responsibility for grounding the shuttle, and the gaps in information dissemination all contributed to the failures of the safety review processes.

Last-Minute Warnings

The *Challenger* was certified for flight on January 15, 1986, and the launch was scheduled for January 27. The events in the hours before launch exhibit some of the confusion we have seen about the status of the O-rings, but raise issues of organizational autonomy, intercenter power struggles, and rivalries as well. The mission management team, which would assume responsibility for flight readiness and guide the mission from two days before the flight to its completion, included three key actors: Jesse Moore, associate administrator for space flight at NASA headquarters and director of the Johnson Space Center in Houston; Arnold Aldrich, the manager of the shuttle program office at Johnson (Level II); and William Lucas, the director of the Marshall Center. They met on January 25 and determined that there were no open problems or technical issues, though they were concerned about the predictions for rain and cold temperatures. When cross-winds came up on the morning of the twenty-seventh, the launch was scrubbed and rescheduled for the next day (Rogers Commission 1987, 85). The mission management team met again at 2 p.m. that day to consider the implications of very cold overnight temperatures, predicted to reach the low 20s. They expressed concern about icing on the launch facilities but did not discuss the O-rings (86). At Thiokol offices in Utah, however, Robert Ebeling, manager for the solid rocket booster motors project, was concerned about the effect of the predicted temperatures on the O-rings, and he called a meeting of some the Thiokol engineers, including Roger Boisjoly, who had worked on the O-ring task force. They expressed alarm that the conditions were "way below what we qualified for" (87). Ebeling contacted others from Thiokol and a teleconference was arranged on the issue with NASA managers from Marshall.

The first teleconference at 5:45 p.m. included the manager of the shuttle projects office at Marshall, Stanley Reinartz, his deputy, Judson Lovingood, and George Hardy, the deputy director of the safety organization at Marshall, as well as others from Kennedy and Thiokol (Rogers Commission 1986, 86). Thiokol engineers presented their data about the loss of resiliency in cold conditions (87) and recommended that the launch be delayed. They also recommended that the Level II program administrator, Arnold Aldrich, be informed of the situation. Reinartz, however, thought that they should "gather the proper technical support people at Marshall for examination of the data" (88) and reconvene for another teleconference later. Charts and data were faxed from Utah to Kennedy for the second conference, which began around 8:45.

At the second teleconference a wider set of actors was assembled from Marshall, including Reinartz' subordinate, Lawrence Mulloy, the NASA manager of the solid rocket booster project at Marshall, who had earlier waived the launch constraint related to the joint seal, and others from Thiokol and Kennedy. Reinartz had decided, however, not to escalate the discussion to Level II in the program hierarchy. Roger Boisjoly, the engineer from Thiokol, presented two charts summarizing concerns about the O-ring seals. The first described the erosion problems with the primary and secondary seals, and the second provided findings from the cold-weather flight the previous January, when the temperature was 53 degrees. On that launch, O-ring charring had been linked to a hardening of the rings by the cold (Rogers Commission 1986, 89), reducing the capacity of the rings to seal the joint. Boisjoly explained that launching with hardened rings "would be likened to trying to shove a brick into a crack versus a sponge" (89). But when asked to "quantify" his concerns, he said he did not have the data to link particular temperatures to the resiliency effects, although he did state that it was "away from goodness in the current data base" (89). Robert Lund, Thiokol's vice president for engineering, also presented his recommendation not to "fly outside our data base" (90), which was down to 53 degrees for the launch. All at Thiokol agreed, including Kilminster, the program manager for the solid rocket booster program at Thiokol (90).

"Listeners on the telecon were not pleased with the conclusions and the recommendations," according to Boisjoly (Rogers Commission 1986, 90). Mulloy expressed exasperation with the notion that Thiokol was proposing to create additional launch criteria based on temperature. He said, "My God, Thiokol, when do you want me to launch, next April?" (96). It was then that Kilminster, Thiokol's program manager for the booster, asked for a five-minute caucus for the Thiokol staff offline. It lasted thirty minutes.

When they resumed the teleconference, Thiokol management had reversed its position and recommended that the launch proceed. While acknowledging that cold temperatures would reduce the resiliency of the seals, Thiokol's assessment was that "temperature data [were] not conclusive on predicting primary seal blow-by" (Rogers Commission 1986, 97). Thiokol now maintained that the current launch would "not be significantly different" from the cold-weather launch a year earlier (97). This was the recommendation that went to the shuttle project manager office at Marshall. We address the dynamics of the meeting between NASA managers and the Thiokol group in the next chapter on contractor relations.

After the Thiokol recommendation was sent, McDonald, the Thiokol liaison at Kennedy who had been one of the first to sound the alarm about temperatures, tried to reopen the launch-delay question because of ice on the launch facilities and bad weather in the recovery zone. Mulloy transmitted this information to Arnold Aldrich, shuttle program office manager at Johnson, but did not mention the discussions they had just completed about the O-rings. Mulloy later testified, "We work many problems at the Orbiter and the Solid Rocket Booster and the External Tank level that never get communicated to Mr. Aldrich or Mr. Moore. It was clearly a Level III issue that had been resolved" (Rogers Commission 1986, 98).

The engineers' concerns were not communicated up the chain of command to Level II or I or to the mission management team that made the final launch decision. This communication failure also had the effect of preventing the incident from being reported to managers at the Johnson Space Center. It also meant that managers at Marshall could not be accused of failing to maintain the flight schedule. William Lucas, the director of the Marshall center and part of that team, only learned about the last-minute temperature controversy through informal channels on the morning of the launch. He testified that Reinartz, manager of the shuttle projects office at Marshall, told him that when he had gone into the control room, "an issue had been resolved, that there were some people at Thiokol who had a concern about the weather, that it had been discussed very thoroughly by the Thiokol people and by the Marshall Space Flight Center people, and . . . he had a recommendation by Thiokol to launch"(101).

Lucas, who resigned a few months after these events, explained his decision not to report the incident up to Level II in this way: "That is not the reporting channel. Mr. Reinartz [solid rocket booster project manager at Marshall] reports directly to Mr. Aldrich [manager of the shuttle program office at Johnson]. In a sense, Mr. Reinartz informs me as the institutional manager of the progress that he is making in implementing his program, but that I have never on any occasion reported to Mr. Aldrich" (Rogers Commission 1986, 101).

This claim was not entirely accurate. Formally, center and program management were separate, but in reality they were closely linked. Lucas was on the mission management team for the launch. The shuttle program was also by far the largest project at Marshall and so the center director was of necessity involved it its management (Dunar and Waring 1999, 294). The Rogers Commission report on the implementation of recommendations showed that in the pre-*Challenger* structure of the shuttle program, program elements such as the solid rocket booster and the orbiter were organizationally located within their centers, and their budgets were funneled through the centers—not the program office hierarchy (Rogers Commission 1987, 30). Lucas's comments do indicate, however, how the dual line of command of the centers and the programs complicated reporting and decision making about safety.

Arnold Aldrich, manager of the shuttle program office at Johnson, Level II in the hierarchy, later identified several communication barriers (Rogers Commission 1986, 102). One was the decision of the Marshall officials not to report the problem up to the next level the day before the launch. Next, as Aldrich stated, "The second breakdown in communications, . . . and one that I personally am concerned about is the situation of the variety of reviews that were conducted last summer between the NASA Headquarters Organization and the Marshall Organization on the same technical area and the fact that that was not brought through my office in either direction" (Rogers Commission 1986, 102).

Further, NASA procedures sent Marshall budget requests for hardware solutions to the seal problems directly to headquarters, bypassing Level II, so that Aldrich lost that opportunity to discover the long-standing joint-seal problem (103). He was not aware, for example, that redesigned solid rocket booster cases with improved linking mechanisms for the segments had been ordered in mid-1985 (Dunar and Waring 1999, 407).

Based on these and past incidents, the Rogers Commission identified the reluctance to communicate between Marshall and Johnson as a serious weakness. In the third of four findings on the organizational causes of the accident, they noted they were

> troubled by what appears to be a propensity of management at Marshall to contain potentially serious problems and to attempt to resolve them internally rather than communicate them forward. This tendency is altogether at odds with the need for Marshall to function as part of a system working toward

successful flight missions, interfacing and communicating with the other parts of the system that work to the same end. (Rogers Commission 1986, 104)

EFFECTS OF INFORMATION-PROCESSING FLAWS ON SHORT-TERM LEARNING

We will shortly examine the changes adopted by NASA after the *Challenger* accident to determine which of them persisted up to the launch of *Columbia*. Learning how to create program-authority structures and safety-tracking systems in the aftermath of the *Challenger* accident would signal, in this context, long-term learning and an occasion for double-loop learning. But in the case of information-processing issues, the shuttle program also provides opportunities for, but failures in, short-term, single-loop learning about the technical problems with the seals. That is, actors did not apply the monitoring and correction procedures that already existed to solve the problems they observed, raising two key questions: Why did the early indications of problems with the solid rocket booster seals not prompt greater action? How did these problems with information dissemination, the launch-readiness review process, and the management structures affect the capacity of NASA over the early years to learn from evidence from flights and laboratory work about the seriousness of the problems with the O-rings?

First, to learn, actors must acknowledge that results are unsatisfactory. In the NASA case, there are many instances of the inability or unwillingness of actors to assemble key information needed to analyze the O-ring failures. There is even evidence of reluctance by the contractors and the Marshall managers to admit to the existence of failures. In later chapters the sources of this reluctance will be seen to lie in the schedule pressures, the ingrained rivalries between the centers, and the harsh oversight practices of managers. The Rogers Commission based part of its recommendations for restructuring on what they called "a tendency at Marshall to management isolation" that led the center to fail to follow procedures for reporting to other vital elements of shuttle program management (Rogers Commission 1986, 200). But clearly, knowledge of the erosion of the seals and even of the impact of the new leak test and cold temperatures on the likelihood of joint failure was available to at least some of the actors some of the time. Nonetheless, actors who were aware of the problems waived launch constraints and approved the shuttle's readiness. This suggests that the lack of problem recognition was due to more than the absence of information. We see examples of managers at all levels avoiding the pursuit of findings about results that would have revealed the seriousness of the problems. The tendency to avoid inconvenient truths is not an unusual or even rare event, as Perrow (1999) and Kaufman (1973) have noted. But it has serious consequences.

Next, to learn, actors must be able to track cause and effect, evaluate results, and compare interpretations to come to better understanding of how to achieve results. We see almost no evidence of this second learning process here. Lapses in reporting and disseminating information about the seals are evident from the start of the program. Over the years, many observations about the erosion of the seals appear in postflight close-out reviews, but these were not evaluated in a consistent manner. Though there is at least one instance of a conference to examine the seal-erosion issue, NASA managers appear to have dealt with the problem in a peremptory fashion. For the contractors, the task force to investigate the causes of the erosion was a low priority. Even the day before the launch, the managers at Marshall guarded information about the Thiokol engineers' reservations about the launch temperatures. Finally, rivalry between the centers appears to have pitted one level in the program hierarchy against the other, with the result that Marshall became unwilling to report on continuing problems with the seals. Instead, managers at Marshall claimed that the problems were under control, even when the evidence was clear that they were not.

These lapses in reporting were in some cases caused by not following established procedures, but in other cases the procedures designed to ensure safe and reliable performance appear to have been so ambiguous that it was possible to either evade or overlook them. In addition, the "streamlining" of problem reports from Level III limited Level II managers' insights into emerging trends. The in-flight anomaly reporting system and the procedures surrounding the critical items list both appear to have been so complex that actors may have disagreed about how to comply or become irritated by what they viewed as excessive and cumbersome procedures. Such ambiguities and lack of observance of rules from the bottom up may have made it difficult for shuttle managers to see how program components operated as a whole. The potential for communication and coordination lapses between the contractors and the program managers was also significant, and this is the subject of the next chapter. In any case, many of these problems were identified by the Rogers Commission and the House Report and efforts to eliminate them comprised a large part of the return to flight strategy after the *Challenger* accident. However, no final resolution or new understanding of the problem with the seals was achieved prior to the launch of the *Challenger*. In the short term, there were no lessons to institutionalize.

The safety-reporting system in the years leading up to the *Challenger* accident illustrates three levels of problems that made short-term learning unlikely. First,

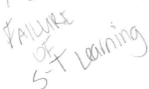

the elaborate nature of the safety systems, the reviews, tests, and classifications illustrates the huge complexity of the program design and the challenge of tracking and resolving an enormous number of unresolved but critical problems. Uncovering "what goes with what" is more difficult with such a large number of potential causes and so many gaps in information about effects. In addition, a history of withheld information and communication breakdown illustrates the flaws in the decisions made about the problem tracking as it was designed. Finally, the case shows the accidental oversights and confusions that plagued the shuttle program. All of these factors blocked the dissemination of information and contributed to the failure of short-term learning. We consider the evidence of long-term learning and the opportunities for double-loop learning in the organizational changes that followed the accident.

THE POST-*CHALLENGER* PERIOD: NASA'S RESPONSES TO THE ROGERS COMMISSION RECOMMENDATIONS

After the loss of the *Challenger*, the Rogers Commission made a number of recommendations related to the immediate causes of the accident. Flights were immediately halted, the improvements in the solid rocket booster seals that had been under development were adopted, and new, strict, weather-related rules for launches were created. New procedures for launch reviews were instituted so that flight readiness reviews at Level 1 had to formally consider all constraints and waivers (Dunar and Waring 1999, 418). NASA also implemented a number of recommended changes in management and communications structures and in safety and problem-tracking procedures. The commission's second recommendation was for NASA to review the shuttle program structure and redefine the responsibilities of the shuttle program manager so that "vital program information" would no longer bypass him or her: "Program funding," the commission advised, "and all shuttle program work at the Centers should be placed clearly under the Program Manager's authority" (199).

As noted earlier, at the time of the accident, the agency overall was operating under the lead-center management approach in which each of the multiple elements of one shuttle program was placed under the command of one of the NASA centers. This administrative structure may have contributed to the communication and coordination problems leading up to the *Challenger* accident. Speaking of how the arrangement worked for the space shuttle program, a former Apollo program executive observed, "the JCS (Johnson Space Center) was the Lead Center, but they weren't in charge of the program . . . the people in the other centers wouldn't even give Houston the courtesy of responding to their communications, much less recognizing them as being in charge" (McCurdy 1993, 131). The decentralization created by this arrangement "elevated bureaucratic barriers for cooperation and communication" (McCurdy 1993, 131).

To break down the communication barriers and reduce intercenter rivalries, the lead-center structure was slated to be minimized, and the shuttle-management structure was centralized under the director of the shuttle program, who was to be a NASA headquarters employee. This design reflected the earlier and much more effective Apollo program structure.

It was thought that the unrelenting pressure to meet the demands of an accelerating flight schedule might have been adequately handled by NASA if it had insisted upon the exactingly thorough procedures that were its hallmark during the Apollo program. An extensive and redundant safety program comprising interdependent safety, reliability, and quality assurance functions had existed during the lunar program to discover potential safety problems. Between that period and 1986, however, this safety program became ineffective, and the checks and balances essential for maintaining flight safety had been seriously downgraded (Rogers Commission 1986, 152).

In response, NASA redesigned the shuttle program's command structure. Lt. General Samuel C. Phillips, formerly the Apollo program director, chaired a study group to reassess NASA's structure and management, and the group's conclusions were published eighteen months after the *Challenger* accident as an implementation report whose major recommendations were "to establish centralized headquarter responsibility for all programs and to restructure the agency to improve the lines of communication" (Rogers Commission 1987, 27). The references in the implementation report to the success of the Apollo-era structures and safety organization show NASA reinstituting a core design based on earlier experience. This is an explicit inference about cause and effect and offers evidence that NASA was engaged in the classic learning scenario. Under the new shuttle program director were two new deputy directors, both headquarters employees, one for project management located at Johnson and one for operations located at Kennedy. But the manager of the shuttle projects at Marshall would now still report directly to the new deputy director at Johnson (Rogers Commission 1987, 29), even though that person was a headquarters employee, a decision that created later problems. New operations-integration offices were also established for each center to report directly to the deputy director for operations to ensure coordination with problem tracking and other operational issues. Funding requests would, after approval at the center level, go to the deputy directors. All these changes were designed to break down intercenter rivalries and communication blockages. The NASA implementation report predicted that the changes would "permit early detection and timely resolution of potential problems" (Rogers Commission 1987, 27).

The safety organization was also redesigned and centralized in the headquarters' Office of Safety, Reliability, Maintainability, and Quality Assurance under an associate administrator who reported directly to the NASA administrator (Rogers Commission 1986, 45). Separate, new offices of safety and mission assurance in each center were also created, and their directors reported to their center director rather than to the program offices they were monitoring (GAO 1996, 19), providing them with more independence. These were to be part of the headquarters safety organization, but as will become clear, centralization of the safety function was not fully implemented. In a further effort to improve their autonomy and professional status, safety engineers were now grouped together more visibly within each center rather than being spread across engineering divisions in different locations. These adjustments did, however, also remove them from the chain of command, a double-edged achievement. The newly organized safety officers were to participate in the flight readiness reviews and independent prelaunch reviews to ensure that safety issues were closed out (GAO 1996, 15–16). The retention of items on the critical items lists would have to be rejustified to headquarters. The number of personnel assigned to the safety reporting systems was also increased (GAO 1996, 19), and the offices were given more resources in hopes of attracting a staff who could serve as an effective "check and balance" (Rogers Commission 1986, 45). The problems with staffing these offices are described in more detail in chapter 6.

Other efforts were aimed at improving the integration of information systems. A unified, intercenter problem-reporting database was to be created to make it easier to spot problems and trends (Rogers Commission 1986, 49). Several new incident-reporting systems were established, including a standardized, agency-wide "mishap reporting and corrective action system" to provide a way to collect and disseminate "lessons-learned" summaries across the organization electronically (50). We will see what happened to these new systems shortly. Some of these recommendations were internalized and developed by NASA administrators. Others, for reasons that will become clear, were never elaborated or implemented.

In some areas real strides were made in the aftermath of *Challenger*. In a GAO study a decade later based on focus groups and questionnaires, respondents "identified multiple channels, both formal and informal, for communicating flight safety information. In some cases, these communication channels represent independent, parallel paths for assessing risk" (GAO 1996, 19). Managers were

also encouraging personnel to speak up about any safety concerns and not to assume that raising a problem meant poor performance (GAO 1996, 20). Finally, new channels to report safety problems confidentially were developed to overcome what we will see was a culture-based reluctance to report deficiencies (Rogers Commission 1986, 50; GAO 1996, 19). GAO concluded that a new openness in addressing safety issues in the agency had been created.

Problems remained, however. The same GAO study found that some NASA officials reported that one of the new automated problem-reporting databases, the Program Compliance Assurance and Status System, was unwieldy because "it [was] based on older technology, some trend and other data is not centralized in the system, and software needed to convert contractor data to NASA database format has not been developed" (GAO 1996, 42). NASA's own investigation showed that criticality level codes were missing from thousands of database entries, blocking their ability to track problems. The other safety-data system, the Problem Reporting and Corrective Action System, was designed to track shuttle problems, but GAO found that its "records are often not reliable and lack uniformity in categorizing problems" (42). NASA recognized these problems but told GAO that decisions about remedies would be made after the upcoming consolidation of its many contracts under a new prime contractor, United Space Alliance (USA) (GAO 1996, 42). This new entity was created by a partnership between Lockheed Martin and Boeing and is described in the next chapter. Similar concerns were raised in another GAO study in 2002, which investigated NASA's Lessons Learned Information System: "[O]ur survey found that lessons are not routinely identified, collected, or shared by programs and project managers. Respondents reported that they are unfamiliar with lessons generated by other Centers and programs"(GAO 2002, 3).

A 1988 report titled *Lessons Learned from Challenger*, commissioned by the newly constituted Office of Safety, Reliability, Maintainability, and Quality Assurance at headquarters, was critical of the lack of management openness to reporting safety violations by front-line personnel. The report also found a "tired and unmotivated work force with a lack of personal commitment to excellence" (NASA 1988, 9) that failed to follow procedures or report dangerous technical conditions. While these criticisms mirrored many of the Rogers Commission findings, the agency was by then impatient with the barrage of criticisms that had followed the loss of the *Challenger* and, at least initially, rejected the report (Klerkx 2004, 247). This suggests that shuttle administrators did not necessarily embrace error or internalize critical investigative reports or panel findings even when they themselves commissioned them.

Furthermore, some of the structural changes were not permanent. The lead-center concept, never fully eradicated, now was openly reestablished. By January

1996 the responsibility for shuttle program management had been tra....
from the headquarters shuttle-project-management director to the Johnson
Space Center director, reestablishing the old pattern (GAO 1996, 18). The 1990
Report of the Advisory Committee on the Future of the U.S. Space Program (the
Augustine Report[4]), commissioned by the White House, also recommended this
change so that projects would be managed close to the site of the "primary
center" involved in the undertaking, freeing headquarters staff for oversight and
policymaking (NASA 1990).

Other announced changes never occurred or were more symbolic than real.
The CAIB later criticized the extent of real change in the safety program, noting
that the safety activities were still functionally dependent on other program and
center offices and were still not truly independent. This was a long-standing
problem. The 1988 report commissioned by the Office of Safety, Reliability,
Maintainability and Quality Assurance had found that

> many dual responsibility roles for in-line program and [safety and quality]
> assurance management systems are necessary due to limitations in availability
> of technical or specialist personnel. Part of the confusion in responsibilities that
> existed prior to [*Challenger*] was a result of these dual roles being inadequately
> defined. Personnel were required in some cases to perform work and then were
> required to make judgments on how well it was done. While this task is not
> impossible, it is one that is contrary to human nature. ((NASA 1988, 8)

SLIPPING BACK: DAN GOLDIN AND
DECENTRALIZATION OF PROGRAM MANAGEMENT

Despite the agency's halting movement toward change, some progress did occur.
A relatively centralized program structure, for example, was established and
remained in place until the 1990s. But at this point a new set of reorganizations
shook NASA under Dan Goldin (Lambright 2001). Some decentralization had
already taken place under Administrator Truly, and we will have more to say
about the external pressures to make these changes in chapter 5, but Goldin took
the trend much further. Responding to a decline in the priority attached to space
exploration with the end of the cold war and to the trend in the 1990s to shrink
the size of government, Goldin strove to remake NASA. His strategy involved
privatizing, decentralizing, and downsizing (Lambright 2001, 21). In 1996 the
lead-center organization structure returned, and management and budget
authority was shifted back to the director at the Johnson Center in Houston as
an efficiency move and, Goldin argued, to improve safety. He charged, "the

layering of bureaucrats obfuscated responsibility" (21). The Kraft Report,[5] NASA's independent review of contractor relations, supported this conclusion, arguing that "the 'safety shield' that has been built has created a difficult management situation. Managers, engineers, and business people are reluctant to make decisions that involve risk because of the fear of persecution" (NASA 1995, 6).

A former astronaut and head of the shuttle program at headquarters, Bryan O'Connor, complained that this reversion to the pre-*Challenger* organization created a "safety issue" (CAIB, 107; Lambright 2001, 21), but Goldin's "faster, better, cheaper" policy won support in the White House and Congress. Downsizing at headquarters and in the field followed, and much of the shuttle operations' work was "privatized" under contracts with the United Space Alliance, the new business partnership of Lockheed Martin and Rockwell. Shuttle resources were cut as budgets once again leveled off and funding began to be shifted to the International Space Station in 1993. The number of civil servants working on the shuttle also declined by more than 50 percent to only 1,718 by 2002 (CAIB 106).

The Augustine Report on NASA's role in U.S. space policy had also earlier criticized the decentralization and increase in number of offices, linking these changes to the problems created by the lead-center strategy that divided projects among centers to preserve the separate facilities:

> It is said that, on occasion, projects appear to have been tailored to help perpetuate the work force, rather than the work force having been tailored to meet the needs of the project. One by-product of any such practice is that it tends to maximize the number of organizations, and therefore interfaces, involved in a task—exactly the opposite of generally accepted management philosophy that argues for minimizing interfaces, the "nooks and crannies" where problems seem to breed. (NASA 1990, subsection "Institutional Aging")

There were indications even before the *Columbia* accident that the reforms in the communication system, the problem-reporting system, and the safety organizations instituted after *Challenger* departed from what may have been lessons learned after the accident. The changes brought in under Goldin created new coordination challenges from increased outsourcing of the shuttle program. These contracting issues are taken up in more detail in the next chapter, but the immediate effects on the safety system were major:

> The contract . . . involved substantial transfers of safety responsibility from the government to the private sector; rollbacks of tens of thousands of Government

Mandated Inspection Points; and vast reductions in NASA's in-house safety-related technical expertise. . . . In the aggregate, these mid-1990s transformations rendered NASA's already problematic safety system simultaneously weaker and more complex. (CAIB, 179)

Under this new plan, NASA had only indirect "insight" into safety through a system of reviews and "metrics" provided by contractors. In addition, with much of the safety system in the hands of contractors, the potential for conflict of interest arose again. Thus the real independence of the safety system again became problematic. In 1999, the Shuttle Independent Assessment Team created by NASA to investigate several "close calls" (CAIB, 179) criticized this arrangement and strongly recommended that the previous, more independent safety office design be restored (188).

NASA had been warned of these issues in internal and external investigations. In 1990 a GAO study following up on the Rogers Commission recommendations found that only the safety office at headquarters was independently funded; funding for the safety operations in the centers was still tied to the programs and centers they were to oversee (CAIB, 179), and this remained the case through 2003. The 1999 Shuttle Independent Assessment Team concluded that after Goldin's efficiency drive, the program was becoming a "slimmed down, contractor-run operation" and that the relationship between NASA and its contractors demanded "better communication practices" (179). The team warned about the potential for conflict of interest among contractors given the charge of problem-tracking systems. These concerns were echoed in the report of the integrated action team established to carry out these recommendations, with team members noting particularly the need for "multiple processes to get the messages across the organizational structure" (179).

Under the redesigned safety programs headquarters was to set the overall safety policy, monitor anomalies or "out of family" events (an event outside the range of performance seen previously), and sign off on the flight readiness reviews. But in practice, the shuttle safety program was now again decentralized and operated differently for each center or project (CAIB, 185–86). At Johnson, the director of the space shuttle division assumed program and center management duties combined with three safety roles: representing the center, the shuttle program, and the NASA headquarters safety program. This resulted in a bewildering arrangement of authority and accountability that "almost defies explanation," according to the CAIB, which noted that the director assessed the safety of his own activities, effectively eliminating "checks and balances" (186).

The agency's many reorganizations were also taking their toll on the clarity and costs of shuttle program management. In 1990, the Augustine Report on the future of the space program detailed the costly impacts of continued "management turbulence, defined as continual changes in cost, schedule, goals" (NASA 1990, subsection "Managerial Turbulence") that resulted from design changes to the shuttle components, budget forecasting problems, and reorganizations. They note further, "Each change induced has a way of cascading through the entire project execution system, producing havoc at every step along the way." Similarly, the Kraft Report on NASA's contract management cited reorganizations that followed the *Challenger* accident and the ramping up of the International Space Station program as generating "confusion within and among NASA Headquarters, the centers, and the contractors as to responsibility and decision making. It is now increasingly difficult for center management to provide the classical technical inputs to program management and to provide the customary checks and balances that were essential in previous programs" (NASA 1995, 6).

Other fundamental weaknesses in information processing further compromised the ability of shuttle managers to track programs and monitor events. Though the Rogers Commission recommended the integration of information systems and some progress was made in that direction, a system for integrating information about the safety of the shuttle as a whole, across all its components and centers, was absent at the time of the *Columbia* accident (CAIB, 187–88). Despite the creation of an array of program integration offices designed to try to prevent the isolation of program components, the Space Shuttle Systems Integration Office did not, in fact, cover the orbiter, limiting its real ability to merge information or management. After 2001, hazard analyses were conducted of components but not of the entire shuttle system, providing no precise "top-down" hazard analysis for upper-level managers to use in looking for trends or interactions (188). Nor, as noted earlier, was there an effective integrated database of hazards reports from which to generate performance trends (189). Even the Lessons Learned Information System, ironically, was also flawed because it was only used on an ad hoc basis (184, 189).

The effects of these weaknesses in the collection, storage, and retrieval of information about past flight experience rippled across the organization. CAIB observed that "sometimes information gets lost altogether, as weak signals drop from memos, problem identification systems, and formal presentations" (190). The flight readiness reviews and the critical items list that rested on these analyses were in turn compromised. After the *Columbia* disaster, the CAIB observed that of the 4,222 components designated criticality 1 or criticality 1R, 3,233 of them had gotten waivers because they could not at that point be redesigned or replaced. More than one-third of those had not been recertified in over ten years

(CAIB 189), as required by the Rogers Commission for the return to flight after the *Challenger*.

In sum, even after the changes made following the loss of the *Challenger*, ambiguous and uncertain reporting relations limited NASA's capacity to track safety problems in a very complex and hazardous technology.

THE SEQUEL: *COLUMBIA*

As in the *Challenger* case, the problems that led to disaster were not new ones. Though formal shuttle specifications explicitly precluded the shedding of foam debris from the external tank (CAIB, 122), the divots produced in the orbiter tiles from the foam strikes had become so common that they became accepted by contractors and NASA engineers as problems of maintenance or turn-around issues. Problems with foam shedding were well-known and had been seen in sixty-five of seventy-nine launches in which photographic records were available, including seven at the left bipod ramp area, where the foam that downed the *Columbia* originated (123). In one of two foam-loss incidents just preceding the *Columbia* flight, the problem was categorized as an in-flight anomaly but was closed out prior to the next flight. The tile damage was repaired, but the underlying cause of the foam loss was not uncovered and no solution was identified. NASA managers assigned the task of determining the "root cause" (125) to the external tank project at Marshall, meanwhile scheduling two more shuttle launches, including *Columbia*, before the report was due. The CAIB drew attention to the differences in how the various parts of the shuttle-safety organization classified one of these incidents. The Marshall external tank office declared it not to be a "safety of flight" issue, whereas the integration office at Johnson declared it to be an "accepted risk," again illustrating the lack of an integrated problem-tracking system (124). Nor could the integration office clarify the locus of responsibility for dealing with the foam-shedding problem. Sometimes it was seen as the task of the external tank office, sometimes that of the orbiter office (193).

Two flights prior to the *Columbia*, mission STS-112, particularly serious damage was caused by foam debris, but it was not classified as an in-flight anomaly and so required only an "action report," calling on the external tank project to resolve the problem in the future. Nor was the foam-shedding problem raised in the flight readiness reviews for the flight just prior to the *Columbia*. The Columbia Accident Investigation Board later speculated that this decision, which formally accepted that it was safe to fly with foam shedding, made it possible for actors to use the same rationale to dismiss reports of foam loss during the *Columbia* flight (CAIB, 125). This pattern of avoiding the rigorous application of safety procedures designed by the shuttle program itself mirrored the events seen before the loss of the *Challenger*.

Misdirected Warnings In-Flight

On January 16, the day after the final launch of the *Columbia*, the Marshall Intercenter Photo Working Group, responsible for launch videos, first recognized the large piece of foam hitting the orbiter. It notified its counterparts at Kennedy Space Center, and they in turn e-mailed digital images of the strike to a wide, informally constituted circle of NASA managers and contract engineers. Though the image revealed the largest-yet debris event so late in flight when speeds are great (CAIB, 140), the image was poor, at least in part because of camera problems and staff cuts, and could not reveal the extent of the damage. The mission evaluation room, the group of NASA engineers and contract engineers from United Space Alliance (USA) assigned to troubleshoot problems that might arise during the flight, was notified. A debris assessment team, cochaired by Pam Madera from USA and Rodney Rocha, chief engineer for thermal protection at Johnson, was created to pursue the analysis of images. The head of the Intercenter Photo Working Group next contacted Wayne Hale, then the launch integration manager at Kennedy, to request more detailed images of the area of the strike on the left wing (CAIB, 140). Hale had a top-secret clearance and understood the procedures for requesting military imaging of the shuttle on-orbit as a result of his experience as a mission-control flight director. Hale in turn notified Linda Ham, chair of the mission management team responsible for the *Columbia* in flight, and Ron Dittemore, the shuttle program manager, of the strike and the group's request for images.

Informal e-mail conversations among the group members and with other NASA and USA contract engineers seemed to indicate that the impact would likely have created only shallow damage to the leading edge of the wing (CAIB, 141). This early assessment, according to the CAIB investigators, "contributed to a mindset that the foam hitting the (wing tiles) was not a concern" (141), a mental model of the strike that guided later actions.

Nevertheless, one USA engineer classified the debris strike as "out of family" (CAIB, 143, 171), that is, an event outside the known performance range and experience and so of particular seriousness (122). This action at least offers a clear contrast with events leading up to the loss of the *Challenger*. However, under NASA procedures in place in 2003, this classification of the event required

NASA engineers to coordinate with contractors to form a "tiger team," under the direction of the mission evaluation room. However, in this case, the individuals who formed the debris assessment team were not constituted as the tiger team, which meant they did not have a place in the chain of command that would give them frequent and direct access to shuttle managers. Further, program managers did not provide direct support for the team, nor did they regularly consult with the team about their findings. These lapses later led to serious communication failures.

The circulation of the Intercenter Photo Working Group reports prompted a burst of informal communication. To assess the effect of the strike, USA/Boeing contract engineers worked with Boeing's computer model for predicting tile damage, Crater, through the Martin Luther King holiday weekend. This tool was remarkably accurate, according to the CAIB (143), despite the fact that it was not designed for anywhere near such large pieces of debris as had been seen in this case. The model predicted damage deeper than the thickness of the tiles, suggesting that the aluminum frame of the shuttle could be exposed to high enough re-entry temperatures to burn thorough the frame (145). The direst implications of this assessment were discounted by the debris assessment team, however, who met the next day, day 5 of the flight. They based this view on their estimate that the angle of the strike would likely be shallow and their belief, later revealed to be unfounded, that the Crater had made a conservative estimate. The assumptions made at this point and the uncertainties built into those assumptions were never conveyed to the mission evaluation room or to the mission management team (145).

An informal meeting of the debris assessment team was called for Martin Luther King Day, January 20. For this session the group was expanded to include tile experts from NASA and Boeing, and a representative from the safety contractor, Science Applications International (CAIB, 146). The meeting ended with an agreement that on-orbit images of the left wing were needed to determine where the hit had occurred and whether damage to the landing gear door had occurred (146). *This request, and similar requests that followed, were never honored.* The request did not adhere to the unevenly applied procedures, at least in part because the group was never given the "tiger team" designation that would have placed it clearly in the chain of commend. Even before this meeting, Rodney Rocha, cochair of the debris assessment team heading up the review, asked the Johnson engineering directorate whether the crew had been advised to visually inspect the wing, but he never received an answer (145). Based on the team's assumptions about the strike, the log entry for day 5 by the mission evaluation room reported that the size of the debris strike was similar to the strike seen in

STS-112, two flights earlier. The implication, of course, was that the strike should be reclassified as an "in-family" event (146), which would not require that the foam-shedding problem be fully resolved, a requirement that could delay future shuttle flights.

The next day, day 6 of the mission, the debris assessment team briefed Don McCormack, manager of the mission evaluation room, about the findings, which he relayed to a mission-management-team meeting chaired by Linda Ham. The CAIB report of this critical meeting notes that her principal concern appears to have been to find an acceptable rationale for the flight. Since the previous shuttle flight returned despite serious foam loss, it seemed to justify the subsequent flight without resolution of the foam issue: "What I'm really interested in is making sure our flight rationale to go was good" (CAIB, 147). But in a later e-mail she noted that the rationale to fly without a resolution of the problems was "lousy" for the previous flight, and that nothing had changed (148). Hers seems an odd response, but she was scheduled to be the launch-integration manager for the next mission, which was a critical one for NASA's effort to finish a key component of the International Space Station upon which all felt NASA's credibility rode (137–39). This launch would be delayed if the rationale were not deemed acceptable. Later e-mails make the point that foam losses in the past had not been classified as "safety-of-flight issues, and so they should not be classified that way in this case either" (150). The motivations for this pattern of rationalization and the source of the heavy schedule pressures will be taken up in subsequent chapters, but here it is important to note that these rationalizations, especially the concern with maintaining the launch schedule, led to a reluctance to collect information about the status of the strike area.

At the same time, the requests for imagery were being pursued by several groups along formal and informal pathways. In all, the CAIB documented three sets of requests by various actors to obtain images of the wing. None of the requests were successfully processed up the chain of command. On day 2, the chair of the Intercenter Photo Working Group, Bob Page, asked Wayne Hale, the shuttle program manager for integration at Kennedy, for images of the wing. On day 7, Hale carried this request to NASA's DOD representative. Although his contact was not the proper DOD official for coordinating NASA imagery requests, the representative conveyed the request to the U.S. Strategic Command in Colorado (CAIB, 152). Hale had also skirted correct procedure by failing to obtain authorization from the mission management team. Meanwhile, on day 6, the USA manager, Bob White, supporting his employees on the debris assessment team, had requested Lambert Austin, the head of the space shuttle systems integration at Johnson Space Flight Center, to find out if imagery could be obtained. Austin pursued the request though a different DOD office, showing he was not aware of NASA's procedures for requesting images from the National Imagery and Mapping Agency (150).

On the same day, NASA's cochair of the debris assessment team, Rodney Rocha, made another, independent request for images in flight: "Can we petition (beg) for outside agency assistance?" (CAIB, 152). He also made the request through incorrect procedure, using the only communication channel with which he was familiar, the engineering directorate at Johnson. The correct procedure would have been to go up the chain of command to the mission management team, but they had shown no interest in working on this issue with debris assessment (151). The CAIB attributes this lack of procedural knowledge to the lack of "participation" by the mission management team (151), but because even relatively senior managers did not appear to use the correct procedures, the errors may also reflect the arcane structure for safety tracking and reporting that emerged after the agency's multiple reorganizations (187). All three of these requests were dismissed by the mission management team on day 7 (152).

The ostensible rationale for canceling the three requests was that they had not gone through the proper channels and the images were not needed. The need for DOD assistance was also dismissed (CAIB, 151). Later, in thanking the DOD for its prompt offer of help, NASA managers said that the situation pointed to the need for more coordination to ensure that requests are "done through the official channels" (159). But few seem to have known in practice what those official channels were (159). Austin's formal request was cancelled by Ham after she determined that there was no documented "requirement" for the images from the mission evaluation room, to whom the debris assessment team reported, or from the shuttle engineering office, or from other NASA program offices. Ham also believed, erroneously, that the resolution possible for images would not be detailed enough to detect the kind of damage they were looking for. But almost none on the *Columbia* team had the security clearance to know the actual capacity for imagery that was available to NASA (154). Here once again is evidence of a faulty design for information systems and safety procedures. Several members of the Safety and Mission Assurance Office from headquarters and Johnson Center were informed of the pending imaging request but were told that the strike was an "in-family" event and so deferred to shuttle management decisions on the matter (153).

Other evidence of miscommunication about the images also exists. Although shuttle program management had turned down the multiple requests from the debris assessment team, neither side ever fully understood the other's actions.

Communications between the debris assessment team and the mission management team had been so sporadic and indirect that the reasons behind the decision to cancel the imagery requests were not conveyed to the debris assessment team (CAIB, 157). Rocha, who had begged for outside help, was told that NASA's orbiter office was not requesting imagery (157), and so he declined to pursue an earlier request still in the system because the program managers had already turned down this later request (158). He privately circulated his worries about the effects of the strike, even invoking the safety slogan "If it is not safe, say so." But he did not want to "jump the chain of command" (157), and he did not pursue the requests further.

We see here weak communication among the several teams who were supposed to be in daily contact and close coordination. Instead, the mission management team met sporadically, only five times instead of daily over the sixteen-day mission, and did not actively pursue better understanding of the problem. Neither of the cochairs of the only group of engineers and managers devoted to the foam-strike problem knew how to go about requesting imagery or knew what the imagery resources really were. The formal and informal requests from the group that had been assembled to look at the problem were dismissed for lack of concrete evidence of the severity of the strike damage. Meanwhile, the members of this group were frustrated at having to establish a "mandatory need" for the images when the images themselves seemed to be the best evidence of the need (CAIB, 156). As in the case of the *Challenger*, engineers were being forced to demonstrate that a situation was *not* safe, a task made more difficult by the absence of clear, well-observed procedures for identifying a crisis.

At the third meeting of the debris assessment team on day 8, engineers expressed puzzlement at being denied their request for images. CAIB testimony identifies Boeing engineering analysts specifically as failing to understand why their "original justification was considered insufficient"(CAIB, 160). The concern this issue generated among working engineers was illustrated by the large numbers who crowded into the briefing room and lined the hallway (160) when the debris assessment team's findings were presented to the mission evaluation room the next day, day 9. The debris assessment team, forced to make a forecast without the images, concluded their formal assessment by stating that their limited analysis "did not show that a safety-of-flight issue existed" (160). Ignored was the stress they placed on the many uncertainties remaining (160). As in the *Challenger* case, the burden of proof appears to have lain with the engineers to prove danger rather then to prove safety. The Columbia Accident Investigation Board noted, "the Debris Assessment Team was put in the untenable position of having to prove that a safety-of-flight issue existed without the very images that would permit such a determination" (190).

A viewgraph presentation by Boeing and USA contract personnel at the day 9 meeting has been criticized in the CAIB and by Edward Tufte (2003) for its lack of clarity and for obscuring "key assumptions and uncertainties" (CAIB, 160). The main conclusion from this meeting was that there was no clear evidence of a "potential for burn-through," which Ham took to rule out "catastrophic damage" (161). The mission management team appears to have accepted this conclusion without probing further into the evidence or into minority views among the engineers (161). Nevertheless, debris assessment team leader Rocha was still very uncertain about the real state of the tiles, and he continued to collect analyses of the likely effects of the strike (163).

Once again, the safety organization was silent. Safety personnel, including both contract and NASA staff, were present but passive in the meetings of the debris assessment team, the mission evaluation room, and the mission management team. Safety contractors were only marginally aware of the debris analysis. The CAIB found that "the highest-ranking safety representative at NASA headquarters deferred to Program managers when asked for an opinion on imaging of *Columbia*" (170). No images were obtained, and the *Columbia* began its return to Earth.

LEARNING ABOUT SAFETY SYSTEMS

We began this book by asking what evidence there was for the CAIB's finding that NASA did not learn from the *Challenger* accident. Comparing the two shuttle disasters, it is clear that, though there were some important changes adopted after the *Challenger* accident, in too many ways the loss of the *Columbia* exhibits the same structural, information-processing, and safety-program problems seen in the *Challenger* case. We can summarize the case so far by comparing these failings to identify the degree to which learning did or did not take place.

A number of similarities present themselves. As we saw in the *Challenger* case, the problem with eroding seals in the solid rocket booster was long-standing. Nevertheless, information about seal performance was not reliably communicated upward beyond the Marshall center management or was given only passing attention and not acted upon. Intercenter rivalries meant that findings about unresolved problems or indications of trouble were not shared. Important information about anomalies was not considered in the flight readiness reviews, the key mechanism for integrating information about problems for a shuttle launch.

Lower-level engineers' concerns were not seen as a priority even when they were communicated. The safety offices were not organizationally independent, were underfunded, and had had difficulty filling their positions. All of these flaws limited the ability of actors throughout the organization to embrace error, seek out evidence for the trends in O-ring performance, or insist on a resolution of the problems with the seals.

We see a similar pattern in the *Columbia* case. Like the erosion of the O-rings, loss of foam was a known problem, but by the time of the *Columbia* launch it was no longer regarded as an in-flight anomaly. That is, NASA managers were inured to the issue and no longer regarded it as a problem to be addressed before the shuttle program could proceed. Despite the damage caused by foam in the flight just preceding *Columbia*, the problem was not included in the *Columbia*'s flight readiness review, just as the O-ring problem had been dropped from consideration. Moreover, information about the past effects of foam debris seems to have been lost. The unwieldy problem-tracking software, the reduced flow of rich information about safety issues from contractors, the decentralized, dependent safety structures, and the lack of a mechanism for integrating safety information about the shuttle all contributed to reduced attention to the dangers posed by foam shedding both before the flight and in flight.

The weaknesses of information processing were especially evident in the *Columbia* case in the difficulties encountered by engineers trying to determine the size and position of the debris strike and the threat it posed. Here the great complexity of the problem-tracking and safety-reporting systems defeated even veterans. The legacy of multiple reorganizations combined with the very large number of critical items to be tracked seems to have overwhelmed the information-processing capacity of the organization. Important requests for images of the wing by midlevel managers using formal and informal communication channels were misdirected and misinterpreted.

Again, as in the *Challenger* case, blocked communication can be traced to poorly designed structures and procedures, as well as to lapses in the use of existing procedures, such as the failure to create the tiger team or to meet regularly with the members of the debris assessment team. As in the *Challenger* case, these lapses were partly due to the design of the various information-processing systems but also to the disinclination of managers to disrupt the launch schedule to investigate a possible defect, a factor we will look into further in later chapters. Finally, as in the case of the *Challenger*, short-term learning about the foam problems was blocked when the problem was not acknowledged as important and when each forum for the analysis and interpretation of the foam strike was overshadowed by the assumption that the strike could not cause significant damage.

Our examination of the evidence about the similarities in the management failings behind the two accidents leads us to conclusions similar to those of CAIB. At first glance, the absence of many of the management changes recommended by the Rogers Commission by the time of the *Columbia* accident is puzzling. It does appear that a classic learning scenario—adopting the centralized administrative structure from the successful Apollo program era—had occurred. NASA had also accepted and appeared to have implemented many other recommendations from the commission and other internal and external studies, such as providing independent authority and funding for the safety organization, making efforts to create an integrated safety-information system, and encouraging staff to come forward with safety concerns. But despite these changes, many of the problems in the safety organization, the communication patterns, and information processing seen before *Challenger* re-emerged before *Columbia*.

The second question posed in this chapter is why these flaws in information processing and safety systems persisted or reappeared. Why did the agency fail to learn from the first accident? In chapter 7 we will look further at how all the factors—structural, contractual, external pressures, and culture—together account for this disastrous and perplexing outcome. Here we examine only what happened to block the learning efforts about the design of the safety-information systems in the return to flight after *Challenger*.

Opportunities for Double-Loop Learning

Examining the aftermath of the *Challenger* case, three patterns of failed long-term learning about the management structures and the design of the safety and problem-tracking systems seem apparent. In some cases, changes were made in line with Rogers Commission recommendations but genuine learning does not seem to have taken place. Second, some changes were agreed to but never fully institutionalized. Finally, some important structural changes were quite clearly the product of learning but then appear to have been forgotten or displaced.

Lessons Not Learned

First, for some of the recommended changes, it does not appear that the analysis and inference process went far enough to allow NASA managers to identify the underlying organizational flaws, explore alternative cause-and-effect interpretations, and determine what experience could tell them about the organizational and procedural arrangements that had worked well. In other words, NASA managers did not actually get through the second phase of learning. While they clearly recognized after the accident that authority structures, communications, and safety systems were flawed, they did not themselves undertake the kind of cause–effect analysis that would allow them to uncover their own solutions to the problems. The recommendation for restructuring the safety system is a case in point. The Rogers Commission made a number of recommendations for establishing more effective and independent safety programs. NASA complied within the letter of the recommendations but did not develop solutions beyond minimum compliance, suggesting that agency officials were not themselves convinced of the need for the changes or that they were unable to satisfy themselves that the proffered solutions were acceptable.

For example, the Rogers Commission recommended that the safety systems be centralized, reorganized, and given separate budget lines:

> NASA should establish an Office of Safety, Reliability and Quality Assurance to be headed by an Associate administrator, reporting directly to the NASA Administrator. . . . The office should be assigned the work force to ensure adequate oversight of its functions and should be independent of other NASA functional and program responsibilities. (Rogers Commission 1986, 199)

NASA complied, but only up to a point. The new safety office was created with a separate budget line, but only at headquarters. The offices at the centers, close to the action, were still tied to center directors and budgets. Later, when safety monitoring was contracted out to United Space Alliance, the independence of the overall safety function became again questionable.

The Rogers Commission also recommended that intercenter rivalries be dampened by having the Marshall shuttle projects director report to a headquarters official in the role of deputy director for shuttle projects. This would take the Marshall managers out of the Johnson center's line of authority and relieve turf struggles. But again, this change was only partly carried out and quickly scrubbed. The headquarters official was stationed at Johnson, and by 1996 the responsibility for shuttle program management was transferred back to the Johnson Space Center director, re-establishing the old problem. The separation of safety management to ensure the independence of safety personnel was similarly compromised by that change so that the Johnson program director became the safety representative for the center, the shuttle program office, and headquarters.

Part of the problem with learning from the recommendations of the Rogers Commission may have been that they were, in essence, imposed on NASA: NASA

was required to adopt the changes and the agency's progress in implementing the recommendations was monitored. True learning, as noted in chapter 2, requires some kind of cognitive change on the part of the learners, not just adaptation to necessity. Vicarious learning, in which lessons based on the experience of others are observed and adopted, still requires cognitive change. Though notoriously difficult to observe, this kind of change is not consistent with the half-hearted efforts just described. The question then becomes whether the managers really accepted the recommendations as valid inferences from the past results. Did at least some managers embrace error and change their minds about how to manage the shuttle enterprise? We take up in detail such questions about the motives and beliefs of NASA managers in later chapters as we explore the leadership and culture of the organization, but the case so far suggests some reluctance to fully adopt the Rogers Commission recommendations and undertake large-scale changes in the chain of command and the safety-information systems. That is, NASA managers did not engage in turnaround or double-loop learning about the overall organizational structure or the design and staffing of safety offices.

Lessons Espoused but Not Institutionalized

A second pattern of learning failure in the aftermath of the *Challenger* accident was that some of the recommendations of the Rogers Commission were adopted and agreed to in principle but could not be institutionalized. These recommendations were genuinely embraced by NASA, and managers both agreed with the ideas proposed and themselves worked to elaborate them with further analysis and solutions. However, the organization was unsuccessful in implementing these changes because of resource constraints or because of its own robust, well-institutionalized, but incompatible structural and cultural features. For example, efforts to establish an open-door management policy for reporting safety concerns ran into the entrenched cultural belief that reporting on perceived safety issues indicated poor performance or a lack of proper solidarity (GAO 1996, 20).

For example, the Rogers Commission recommended that NASA's new safety organization document and report "problems, problem resolution and trends associated with flight safety" (Rogers Commission 1986, 199). This recommendation was acknowledged by NASA in the *Rogers Commission Implementation Report* in 1987 but it was never fully implemented. The Lessons Learned Information System also seems to have run into problems with resources, entrenched rivalries among centers, software problems, and lack of participation by staff with other priorities. Stove-piped data systems could not easily be integrated.

Plans to establish an intercenter problem-reporting database with common data elements (Rogers Commission 1987, 49) and to centralize and disseminate information on safety procedures agency-wide were not in place when administrators were struggling to find ways to collect images of the wing.

By 2001, NASA's own Office of Inspector General had identified a number of problems with safety-information tracking systems:

> NASA's OIG has reported that safety and mission assurance has become a serious challenge for NASA. Key considerations to ensure safety in future NASA operations include (1) ensuring an appropriate level of training for staff who conduct safety reviews and evaluations; (2) maintaining adequate safety reporting systems; (3) ensuring variances to standard safety procedures are appropriately justified, reviewed, and approved; (4) maintaining an effective emergency preparedness program; (5) ensuring NASA and contractor compliance with safety standards and regulations; (6) ensuring product safety and reliability; and (7) ensuring the space shuttle and the ISS maintain crew safety. (GAO 2001b, 17)

New, willingly learned lessons could not be institutionalized without unlearning the painful post-Apollo lessons about how to survive on lean budgets and threats of center retrenchment. For example, it appears that the return to decentralized program structures in the period between the accidents contributed to the uncertainty and confusion about reporting safety information as new procedures imperfectly meshed with older, entrenched ones (CAIB, 187). In other cases, it appears that the recommended changes were agreed to but not actually or fully implemented.

Lessons Forgotten or Unlearned

Some genuinely learned and institutionalized changes did emerge but for reasons to be explored in subsequent chapters, they were either forgotten or unlearned. That is, they were unintentionally displaced by reorganizations, downsizing, or the latest crisis, or they were intentionally supplanted by new management strategies. For example, post-*Challenger* efforts to create an integrated problem-tracking system and establish procedural knowledge about crisis response were at least in part casualties of multiple reorganizations and downsizing. Known safety routines were inadvertently obscured, complicating efforts to get images of the *Columbia*'s wing. Knowledge and institutional memory had been lost.

In contrast, some successful lessons were unlearned. NASA seemed to have engaged in a classic learning scenario when it brought in the successful Apollo

program director to head up the redesign of the agency and when explicit reference was made to returning to that program structure. This design moved the
agency to a relatively centralized structure but it retreated from this change with
the advent of streamlined organizational designs in the 1990s. It does not appear
that new indigenous lessons or inferences about how to better achieve program
goals replaced *Challenger*'s lesson about the need for centralization. Rather,
structural lessons were unlearned or displaced by the new administrator's project
priorities and the new government-wide reforms for doing more with less. The
sources of these new ideas are the particular subject of chapter 5, the outside
forces that influenced NASA, and chapter 6, NASA's culture.

In sum, the *Challenger* accident did not lead to the adoption and institutionalization of many valuable lessons about the design of management structures,
information processing about threats to safety, or monitoring systems to prevent
the recurrence of many of the flaws that caused the accident. The shuttle program did not learn these lessons in part because the character of the information-
processing problems themselves blocked the capacity of NASA to learn in the
short term or in the longer interval between the accidents. But key shuttle program managers also failed at crucial points to pursue information about threats
to safety. This pattern, seen before the *Challenger* accident, was repeated in the
short and long term before the loss of the *Columbia*. Pressures on program staff
to maintain the shuttle launch schedule and the cultures and subcultures of the
centers also contributed to these failures. We turn now to how increased reliance
on contractors may have magnified the problems in constructing and maintaining effective information systems for safety.

CHAPTER 4

Contractor Relations

THE SHUTTLE PROGRAM is the result of the contributions of a large number of contractors who design, construct, and maintain its components. In this chapter we investigate what part the heavy reliance on contractors and the complexity of synchronizing and communicating with numerous contractors might have played in the accidents. More to the point, might the fact that so many portions of the shuttle project were in the hands of contractors, which are separate organizations with different pressures and motivations, have inhibited NASA's capacity to monitor and correct the flaws that caused the accidents? Learning in this case would mean figuring out how to manage contracts to overcome problems with communication and coordination. The key questions here are these: Did lessons about how to manage contracts emerge from the *Challenger* investigations? Were these lessons still in evidence at the time of the *Columbia*?

Various past incidents arising from contractor relationships provide some reason to suspect that NASA's contract-management capacities may have played a role in the shuttle accidents. Flaws, for example, in one of the Hubble Space Telescope's mirrors that diminished the clarity of its images and required a later, elaborate in-space fix, were directly linked to imperfect grinding by the contractor, Perkin-Elmer Corporation, and went undetected by NASA until after launch. It was unclear who was responsible for the prelaunch failure to test the assembly: The university contractors who were in charge of the mirror assembly assumed that Marshall was overseeing testing of the primary mirror (Levine 1992).

More recently, in 1999, NASA lost the Mars climate orbiter, which was designed to scout the terrain and relay messages from the Mars polar lander to Earth. The orbiter crashed into Mars "because of poor management, inadequate staffing, and the failure of the prime contractor, Lockheed Martin Astronautics, to convert critical navigation data from English units into metric as specified in its contract" (Naeye 2000, 24). Three months later, the $165 million lander was due to touch down on Mars but was never heard from. The causes of the lander's failure were investigated by an independent panel headed by Tom Young, a former Lockheed Martin manager, who specifically targeted NASA's "Jet Propulsion Laboratory (JPL) in Pasadena for failing to manage the last two Mars missions adequately, [and took] both NASA headquarters and Lockheed Martin to task for their respective roles in the botched orbiter and lander projects" (Lawler 2000a, 32). In 2001 the delicate *Genesis* space probe designed to sample solar wind atoms crashed in the Utah desert (Malik 2004). The mishap investigation board inquiring into the crash traced it to a flaw in the deployment of parachutes and parafoils that might have been detected by the contractor. But Lockheed Martin skipped a preflight procedure, opting for a simpler test (Associated Press 2006). NASA's own independent review of contractor relations, the Kraft Report released in February of 1995, was very critical of contract management: "Many inefficiencies and difficulties in the current shuttle program can be attributed to the diffuse and fragmented NASA and contractor structure" (NASA 1995, 8).

The GAO had also been critical of NASA's systems for managing contracts and acquisitions at least since 1990. It noted, "there was little emphasis on end results, product performance, and cost control; the acquisition process itself was awkward and time-consuming; and NASA found itself procuring expensive hardware that did not work properly" (GAO 2001a, 7). In 2000 NASA implemented its third attempt at a new, integrated contract-management system. But GAO found that serious problems with integrating contract requirements remained. The GAO report took care to point out that when "building a system from commercial components, it is essential to understand the characteristics and credentials of each component to select ones that are compatible and can be integrated without having to build and maintain expensive interfaces" (GAO 2003, 3). GAO also found that the new system for tracking the details of budgets and contractors' actual cost data as implemented ignored the needs of NASA's own program managers:

> According to . . . program officials, they chose to defer certain system capabilities and related user requirements in order to expedite implementation of the core financial module. As a result, program managers and cost estimators told us that they will not rely on the core financial module and instead will continue to rely on other systems or use other labor-intensive means to capture the data they need to manage programs such as the International Space Station. (2003, 4)

Students of public management have also been suspicious of problems with organizational feedback and learning in the current climate of outsourcing. Kettl (1994) argues that when services are contracted out, critical information about the workability of programs is imperfectly passed on to the contracting agency.

Public agencies are, in effect, cut off from direct experience with the programs, and the contractors who are experiencing program effects do not have the authority to make program or policy changes. In addition, there is the problem of perverse incentives. It may be too much to expect that a contractor, whose continued funding or profitability depends on successful service, will report problems at the level of detail or with the interest in longer-term outcomes that actors in the agency themselves might do.]

So for both historical and theoretical reasons, we might expect that the reliance on contractors for many shuttle components and services might have both contributed to the loss of the shuttles and made learning more difficult. We first investigate the *Challenger* case to determine how poor contract management contributed to the accident and what changes were instituted afterward to deal with identified flaws. We then examine the *Columbia* case to determine if the same problems with contract management appeared.

NASA–CONTRACTOR RELATIONS

NASA has always relied on contractors, early on for hardware and propulsion systems and more recently for operational services for the shuttle as well. Even before 1958, when NASA was created from the National Advisory Committee for Aeronautics, contract engineers and scientists in the aeronautics and aerospace industry have been essential to the agency's workforce. Early administrators favored contracting as a conservative management strategy to avoid increasing the size of government and to create a viable space technology industry (Bromberg 1999, 40). Contracting has also been a political resource for NASA, offering a way to garner congressional support when contracts are awarded to firms in key states. A map of NASA contracts in 2003, for example, shows that the agency boosts the economy in every state, from a low of $1.3 million in South Dakota and Montana to a high of $3.79 billion in Texas (Wikipedia, NASA budget). On occasion, the political ties between some firms, Congress, and NASA officials may have influenced the selection of one contractor over another. NASA administrator James Fletcher from Utah was the center of controversy when NASA awarded the solid rocket booster contract to Thiokol, also from Utah (Dunar and Waring 1999, 219). These kinds of ties also made large contractors into stakeholders with influence and leverage in their own right. NASA and the military needed them. They could "push back."

The dependency of NASA on contractors has grown in recent decades so that by the time of the *Columbia* accident over 90 percent of the shuttle workforce were contract employees (CAIB, 106). Contract personnel were directly involved in the events surrounding both accidents and were among the first to express concern about the shuttle program elements that destroyed both the *Challenger* and the *Columbia.* After the *Challenger* disaster, the Rogers Commission uncovered disagreements between contractors and NASA officials over how information about the reliability of the seals in cold weather had been clearly conveyed from Thiokol, the contractors for solid booster rockets, to NASA managers. The Columbia Accident Investigation Board reports that warnings and concerns of lower-level contract engineers about the need for in-flight images to determine the damage from foam debris were not heeded.

By 1986, the Marshall Space Flight Center in Huntsville, Alabama, managed the contracts with Thiokol in Utah for the solid rocket boosters and solid rocket booster motors, and the contract with Martin Marietta Denver Aerospace in Michoud, Louisiana, for the external tank. The Kennedy Space Center in Florida managed the contracts for shuttle-launch processing, and the Johnson Space Center in Houston managed the contracts for the orbiter. The engineers and managers in the contracting organizations formed Level IV in the flight-readiness-review hierarchy described in the previous chapter.

Relations between Marshall's managers and its contractors were often difficult. In the 1960s and '70s a number of episodes raised suspicions about contractors. Since the early 1960s, NASA had practiced what is called "penetration," whereby agency engineers were permanently stationed in contract facilities to monitor quality and costs. With increased downsizing and reductions in force in the late 1960s, however, NASA lost some of its capacity to oversee contractor performance. Nevertheless, by 1978 Marshall was still assigning three shifts of its own engineers to the Thiokol facility to monitor operations. The NASA engineers identified twenty-six incidents leading to damaged components and other problems with quality control in 1977 and '78, and Marshall blamed Thiokol management for the problems. Marshall was also critical of work by Martin Marietta and McDonnell Douglass on account of work errors, cost overruns, and schedule delays (Dunar and Waring 1999, 311). For their part contractors viewed Marshall's oversight stance as overly critical, leading managers at all of the contractor facilities to become reluctant to report problems to their overseers (311).

CONTRACTOR RELATIONS IN THE *CHALLENGER* ACCIDENT

Thiokol conducted the lowest-level flight-readiness review of the solid rocket booster for the fatal *Challenger* flight, making a presentation to NASA managers at the Marshall center on December 11, 1985. They also participated in the presentation to the next level of NASA managers at the Solid Rocket Motor Booster Project Office at Marshall a week later. After that, in the six-week run-up to the launch, six more reviews were conducted at successively higher levels in NASA, ending with the signing of the flight readiness certificate.

[Long before this final review process, however, as early as 1977, test findings led a pair of NASA engineers to call for immediate attention to the potential for hot gas leaks between segments of the solid rocket boosters from the rotation or twisting of the joints. The engineers argued that Thiokol was lowering the technical requirements for the seals, but managers at both NASA and Thiokol rejected these claims](Dunar and Waring 1999, 345), observing that Thiokol was the expert in solid-rocket technology while Marshall's work had been almost exclusively with liquid propellants. By 1982, NASA managers came to agree with their own engineers about the need to redesign the seal, but as noted in chapter 3, still believed the joint to be safe (Dunar and Waring 1999, 352).

Thiokol first denied that the early tests had revealed inherent flaws that would oblige them to undertake a costly redesign of the seal (Dunar and Waring 1999, 344; Rogers Commission 1986, 84). NASA, however, insisted that they wanted further tests as more launch experience demonstrated O-ring charring and seal erosion. Roger Boisjoly, a Thiokol expert on the joint seal, wrote a memo also expressing concern about test results and predicted that "NASA might give the motor contract to a competitor or there might be a flight failure if Thiokol did not come up with a timely solution" (Rogers Commission 1986, 139). He convinced the firm to set up an O-ring task force to recommend short- and long-term solutions (139). But the team made little progress, and internal memos from Boisjoly complain about administrative delays and obstruction in getting cooperation with Thiokol divisions that had other priorities. NASA, too, complained about the slow pace (141).

Meanwhile, Thiokol engineers assembled more information about the O-ring erosion and charring. Their data were used to determine that the seal mechanisms were no longer officially considered redundant because the secondary seal was not reliable. Thiokol engineers had also assembled laboratory data on the relationship between cold temperatures and the resiliency of the seal, and it used these data to brief Marshall and Level III officials in February 1985. As noted in the previous chapter, in August 1985, the erosion problems with the seals were presented at a meeting of Level 1 and Level III shuttle managers by NASA officials from the solid rocket booster program and the Thiokol seal experts. All of the later external investigators of the accident agree that this information was available across the organization (Rogers Commission 1986, 148; Dunar and Waring 1999, 349).

However, disagreement surfaced in testimony before the Rogers Commission about how clear Thiokol engineers had been about the connections between cold temperatures and the resiliency of the O-ring seal, and it does not appear that the laboratory data were included in the August 1985 briefing documents (Rogers Commission 1986, 158). Roger Boisjoly, the Thiokol engineer who made the presentation and who had been a member of the solid rocket booster seal task force, however, argued that in at least one of the charts he had prepared for the briefing, the connection was clearly made (Rogers Commission 1986, 88–89).

Perverse Incentives: The Eve of the Challenger *Liftoff*

The case was certainly made in the teleconference with NASA managers from Marshall and Kennedy and the Thiokol engineers and managers on January 27, 1986, the day before the *Challenger* launch. Boisjoly and his colleague Arnie Thompson expressed serious reservations about the launch based on the continued cold weather at the Cape. At past launches in cold weather, temperatures had moderated by launch time. Boisjoly reported that he and Thompson had been successful in convincing the other Thiokol engineers and managers of the problem. Bob Lund, who was a Thiokol vice president and director of engineering, summarized the findings with a recommendation that the *Challenger* not launch the next day because the O-ring temperatures predicted at launch time would be lower than on previous launches, that is, below 53 degrees Fahrenheit (Rogers Commission 1986, 91). He said, "Gee, you know, we just don't know how much further we can go below the 51·or 53 degrees or whatever it was. So we were concerned with the unknown" (94). No one at this Thiokol meeting recommended launch. Boisjoly later testified, "There was never one positive, pro-launch statement ever made by anybody" (90).

But as we saw in chapter 3, NASA managers resisted this conclusion. George Hardy, deputy director of science and engineering, the safety organization at Marshall, said he was "appalled" at Thiokol's decision because it would cause delays (90), but he said he would not support a launch against Thiokol's recommendations. Lawrence Mulloy, manager of the solid rocket booster project at Marshall, was at Kennedy Space Center for the launch. He was obviously unhappy, and said he feared Thiokol was trying to "generate a new Launch Commit Criteria on the eve of launch" (96).

The arguments that Marshall shuttle managers used to resist another shuttle-launch delay were that there were, in effect, margins of safety in the seals because they had withstood erosion in the past. Mulloy later testified, "My assessment at that time was that we would have an effective simplex seal, based upon the engineering data that Thiokol had presented, and that none of those engineering data seemed to change that basic rationale" (Rogers Commission 1986, 91). In addition, they had seen erosion in both cold and warm temperatures. Unnoted were the larger number of instances of warm-weather launches where no erosion was found. But all this ignored the fact, clearly articulated by Richard Feynman in an appendix to the Rogers Commission report, that there was no margin of safety. "O-rings of the Solid Rocket Boosters were not designed to erode. Erosion was a clue that something was wrong. Erosion was not something from which safety could be inferred" (Rogers Commission 1986, vol. 2, F-2, 2).

At this point, one of the Thiokol managers, Joe Kilminster, who was vice president for space booster programs at Wasatch, Utah, called for a caucus of Thiokol staff "off the loop" (Rogers Commission 1986, 93). It was after this meeting that Thiokol management changed its position.

The dynamics of the thirty-minute caucus are instructive. It opened with a statement by Jerald Mason, the senior vice president for Thiokol in Utah, who said that because the matter boiled down to a judgment call, a management decision was required (Rogers Commission 1986, 92). Bob Lund, who earlier supported a launch delay, testified that he was asked by Mason "to take off his engineering hat and put on his management hat" (94). But Roger Boisjoly and Arnie Thompson continued to argue for a delay: "I tried one more time with the photos," Boisjoly recalled. "I grabbed the photos, and I went up and discussed the photos once again and tried to make the point that . . . temperature was indeed a discriminator and we should not ignore the physical evidence" (92). As the meeting progressed, however, the consensus shifted to support Mason and the other managers in recommending launch. None of the other Thiokol managers maintained their support for delaying the launch.

The Rogers Commission reports, "At approximately 11 p.m. Eastern Standard Time, the Thiokol/NASA teleconference resumed, the Thiokol management stating that they had reassessed the problem, that the temperature effects were a concern, but that the data were admittedly inconclusive" (Rogers Commission 1986, 96). Kilminster formally released the Thiokol recommendation to launch.

Thiokol engineers said afterward that the decision had already been made by management, and that the normal burden of proof to demonstrate safety was, in this case, reversed so that they were being asked to prove conclusively that the launch was *not* safe. According to Lund,

> I guess I had never had those kinds of things come from the people at Marshall. We had to prove to them that we weren't ready, and so we got ourselves in the

> thought process that we were trying to find some way to prove to them it wouldn't work, and we were unable to do that. We couldn't prove absolutely that that motor wouldn't work." (Rogers Commission 1986, 94)

Boisjoly also testified:

> Mr. Mason said we have to make a management decision. . . . From this point on, management formulated the points to base their decision on. There was never one comment in favor, as I have said, of launching by any engineer or other non-management person in the room before or after the caucus. I was not even asked to participate in giving any input to the final decision charts. (92–93)

Lawrence Mulloy, who was NASA's manager of the solid rocket booster at Marshall, insisted that there was no management pressure and Thiokol had just wanted time to discuss the comments he and Hardy had made earlier (95).

SHORT-TERM LEARNING ABOUT CONTRACTOR MANAGEMENT

Several questions arise at this point. Why did the Thiokol managers accede to NASA management's urgings? And why did Thiokol not act sooner to investigate and resolve the seal-erosion issues? We must also ask why NASA managers resisted Thiokol's original advice on the eve of the launch. It is puzzling that no indications of learning by the participants emerge from the early indications of problems with the seals.

First, Thiokol managers were clearly daunted by NASA management's reaction to their cautions about the launch. Mulloy's rejection of each of the arguments offered by the engineers about the dangers of the launch left Thiokol managers without a rationale NASA would accept for refusing to fulfill their contract. Only with heroic self-sacrifice could they be expected to face the consequences of refusing their employer's requirements. The Rogers Commission, in fact, offers as its fourth conclusion about the contributing organizational causes of the accident this statement: "The Commission concluded that the Thiokol Management reversed its position and recommended the launch of 51-L, at the urging of Marshall and contrary to the views of its engineers *in order to accommodate a major customer*"(Rogers Commission 1986, 104, emphasis added).

However, there was also a reluctance on Thiokol's part early on to make changes to the seal. A redesign would have taken time and could have led to delays. Pertinently, the contract specifications under which Thiokol operated provided no incentives to fix problems that were unlikely to significantly affect the mission; at the same time, the contract rewarded on-time delivery with incentive fees worth up to 14 percent of the value of the contract (Dunar and Waring 1999, 365) so that delays for redesign were costly. The report of Thiokol's seal task force still was not available at the time of the accident. Robert Ebeling, a Thiokol manager overseeing the project, said the seal task force was "constantly being delayed by every possible means" and "Marshall Space Flight Center is correct in stating that we do not know how to run a development program" (Rogers Commission 1986, 141). Being unresponsive to the seal issues could also be costly, however, as Boisjoly feared.

The next question is perhaps harder to answer. Why did NASA not make better use of its contractor's expert information? Thiokol engineers were not in the chain of command, and if NASA chose to downplay their warnings, it could. That the information needed to monitor performance depended on reporting from the contractor who had incentives to present positive results is one of the circumstances that makes learning through contractors particularly difficult. The more typical situation is that contractors are unwilling to provide performance information in order to maximize their autonomy as agents, and this may have been the case earlier as Thiokol chose not to redesign the seal. In the end, however, the situation appears to have been reversed: The contractor had information that the principal appears to have been reluctant to accept.

Thiokol engineers had collected data on precisely the problem at hand, launch in cold temperature. A year before the accident, they had put together charts showing the relatively greater chance of serious erosion in cold temperatures, but this information, presented at reviews at every level in the months prior to the launch, was not factored into decisions about launch readiness.

Several factors appear to explain NASA's, especially Marshall's, decisions. First, program managers believed that the seals, though flawed, were safe. While this assessment appears highly questionable in hindsight, it seems to have been the consensus at the time. As noted in chapter 3, NASA managers were encouraged in this assessment by internal rivalries, defects in incident-tracking and safety systems, and external pressures to increase the rate of launch. We will examine NASA's motivations in pushing the schedule ahead for launch in the chapters that follow, but it is clear that whatever the agency's motives, warnings by contract engineers in the months and days before the launch were not given high priority.

All of this compromised short-term, single-loop learning. We saw in the last chapter that NASA's own problem-tracking systems were flawed, but the dependent position of the contractors and their willingness to alter their recommendations based on what NASA managers wanted to hear made it easier for these managers to ignore the early results about the charring and erosion of seals. NASA management's ability to control contractor recommendations allowed managers to insulate themselves from the results of bench tests and postflight reviews, making it less likely they would openly confront problems and seek solutions. They did not take these warnings seriously, did not acknowledge the gravity of the erosion problem, and did not make the analysis of how to prevent erosion a high priority. Neither the managers at Thiokol nor those at NASA were willing to openly acknowledge the problems and make the search for new solutions a high priority.

AFTER THE *CHALLENGER*: LEARNING ABOUT CONTRACT MANAGEMENT

The management reforms that followed the *Challenger* accident, as noted in the last chapter, focused on restructuring the agency and establishing more independent and authoritative safety reviews. Other changes addressed the issue of contractor independence. Did NASA learn to insulate contractors from undue pressure and improve its willingness to hear contract-engineer concerns? If the front-line experience of agency members is not sought out (or, even worse, is actively repressed), the feedback that makes learning possible will be lost. Any attempt to learn from the past, compare results, and explore promising cause–effect inferences builds on just this kind of information.

The Rogers Commission concluded that the contractors were, in fact, reluctant to report problems that might delay the launch. Incentives built into contracts discouraged time-consuming data collection, analysis, and the kind of reflection upon which new inferences about cause and effect may arise. Motivation problems judged to lie behind shoddy work and errors in shuttle preparations were tracked in turn to other lapses, including the absence of an error-forgiveness policy that might have encouraged reports of problems. A 1988 report titled *Lessons Learned from Challenger*, commissioned by the Office of Safety, Reliability, Maintainability and Quality Assurance, was very critical of the lack of protection for contractors from reprisals for reporting errors or safety violations (NASA 1988). The report further notes:

The fear that punishment will result from an employee reporting a problem, as well as all other obstacles to proper problem reporting, must be minimized. NASA must encourage its contractors to devise effective policies for forgiving or mitigating truly accidental damage. All operations and assurance personnel must understand that their contributions are vital to a safe and successful program. Problem reporting and good procedural discipline must be rewarded. (NASA 1988, 56)

In response to the Rogers Commission report and the *Lessons Learned* report, NASA adopted several changes that were designed to make contractors more willing to report problems and to improve the flow of information between the agency and its contractors. The mission management team responsible for the shuttle from just before launch to the end of mission would now include project managers from the major contractors. This team would have the power to stop the countdown (Dunar and Waring 1999, 418). New contracting rules included incentive and performance criteria for mission safety as well as on-time work. Explicit attention was paid to designing a new safety- and quality-assurance program to include oversight into the safety practices of contractors. Additional staff were to be placed at large contractor facilities to monitor safety (Rogers Commission 1986, 48). The "penetration" system of earlier periods at Marshall gained staff, and a resident quality office was established at the Thiokol facility in Utah (Dunar and Waring 1999, 414). These changes show NASA looking back to earlier practices and forward to new techniques for improving the information flow with contractors.

Other changes were made to directly address the issues in the overall shuttle-program structure and in the procedures for safety reviews. As noted in the last chapter, safety offices were moved outside the offices of the program component they were to oversee. They were relocated as separate center organizations that gave them greater visibility and autonomy. For contractors, this change meant that their concerns would be heard by officials who were not their managers or supervisors in the contract relationship. Contractors were encouraged to enter information in a new agency-wide, standardized mishap-reporting and corrective-action system, but special provision was also made to insulate contractors from reprisals for reporting problems. In its implementation of actions after the *Challenger*, NASA described a supplemental safety-information channel created to allow contractors to

communicate safety concerns to an independent agent when, in their opinions, standard reporting channels lack the proper degree of response to a critical problem. This system, patterned after the FAA's aviation safety reporting system, is not intended to replace normal management channels for reporting hazards or safety concerns. (Rogers Commission 1986, 50)

These changes should have given the contract firms more independence to report bad news on the safety front. Though the Rogers Commission did not make detailed recommendations for changes in contract management *per se,* it did require NASA to create an independent safety program that would insulate contractors. These would seem to be reasonable solutions for at least some of the problems with contract management. They are based on an explicit analysis of the flaws of the previous management of contractor relations, and they appear to indicate that learning has occurred. They were built in part upon vicarious experience, a best practice developed at the FAA to cope with similar problems with error reporting by pilots.

Because of the *Columbia* accident, however, we must ask whether these recommendations were in fact fully institutionalized and whether they were still in place at the time of the *Columbia.*

CONTRACT MANAGEMENT BEFORE THE *COLUMBIA* ACCIDENT

NASA's reliance on contractors was even greater in 2003 than it had been in 1986. Yet both the number of civil service employees at NASA and the number of contract workers had shrunk under relentless budget pressures and downsizing strategies of Administrator Goldin, taken up in detail in the next chapter. Goldin used these budget constraints to undertake other major changes in program structures and to begin the development of long-term projects, including the replacement of the shuttle technology (Lambright 2001, 9). Under his policy of "faster, better, cheaper" and inspired by his past success with TQM and the government reinvention strategies supported by the Clinton–Gore administration, NASA's total workforce had gone from just over 30,000 in 1993 to 17,462 in 2002 (CAIB, 106). By 2002 only 1,718 members of the shuttle workforce were NASA civil service employees, and the proportion of the workforce that worked under contract rose from 87 percent to just over 90 percent.

Ten years after the *Challenger* accident, critics inside and outside NASA were demanding cost containment and management streamlining. In 1995, NASA commissioned the Space Shuttle Independent Review Team, composed of aerospace executives, former astronauts, and former NASA executives, to examine 's management structure and, particularly, its relationships with its contractors. Most of the team's conclusions, including a recommendation to assemble multiple contracts and subcontracts under one "business entity," were adopted. The review team's report, commonly referred to as the Kraft Report, viewed the increasing reliance on contractors as inevitable but not without pitfalls, among those the loss of internal expertise and prestige. According to the team, "One highly regarded NASA scientist recently put it this way: 'People used to come to NASA for information, now they come for a contract'" (NASA 1995, 10). The report did, however, also support the next major change in the contract environment at NASA: the consolidation of contracts and subcontracts to reduce the number of "NASA-contractor interfaces" and simplify program management (11).

In all, NASA moved from a series of eighty-six separate agreements with as many as fifty-six firms to one major contract with the United Space Alliance (USA), created by Boeing and Lockheed Martin (CAIB, 107). In 1996, USA was awarded a sole source agreement to conduct the day-to-day operation of the shuttle program (107–8). The contract gave USA responsibility for shuttle hardware, mission design and planning, crew training, software design, flight operations, and facility maintenance (109). The contract was performance-based and offered incentives to USA for cost reductions. Performance was to be evaluated on "safety, launch readiness, on-time launch, solid rocket booster recovery, proper orbital insertion, and successful landing" (109). Renewed and revised many times, the original contract ran out in 2006. A new, final contract was implemented in October of that year to run through the planned retirement of the shuttle in 2010 and established "USA as NASA's primary industry partner in human space operations, including the Space Shuttle and the International Space Station" (United Space Alliance 2006).

The contract also gave added responsibilities to USA for safety inspections, requiring the contractor to meet a "series of safety gates" (CAIB, 108). NASA retained ownership of the shuttles and their launch components and was still in charge of safety procedures, performance audits, and "commit to flight" decisions (109). But the change in contract responsibilities had the effect of distancing NASA from safety information. NASA now had only "insight" into safety through a system of reviews and "metrics" provided by contractors (179). According to the Columbia Accident Investigation Board, "Collectively, this eroded NASA's in-house engineering and technical capabilities and increased the agency's reliance on the United Space Alliance and its subcontractors to identify, track, and resolve problems" (CAIB, 179).

The object of consolidating contracts was to reduce overhead and inefficiencies "attributed to the diffuse and fragmented NASA and contractor structure . . . [with] ambiguous lines of communication and diffused responsibilities" (NASA 1995, 11). The same NASA-commissioned analysis criticized the existing safety system as "duplicative and expensive" (10). It claimed that the safety, reliability, and quality-assurance effort had become overgrown after *Challenger* and now stifled innovation and decisions involving risk. "Indeed," the report ran, "the system used today may make the vehicle less safe because of the lack of individual responsibility it brings about" (10). The Kraft Report recommended that safety monitoring be restructured "to minimize parallelism and delegate greater responsibility to the contractor . . . to establish clear lines of responsibility with only the necessary checks and balances in place" (NASA 1995, 18–19).

The *Columbia* accident investigators later noted that these new contracting arrangements created structural constraints that "hindered effective communication" (CAIB, 182) and created a complex system of joint review and oversight that complicated the task of supervising contractors. The new contract made NASA decision makers more dependent on contractors for technical expertise (179), and, as noted earlier, because of the rollback of many safety checkpoints, it made the safety system "simultaneously weaker and more complex" (179). The contracts created a demand for "better communication practices" (179) that was not met. Best practices seen in other high-risk programs, such as the Navy's nuclear submarine programs, require that contractor recommendations be independent and peer-reviewed, a pattern at odds with the way contractor reports were handled at NASA (182). In contrast, the shuttle program essentially bought the safety services under contracts with the centers, decentralizing the safety systems and making the safety experts dependent on the continued viability and funding of the shuttle program (186). A study by the General Accounting Office, as it was then called, conducted in 1993 also characterized NASA management as decentralized, a reversal of the earlier lesson learned after *Challenger* about the value of centralization. It further noted that NASA's centers had "considerable latitude in many areas, including the award and administration of almost all of the agency's contracts. For this approach to be effective, headquarters must set clear expectations and carefully monitor and measure the centers' management of their own activities, as well as those of NASA's contractors" (GAO 1994, 14). All of these changes reduced the level of contact and interface between NASA managers and contractors, further limiting their ability to communicate their concerns.

At the end of the Clinton administration, agency officials considered taking contracting further to privatize the shuttle operation entirely. Shuttle Program

Manager Dittemore argued for privatization, noting that merging the "skills bases" was necessary if the shuttle was to remain "safe and viable"(CAIB, 109). But some NASA personnel objected to the downsizing and shift of responsibility within the agency. A senior Kennedy center engineer wrote to the president in 1995 that the shrinking of the NASA civil service force threatened safety and that the long-standing use of two teams of engineers—NASA's and contractors'—was necessary to "cross check each other and prevent catastrophic errors." He also claimed that only a hidden agenda or fear of job loss deterred others from saying so, too (108). The director of the Kennedy Space Center threatened to resign over personnel cuts he considered too deep, and both internal and external studies convinced top NASA officials to halt the cuts and hire several hundred more workers (110).

Some positive developments in creating richer communication pathways between NASA and its contract workers did, however, emerge. A GAO study of communications in the shuttle program in 1996, after the consolidation of the contracts, finds two important changes that derived directly from findings about the management of contractors before the *Challenger* accident. Relying on focus groups, GAO researchers reported: "One manager noted that the *Challenger* accident prompted a change in his contractor's management approach. Before the accident, company meetings were closed to the NASA site representatives. Since the accident, NASA representatives attend all technical meetings" (GAO 1996, 20).

In addition, efforts were made to induce contractors to be more forthcoming about reporting safety issues on their own. The purpose was to address the concerns expressed in the 1988 report for the Office of Safety, Reliability, Maintainability and Quality Assurance (NASA 1988). These changes were also part of a larger attempt at culture change covered in chapter 6. Working engineers in contract organizations noted that they were encouraged to report problems:

> For example, at one contractor facility, program teams are structured so that minority opinions about the handling of safety problems can be elevated to a higher level board. At another contractor facility, the work environment was described as one that encourages debate, discussion, and never keeping a safety concern quiet. At the third contractor plant, the formal reporting process ensures that NASA and contractor managers are continually apprised of issues, review how issues are resolved, and can request more work if they do not agree with the resolution of a safety issue. (GAO 1996, 21)

In sum, of the numerous post-*Challenger* changes in the design and functioning of the safety system, many targeted relations with contractors, including changes in flight-review procedures, monitoring of contractors, and contract cost provisions.

To implement one of the commission's recommendations, an official from the new safety organization, the Office of Safety, Reliability, Maintainability and Quality Assurance, was detailed to participate in revising contractor fee incentives so that work to improve safety was given higher priority (Rogers Commission 1987, 51; Dunar and Waring 1999, 410). To encourage contractors to report problems, they were given the option to report their concerns to safety offices outside the chain of command of the program offices whose decisions they were questioning (Rogers Commission 1987, 50). This last set of changes was not long-lived, however. By the mid-1990s, as noted in the previous chapter, under pressure for downsizing and streamlining, the real independence of the center-level safety offices had been eroded.

Other changes as well were designed to ensure more open and complete information sharing between contractors and NASA management. After *Challenger*, Marshall replaced site visits to contractor facilities with an on-site quality office at Thiokol's Utah facility (Dunar and Waring 1999, 414–15), a system used also in the earlier years of Saturn rocket development when the center had higher levels of personnel and funding (Dunar and Waring 1999, 44). We will see how these changes affected the ability of contractors to voice their concerns in the run-up to the *Columbia* accident. The role of contractors in the *Columbia* accident suggests that these changes were in some respects durable and effective.

Contractor Concerns about the Foam Strike

Contractors were important in the events that led to the loss of the *Columbia*. The external tank was manufactured by Lockheed Martin Space Systems at the Michoud assembly facility outside New Orleans under contracts managed at the Marshall Space Flight Center, and the major part of the foam insulation was installed there. As noted in the previous chapter, problems with foam shedding were well-known and had been seen in sixty-five of seventy-nine previous launches, including many from the same area of the external tank (CAIB, 122). In the flight prior to the *Columbia*, ST-112, particularly serious damage had been caused by foam debris. Though the formal shuttle specifications explicitly precluded debris shedding (122), the divots in the thermal tiles produced when foam pieces struck the shuttle had become so common that they were accepted by contractors and NASA engineers as problems of maintenance or "turnaround."

During the launch of the *Columbia*, the Intercenter Photo Working Group captured the blurred image of the foam strike and distributed it to a wide circle of NASA and contract personnel. As noted in chapter 3, it was a USA engineering manager who, observing this largest yet debris strike, classified it as "out of family" (CAIB, 143, 171), that is, an event outside the known performance range and experience (122). According to the CAIB, "In the case of the foam strike on STS-107 (*Columbia*), which was classified as out-of-family, clearly defined written guidance led United Space Alliance technical managers to liaise with their NASA counterparts" (142). Under NASA procedures designed to ensure coordination between NASA and its contractors, the classification of the foam strike event as out-of-family required NASA engineers to coordinate with contractors on the investigation, first as a debris assessment team, and then as a "tiger team" (142), cochaired by NASA and USA representatives. The assessment team was formed with members from both NASA and USA, but the group was never designated as a tiger team. The CAIB notes, "This left the debris assessment team in a kind of organizational limbo, with no guidance except the date by which Program managers expected to hear their results: January 24th" (142). In consequence, communication problems between this team, designated to pursue the problem, and the mission management team, which had the authority to order the necessary better imagery, plagued the rest of the flight, as noted in the previous chapter.

We begin to see at this point in the *Columbia* case the same kind of differences in level of concern between the managers and working engineers that had occurred in the *Challenger* case. Engineers from the Intercenter Photo Working Group thought the orbiter had sustained damage from the strike (CAIB, 142), while Ralph Roe, from NASA's Shuttle Office of Vehicle Engineering, and Bill Reeves, the USA manager, thought it unlikely that the strike threatened the safety of the flight. They planned to reconvene for a review of the evidence after the Martin Luther King weekend. But USA/Boeing contract engineers, without even encouragement from higher-level management, much less orders, worked through the holiday weekend on the analysis of the strike with their computer model for predicting tile damage, Crater. Unfortunately, the team of contract engineers at Johnson Space Center who performed the analysis was relatively new to the task, because the Boeing contract had just been shifted from California to Houston, and the transition was incomplete. This was the first mission to be undertaken by the engineers at Houston without the guidance of the more experienced analysts in the Huntington Beach facility (190). The CAIB said, "NASA failed to connect the dots: the engineers who misinterpreted Crater—a tool already unsuited to the task at hand—were the very ones the shuttle program identified as engendering the most risk in their transition from Huntington Beach" (190).

The debris assessment team did meet informally on Monday, cochaired by Pam Madera from USA and Rodney Rocha, NASA's designated engineer for the shuttle's thermal tile system. This meeting included an expanded list of participants, including tile experts from NASA and Boeing, and a representative from the safety contractor, Science Applications International. The composition of this group, particularly in its larger form, illustrates the efforts NASA made to foster communication and coordinated action between itself and its contractors. The meeting ended with an agreement that images of the wing were needed. As noted in the previous chapter, this and other requests were never granted. The formal and informal petitions from the group that had been assembled to look at the problem were dismissed for lack of concrete evidence of the severity of the strike damage. In examining the role of contractors, it is important to note that the requesters included, by design, both NASA and contractor employees.

The safety contractor Science Applications International agreed with the shuttle program managers and introduced little into the electronic safety log over the duration of the flight (CAIB, 166). Safety personnel, including both contract and NASA staff, were present but passive in the meetings of the debris assessment team, the mission evaluation room, and the mission management team (170). The safety contractors in the mission evaluation room "were only marginally aware of the debris strike analysis" (170). They deferred to shuttle program managers and failed to act as an "independent source of questions and challenges" (170). Having been told that the mission management team had classified the strike as an "in-family" event, they took their inquiries no further (153).

What we see in this summary of evidence about the role of contractors in the *Columbia* case is that engineers at the lower levels of both NASA and contractor hierarchies were typically more worried about the effects of the strike, more apprehensive about the limitations of their models and projections, and more concerned about the need for imagery than most (but not all) of the higher-level NASA project managers. The classification of the strike as out-of-family was initially made by a USA manager, and that classification was resisted by the NASA managers in the mission evaluation room and the mission management team. After that, various requests for images by both lower-level NASA and USA engineers were miscommunicated or misrouted and eventually turned down. In contrast to what occurred in the case of the *Challenger*, however, the fault line for information was not usually between contractors and NASA personnel, but between levels of NASA management. Resistance to investigating the size and location of the strike came from mission managers who were reluctant to question the rationale to launch and thus delay the next flight.

CONTRACTOR RELATIONS AND ORGANIZATIONAL LEARNING

The CAIB concluded that NASA was not a learning organization because of the similarities overall in the organizational patterns and management actions that led up to the two shuttle accidents. However, a comparison of the role of contractors and the course of contractor management in the accidents suggests that NASA did learn to avoid the agency–contractor communications and incentives problems that had emerged in the *Challenger* case. That is, there were some important similarities but also significant dissimilarities between the two cases in the relationship between contract engineers and managers. By 2003 better communication across NASA–contractor lines and written guidance for joint decision making in the case of an out-of-family event were in place. Not all of the guidance was followed, but the parts relating to the constitution of the debris assessment team did operate successfully.

The two accidents are similar, however, in that neither contractors nor NASA officials stopped the launches to remedy known problems that violated formal shuttle specifications. And in both cases, upper-level NASA managers disregarded the sometimes diffidently expressed concerns of both contract and NASA engineers during the flight. In neither case was critical information about safety fully and unambiguously communicated. Questions remain about whether Thiokol's graph communicated the pattern of cold-weather failure of the O-rings adequately to NASA managers on the eve of the *Challenger* launch. Similarly, in the *Columbia* case, the "viewgraph" slide meant to summarize the findings of the USA and Boeing engineers about *Columbia* tile damage failed to clearly convey the engineers' real uncertainties.

But it is also true that the decision makers to whom the engineers' reservations were, perhaps imperfectly, conveyed were not actively looking for evidence that could challenge the conclusions they had already drawn. The Rogers Commission found fault with the insularity of the Level III NASA administrators at the Marshall Space Flight Center and their unwillingness to pass along critical information (Rogers Commission 1986, 200). Similarly, the CAIB report noted several times that the *Columbia* project managers "resisted new information" and had determined that the foam strike did not pose a safety issue long before analysis began (CAIB, 181). It is also clear that oversight and support for the debris assessment team, which the mission management team should have provided, was missing. The effect of this neglect was to allow requests for imaging to go astray. These lapses in communication, however self-inflicted, also reduced the ability of the mission management team to detect the debris assessment team's real level of uncertainty. Furthermore, the contract organization assigned to monitor safety was largely absent from the scene. Only two comments on the foam strike situation, both minor, were lodged by this contractor (170).

Though the evidence seems to point to the contributory effects of poor contractor relations in the *Challenger* case, contractor management does not appear to have played a major role in the *Columbia* accident. Both USA and NASA engineers in the debris assessment team sought images, and both submitted to pressure to provide an estimate of damage that ignored uncertainties. Even if they had persisted in calling for images of the damaged wing, it is far from clear that upper-level program managers would have acceded to their request. Though the CAIB does not exonerate miscommunication across NASA–contractor lines in the *Columbia* accident, neither do they identify contractor relations effects as a significant cause.

LEARNING, UNLEARNING, AND FORGETTING

What does this tell us about whether NASA learned lessons from the *Challenger* accident about managing contractors? The answer, not surprisingly, varies depending on the lesson. First, some learning clearly did occur. Changes to coordinate contractor and agency crisis decision-making procedures and to share information more completely were made after the *Challenger* accident, and they were largely in place at the time of *Columbia*. These changes were invented and designed by NASA. They were not simply the recommendations of an outside body, and their institutionalization is reported in the post-*Challenger* implementation report issued in 1987. Furthermore, we see them in place during the *Columbia* crisis. Thus they appear to meet the requirements for a learned response.

After *Challenger*, contractor incentives and communications issues had been addressed. NASA did change structures and procedures based on past events. The debris assessment team and the mission evaluation room both were staffed by a combination of NASA and USA personnel. The debris assessment team was cochaired by Pam Madera from USA and Rodney Rocha from NASA. Though there were still incentives for cost-cutting and on-time performance in the new

USA contract structure, we do not see the USA management resisting imaging in the *Columbia* case. The communications problems that emerged during the *Columbia* flight were not along NASA–contractor lines but between levels in NASA's own management hierarchy. The impact of the organizational isolation of the Thiokol engineers in the *Challenger* had been noted, and a remedy was designed and instituted, all of which constitute reasonable evidence of learning.

In addition, fear of reprisals for reporting problems had been addressed at least in part by creating separate safety offices that contractors could report to if they felt they were not being heard. Larger numbers of NASA liaisons were also installed at some contractor facilities. These actions provided communication channels outside of the chain of command, though as will be noted in chapter 6, they were not necessarily trusted. Nevertheless, the changes can reasonably be considered as lessons learned. The Rogers Commission had made a general recommendation about the independence of contractors, but NASA elaborated on this recommendation and charged its own Office of Safety, Reliability, Maintainability and Quality Assurance to further investigate the problem.

Unfortunately, more sweeping changes to the design of the safety structures that were to have decentralized safety offices and made them more prominent and aggressive were "unlearned" in the streamlining and downsizing of the 1990s, as noted in chapter 3. There is no indication that these changes were based on a considered decision to reduce unnecessary levels of independence for contractors generally or safety contractors in particular. On the contrary, a GAO report noted the efforts NASA management was making to encourage independent voice. Rather it appears the lessons about contractor independence were dropped as a by-product of the other changes to cut costs, streamline the chain of command, and consolidate offices. The lessons about an independent safety organization were swept aside, justified by the logic articulated in the Kraft Report that a "diffuse and fragmented NASA and contractor structure" (NASA 1995, 8) did not provide accountability.

Some lessons learned after *Challenger* appear also to have been unintentionally lost or forgotten. Despite the initial efforts to remedy contractor relations, the debris assessment team chaired by Madera from USA and Rocha from NASA was isolated at the time of the *Columbia* accident. Two reasons for this appear in the case. The cochairs persisted, but only up to a point, in pressing for images of the wing. In part, their lack of success was due to the fact that downsizing and multiple reorganizations had left the agency with few people who seemed to know the procedures for obtaining images. In addition, however, existing, known procedures were not being observed by program managers. The debris assessment team was isolated because the mission management team did not follow established rules and did not pay attention to the team's requests and analyses. Similarly, the mission evaluation room and the safety offices were not fully engaged. They were caught between the debris assessment team's uncertainty about the severity of the damage and the mission management team's determination to prevent foam strikes from becoming the kind of issue that would delay subsequent flights.]The mission evaluation room did not pass along the debris assessment team's actual degree of uncertainty or its desire for images. Later, Rocha said he regretted not having been more forceful in making the case for images to the mission management team (Wald and Schwartz, 2003). Why he did not is the subject of the next two chapters. But what this failure to follow the rules suggests is that, in practice, NASA's upper management neglected the procedures and the lessons embodied in them. In the face of pressures to avoid delays in the long-term launch schedule and the structural streamlining and downsizing that were part of cost-reduction strategies favored by several administrations, they forgot lessons from the *Challenger* about tracking engineers' concerns.

Though the two shuttle accidents are similar in many respects, the contractor relations played out differently, at least in part because of the changes made between 1986 and 2003. Even though problems with communication remained, and some of them involved contract employees, NASA did learn some lessons about managing their complex contracting relationships after the *Challenger* accident. They learned how to create workable communication opportunities for NASA and contract engineers, though not, apparently, for the safety contractors. We conclude that NASA did learn some important lessons about managing contractor communications, and it did institutionalize these lessons into new rules. But at the critical time, some of these rules were forgotten or displaced by more pressing priorities.

CHAPTER 5

Political and Budgetary Pressures

IN THIS CHAPTER we examine the impact of external forces, especially Congress and the White House, on learning at NASA. More specifically,
we contend that congressional budget constraints and White House policy and
management initiatives were critical impediments to learning during the pre-
Challenger (1983–86) and the pre-*Columbia* periods (1988–2003). According
to the Rogers Commission, NASA failed to match its resources to its launch rate
(Rogers Commission 1986, 177, 201), seriously jeopardizing the space shuttle
program by increasing the flight rate without the resources needed for safe
operations. Even the modest nine-mission schedule of 1985 was a great strain
on program resources, and "the evidence suggests that NASA would not have
been able to accomplish the 15 flights scheduled for 1986" (Rogers Commission
1986, 164). In the implementation report that followed, NASA outlined new
"ground rules . . . to ensure that projected flight rates are realistic. These
ground rules addressed such items as overall staffing of the work force, work
shifts, overtime, crew training, and maintenance requirements for the orbiter,
main engine, solid rocket motor, and other critical systems" (Rogers Commission 1987, 8). Beyond these changes, however, lay problems with the unwillingness of NASA administrators to challenge political overseers with a realistic
appraisal of the launch-schedule capabilities of the poorly funded space shuttle
program. We examine how external political pressures forced the agency to
promise more than it could deliver.

Why NASA could not withstand these pressures or learn in the aftermath of
the *Challenger* how to resist them is the subject of this chapter. In particular, the
role of agency leadership in either resisting or succumbing to these pressures is
illustrated. In fairness, however, maintaining a sufficient supply of resources *over
the long term* to support NASA's ambitious launch rate was not an easy task. The
White House appoints and removes the leadership while Congress appropriates

(with the president's signature) the agency's budget. Such constraints present supreme challenges to the best of politically savvy administrators, who must adjust to changing political environments. They must somehow devise strategies for maximizing budgets and protecting the agency's programs, while neutralizing their opponents, fending off their rivals, and courting their supporters. At the same time, agency leaders are typically dealing with other political issues that can be very distracting but are part of living in the political world of the nation's capital.

There was a short period during the post-*Challenger* recovery, from approximately 1986–91, when NASA, with a generous budget and under the leadership of James C. Fletcher, implemented the recommendations of the Rogers Commission and the U.S. House Committee on Science and Technology. However, by the mid-1990s it was clear that the agency had diverged from its new course and reverted to its pre-*Challenger* days of striving to achieve impractical launch schedules with diminishing resources. By the time of accident in 2003, the Columbia Accident Investigation Board found that the shuttle managers (like their predecessors of the pre-*Challenger* era) were once again burdened with a very heavy shuttle launch schedule that was well beyond the agency's resource capabilities.

We begin this chapter by going back to the Apollo era—the best of all possible worlds for the newly formed NASA—when resources were plentiful and human space exploration was a top priority for the White House and Congress. We then show how the agency's capabilities to learn were critically affected by changes in its political environment, changes that included new policy agendas, changes in leadership, and budgetary constraints.

APOLLO DAYS: POLITICAL AUTONOMY AND AMPLE RESOURCES

In NASA's early life during the Apollo era, the nation's foreign policy capitalized on human space exploration, and NASA was generously funded by Congress and the White House. On April 12, 1961, Soviet astronaut Yuri Gagarin successfully orbited the Earth, and President John F. Kennedy quickly changed his formerly cautious approach to space exploration. Determined to beat the Soviets, he set the goal "before this decade is out [of] landing a man on the moon and returning him safely to earth" (McDougall 1985, 303). Viewed by Kennedy and others as a "national emergency," the race to the moon was a very high priority on both the president's and Congress's policy agenda (McCurdy 1990, 25). Vice President Johnson was equally supportive, defending the cost of the Apollo project with the comment "I for one don't want to go to bed by the light of a Communist moon" (Byrnes 1994, 75); later, as president, his support did not wane (85). The cost, estimated by NASA administrator James Webb at approximately $20 billion, was astronomical (McCurdy 1990, 19). However, even the director of the Office of Management and Budget, David Bell, knew that it was pointless to argue against this project from the standpoint of costs, as he stated: " I was very skeptical [but] I did not argue at all that we couldn't afford it, because we could, did, can" (McCurdy 1990, 18).

Apollo was not without its critics, however, and budgetary pressures to cut back were ever-present (McDougall 1985, 396–97; Lambright 1995, 120–21). Nevertheless, congressional support was strong enough to make the Apollo project a reality (Byrnes 1994, 75–76). This meant that Administrator Webb did not have to "sell" the program to his political overseers with exaggerated claims or by acquiescing to unrealistic budgetary compromises. And so, the freedom of the agency to provide realistic cost estimates and enjoy relatively smooth relations with White House and Congress gave "NASA engineers a fighting chance to accomplish their mission without any cost overruns" (McCurdy 1990, 19).

This meant that the inevitable shortcuts that accompany scarce resources from "trimmed" budgets were minimized. In addition, NASA was a new agency with a research-and-development mission to create innovative technology for achieving a lunar landing, not, as in the *Challenger* era, an agency managing or operating a human space shuttle program that had become "routine." The private sector (universities and industry) played a critical role in this large-scale undertaking, working with NASA to develop the necessary technology for the success of the program (McDougall 1985, 381). With Webb heading the agency and with support from the White House, Congress, and the American public, the agency enjoyed visionary leadership, a clear-cut goal, and plentiful resources. As one source states: "Between 1960 (the final Eisenhower budget) and 1965, NASA's funding grew by 900 percent. When adjusted for inflation, its 1965 budget represented a thirteen-fold increase over that of five years earlier" (Kay 2005, 92).

The 1966 budget (approximately $5 billion), however, saw NASA experience its first reduction (by $75 million) since the Apollo program began. Although it was a minimal decrease in funding, the downward slide had begun, and greater cuts followed. The following year, NASA funding fell below the $5 billion mark and by 1968, the budget had dropped below $4 billion (92).]

THE SPACE SHUTTLE–SPACE STATION ERA

NIXON

Clearly, NASA's fortunes declined as the decade neared its end. Once the lunar landing had been achieved, public support for grandiose space-exploration programs waned. At the same time, the new president, Richard M. Nixon, was pursuing a very different set of national priorities from John F. Kennedy's. The 1967 race riots originating in Detroit demanded immediate attention, while the Vietnam War dragged on, along with the civil unrest arising from war protests. ·All of this took its toll on American morale and the fiscal health of the nation. NASA had to survive politically in a radically different external environment as the 1970s approached. Claus Jensen (1996) observed that NASA had a tremendous adjustment to make. It was no longer able to bask in the luxury of lavish attention and ministering from its overseers:

> This organization had come into being in another age, under different conditions and with a different goal. *It had grown used to being accorded ample resources,* national popularity, and political backing; to enjoying the protection of the President and being above *the wearisome battle for resources* that typified other public enterprises. (134; emphasis added)

Once Neil Armstrong landed on the moon on July 20, 1967, the nation's attention moved elsewhere to other pressing problems, even though NASA made six more trips to the moon: "The show was over and the nation was making its way out of the theater. And on the street, Pain City awaited" (Jensen 1996, 116). The Vietnam War, rising crime, and inflation were receiving increased national attention. While additional moon landings were highly televised, public opinion polls registered an overwhelming number of Americans who wanted less, not more, involvement in space exploration. "It was as if," McCurdy writes, "NASA had been given a mission designed to make the agency self-destruct upon its completion" (1990, 25).

The Space Station System

In this chilly climate, NASA proposed an elaborate and expensive plan for a space station system that would be assembled from materials ferried from earth by a space shuttle transportation system. This idea had excited the space-science community and portions of the American public at least since Wernher von

Braun's 1952 *Collier's* magazine articles and television appearances with Walt Disney. Not surprisingly, however, in this new political terrain of finite resources and waning interest, the agency adapted in order to survive. The space station, the cornerstone for a lunar landing base and mission to Mars, was placed on the shelf (temporarily) for better times, and the agency fought for funding for the first component of this integrated plan: the space shuttle (McCurdy 1990, 27). Gone were the lofty goals and inspiring rhetoric that characterized the Apollo days such as "new knowledge for mankind" or "the inherent urge to seek fresh challenges" (Jensen 1996, 116). Now it was very mundane and practical arguments that NASA administrator James Fletcher pushed: the economy and jobs.

Generating the Launch Pressures

Fletcher won over Nixon and Congress with political compromises that would haunt the agency for decades. He overpromised on what the space shuttle program could accomplish on a greatly reduced budget of $5 billion (the initial projection was between $10 billion and $12 billion). Although the space shuttle had "no longer anything to shuttle to" (Jensen 1996, 140), once the space shuttle was "operational," it was argued, it would pay for itself by hauling satellites into space and carrying out experiments for the scientific community. In this way, NASA was to remain in the business of human space flight.

And yet, it soon became apparent that these projections were not very realistic. In keeping with agency survival instincts, Fletcher and others engaged in political hype to sell their program. In 1971, using a report by Mathematica Inc., Fletcher initially quoted sixty flights a year (with full payload), an utterly unrealistic figure but politically essential if human space flight was to survive and compete with expendable launch vehicles for cost savings, and even turn a profit. Although the flight rates were reduced to fifty, agency personnel were still being asked to support a mythical figure. In the words of one subordinate, "We had to argue that [the shuttle] was cheaper. It would be cheaper than the expendable launch vehicles. It would be better than all the expendable launch vehicles. Well, there was a feeling that we were on the razor's edge. That if we said the wrong thing, or anything like that, the shuttle would be killed" (Trento 1987, 118).

 Indeed, once the shuttle was deemed operational in 1981 and flights were supposedly routine, the pressure was on to increase launch rate to one mission a week (Rogers Commission 1986, 164). A high number of shuttle flights was critical for fulfilling the agency's promise of cost effectiveness. This situation would have put enough pressure on the shuttle managers in and of itself, but in addition, they had to attempt to live up to an image of efficiency and reliability for their payload customers. After all, these characteristics would be the hallmarks of a truly operational program.]

However, the reality was that the agency never came close to achieving the hyperinflated numbers that were given by Fletcher during the early seventies when the future of the space shuttle program was hanging by a thread. Even the drastically revised projected-flight rate of twenty-four by the year 1990 was still beyond reach of the agency according to the Rogers Commission: "Long before the *Challenger* accident, . . . it was becoming obvious that even the modified goal of two flights a month was unattainable"(Rogers Commission 1986, 164).

Effects of Scarce Resources on the Space Shuttle —cannibalized parts

This goal was unrealistic because the agency did not have the resources, even the number of shuttles and spare parts, needed for such an ambitious launch rate (Rogers Commission 1986, 164). Early on in the history of the shuttle program, in 1983, the Office of Management and Budget (OMB) turned down the agency's request for building a $200 million fifth orbiter now that the program was operational (McCurdy 1990, 123). OMB did, however, approve the sum of $100 million for spare parts for the other four orbiters (123). Apparently, according to the Rogers Commission, this gesture from Congress and the White House was still not sufficient to accommodate the 1985 plan to achieve a projected twenty-four flights a year by 1990:

> The spare parts plan to support 24 flights per year had called for completing inventory stockage by June, 1987. By mid-1985, that schedule was in jeopardy. The logistics plan could not be fully implemented because of *budget reductions.* In October 1986, the logistics funding requirement for the Orbiter program, as determined by Level III management at Johnson, was $285.3 million. That funding was reduced by $83.3 million—a cut that necessitated major deferrals of spare parts purchases. (Rogers Commission 1986, 174; emphasis added)

Those actions resulted in a critical shortage of serviceable spare components. To provide parts required to support the flight rate, NASA had to resort to "cannibalization" in which various items in short supply, ranging from "common bolts to a thrust control actuator for the orbital maneuvering system," were taken from one orbiter and installed in another (Rogers Commission 1986, 173). This bad habit soon "became an essential modus operandi in order to maintain flight schedules.[Forty-five out of approximately 300 required parts were cannibalized for *Challenger* before mission 51-L"](174). Cannibalization was a bad habit because it drained the agency's dwindling resources in the form of manpower and because the increased handling raised the risk of damage to the cannibalized part.

Budget reductions also meant that NASA experienced a serious shortfall of skilled personnel critical for the transition from research and development to an operational organization. Recruitment slowed to a standstill because of hiring freezes. Some personnel retired, and still others were transferred to work on the space station program.

Equally if not more important, as the flight rate increased and resources were stretched to the maximum, agency focus became short-term. The most immediate problems were maneuvering scarce resources to get the shuttle launched on time. In addition, the increasing number of launches, even though still a far cry from projected goals, made it more difficult to analyze all the past data on the shuttle's technical performance before the next shuttle launch; for example, the Rogers Commission reported that "Flight Readiness Review for 51-L (*Challenger*) was held while mission 61-C was still in orbit" (1986, 174).

Amid all of this, James M. Beggs, the administrator of NASA from July 1981 to February 1986, would not admit to problems matching resources to launch rates, even when congressional overseers drew attention to the problem. The following exchange between Sen. Patrick Leahy and Administrator Beggs during the annual Senate appropriations hearings in 1985 demonstrates this point:

> LEAHY: We are looking at budgets based on NASA's projections of the number of flights it is going to be able to make per year. Based on that, we determine how much we are going to give them as a commercial payback, how much the military can use it. Is your 24 flights per year thing unrealistic when you consider the fact it does take a while to work it up? During the next 12 months, will you have 24 flights?
>
> BEGGS: Well, the first year we are projecting a 24-a-year rate is 1989.
>
> LEAHY: Will you do it in 1989?
>
> BEGSS: I believe we will, yes, sir. I think we are on that track.
>
> LEAHY: During the next 12 months, how many flights do you project?
>
> BEGGS: In the next 12 months I think we are projecting 11, in the next 12 calendar months.
>
> LEAHY: You will make the 11?
>
> BEGGS: I believe we will now, yes sir.
>
> LEAHY: Thank you. (U.S. Congress, Senate Committee on Appropriations 1985, 33)
>
> And yet Sen. Leahy continued to be concerned about the figure Beggs gave him, saying: "I just want to know how many times it [the Shuttle] is apt to go up.

. . . you would do a disservice to yourselves if you came in with an overly optimistic thing" (33).

Thus during the post-Apollo years leading up to the *Challenger* accident, exceptional external pressures operated upon the agency from the very beginning of the space shuttle project. A new era of budgetary constraints and a changed national policy agenda placed other policy issues above space research and exploration. In an effort to save the program, agency leaders and supporters overpromised on the number of space shuttle launches and the capability of the space shuttle program to be cost-effective. We see similar compromises to preserve agency staff and facilities in the lead-center design described in chapter 3, and in the next chapter we will see other instances of adaptations to preserve the organization's mission. The result in the present case was that the agency generated production pressures to conform to promises made to Congress and the White House in order to "save" human space exploration, which to many was synonymous with the very survival of the agency. These pressures were only exacerbated by the heightened expectations of the agency's political overseers, who expected great results on an ever-decreasing budget. In this kind of environment, the ability of agency officials to analyze and learn from the technical failures of the seal joint was severely compromised. Shuttle managers were single-mindedly focused on the need to increase the shuttle launch rates, and research and experimentation to correct the seal problems required time and resources the agency did not have. Worse, arguing that more time and resources were needed ran the risk of grounding the shuttle entirely, given the promises of cost-effective operations that had been made. An illuminating example was the August 15, 1985, meeting at NASA headquarters when the consensus was to redesign the seal joint but keep the shuttle flying.

AGENCY LEADERS AND LEARNING, 1983–86

How did agency leadership contribute to NASA's impaired learning environment? External pressures on agency leaders made learning difficult. James Beggs was NASA administrator from 1981 to 1986, during the period that the engineers and shuttle managers at NASA were receiving information on the O-ring safety problem. But several kinds of outside pressures served to distract him and other top leaders from monitoring this problem. Making a success of the space shuttle, finding funds for the space station program while maintaining a commitment to the space station, and building a fifth orbiter for the shuttle fleet were some of the most important issues that occupied Beggs's time. Aided initially by Hans Mark, the deputy administrator, Beggs faced extremely strong opposition in the budgetary battles for requisite funding.

We have already seen what Beggs had to contend with from his congressional overseers and their concern that the shuttle could meet its launch-rate schedule. He also had to reassure them of the viability of the space transport system, as the shuttle was called, in spite of the disconnect between promise and reality. But the reality was that the shuttle program was showing no signs of providing routine and cost-effective access to space at a price lower than the cost of expendable launch vehicles (ELVs). At the same time, Beggs was supremely focused on finding funding and support for the space station. In fact, from the very time that he took over the agency, his commitment to the space station was evident. A planning and development group, the Space Station Task Force, was set up at NASA during the summer of 1981 "to worry," as McCurdy puts it, "about a space station" (1990, 46).

And well they might have worried, because budgetary constraints made it impossible for NASA leaders to push both the space station and the space shuttle at the same time. The space station project, however, was not dropped by Beggs, who approved a small budget request in the agency's fiscal year 1984 budget. While he and Mark were committed to making the space transportation system a success, they also pushed hard for long-term support from Congress and the White House for the space station program, in which the space shuttle fleet would be an indispensable component (McCurdy 1990, 118–23).

At the White House, the men faced an uphill battle with an extremely skeptical David Stockman, then director of OMB, George "Jay" Keyworth, White House science advisor, and a president with only a lukewarm interest in space exploration. Keyworth believed (as did many others in the space policy arena) that ELVs could do the same job as the space shuttle but at much reduced cost (Trento 1987, 184–85). He was also very skeptical about a human space station that apparently had no specific purpose when robots and automation were coming into their own. As he stated, "I have asked ever since I came into this office for people to tell me what we will do with the space station. Neither NASA nor the space community has been able to define what these men would do who would be up on that space station" (McCurdy 1990, 129).

According to one source, Keyworth wanted the two men to develop a more imaginative and challenging vision for the human civil-space program, and supported the idea of a moon base for anticipated trips to Mars (McCurdy 1990, 160–61). In Keyworth's words, the space station was "first and foremost a motel in the sky for astronauts. It was not a step toward something that was of comparable magnitude to Apollo. It was not something that captured a major investment or increased public support for the space program" (Trento 1987, 202–3). Yet Beggs and others at NASA believed that acquiescing to Keyworth and scrapping the space station in its current form would seal the fate of NASA, because a moon base and all that would follow would simply not happen any time soon. In a time of severe budgetary constraints, it would be criticized as too grandiose and costly (McCurdy 1990, 161; Trento 1987, 202–3).

Stockman, on the other hand, had ideological reasons for opposing the space station: "Space stations are high-tech socialism," he said, and he characterized the one proposed by NASA as sounding like "big spending to me, sound investment to NASA administrators" (McCurdy 1990, 127, 194). While the Air Force had endorsed the shuttle in the late 1970s, its history with the concept of even a military-operated space station was tortuous, and it was most decidedly hostile towards a civilian operation (Kay 2005, 139; McCurdy 1990, 133). By the early 1980s, it appeared the Air Force was already regretting its commitment to the civilian-operated shuttle because of the lack of control over its military missions (McCurdy 1990, 134).

Beggs and Mark tried unsuccessfully to convince the Senior Interagency Group for Space (with strong representation from the DOD, CIA, and the State Department) of the merits of the space station. However, the ace card that Beggs and Mark played was the space station's commercial appeal. With the support of the Cabinet Council on Commerce and Trade, the NASA leadership was able to achieve access to President Reagan in late 1983. Using models and compelling viewgraphs that symbolized American leadership in space, they illustrated the potential for scientific and technological advances and for commercial endeavors there (Kay 2005, 140–41; McCurdy 1990, 182–85). Beggs won the day, and shortly after the meeting Reagan accepted the space station idea, albeit gaining only a modest initial funding allocation of $150 million for fiscal year 1985, a small part of the eventual $8 billion price tag (McCurdy 1990, 182).

Clearly, the success of the shuttle was critical for keeping the political momentum behind the space station. Beggs's determined stance in the exchange with Sen. Leahy on the ability of the shuttle to achieve its projected launch rates reflected his need to maintain that it would be a reliable, routine, and cost-effective space transportation program. But this had yet to be proven, and payload customers had to be found.

In 1983, the same year that the space station plan was accepted by Reagan, Beggs and Mark declared the shuttle "operational" after only four development flights. At the same time, Beggs was trying to get the Air Force and the intelligence community to sign on as customers. Instead of using ELVs like the expensive Titan rocket, spy satellites, for example, would be "trucked" up to space and deployed by the shuttle. The Air Force, however, was already concerned about shuttle delays and was understandably nervous about relinquishing control to a civilian agency (Trento 1987, 196).

By early 1984, and within this context of constant budget battles, information on the charred O-rings reached Hans Mark. With evidence mounting from post-flight inspections of the solid rocket boosters, Mark took the next step, as he states:

> The O-ring seal problem did gain my attention again just before I left NASA. This phenomenon had been observed once before on the second flight, but when it did not reappear we thought it was a one-time event. When we saw it again on the tenth flight, the question of what should be done was discussed at the Flight Readiness Review for the eleventh flight. After the completion of the Flight Readiness Review, I issued an 'Action Item' asking for a complete review of all solid rocket motor seals and joints. . . . Unfortunately, this review was never held. I made the decision of leaving NASA about two weeks after signing out the 'Action Item' so the matter was apparently dropped. (Trento 1987, 259)

The action item to which Mark referred was dated April 5, 1985, was sent to Lawrence Mulloy, solid rocket booster project manager at Marshall, and was signed by Lawrence Weeks, deputy associate administrator in the Office of Space Flight at headquarters. This action item asked Mulloy to "conduct a formal review of the Solid Rocket Motor case-to-case and case-to-nozzle joint sealing procedures to ensure satisfactory consistent closeouts" (Rogers Commission 1986, 132).

From his own characterization of his response to the safety information, we see that at least Mark recognized the O-ring problem. With his departure, the attention of upper-level administrators appears to have waned. Beggs was distracted by White House politics, even though Mark noted that he "discussed the O-rings and the burn-through with Beggs" (Trento 1987, 259). Beggs denied this conversation, and Mark's response was to say, "I find that hard to believe, but things do slip the memory" (Trento 1987, 259).

With Mark gone, Beggs was very keen to find a replacement. The White House choice of William Graham infuriated Beggs as Graham was an ally of Keyworth, the White House science advisor. In addition, Graham was a nuclear weapons expert with little management experience. The White House was adamant about Graham, and Beggs finally gave in during the summer of 1985.

Within NASA headquarters, Beggs and Graham hardly spoke to each other even when Beggs was indicted—two weeks after Graham came on board—on charges connected with his previous employment at General Dynamics. Graham became the acting administrator while Beggs remained at NASA, ensconced in an office down the hallway. Officially on a leave of absence, Beggs was supposed to provide "continuity and consultation," but in reality this did not happen (Trento 1987, 272–73). According to Graham, he was left out of the communication loop as Beggs undermined him by consulting directly with senior managers such as Phil Culbertson, who remained loyal to Beggs. According to Beggs, Graham deliberately ignored him. The morale at the agency reached an all-time low.

For all intents and purposes, NASA was virtually a leaderless agency at the time of the *Challenger* accident. When Hans Mark signed an action item for the seal joint to be thoroughly reviewed, it seemed like the joint-seal problems might begin to be recognized, but any move in this direction was scuttled when Mark himself resigned. Moreover, the subsequent political tensions and animosities between Beggs and the White House staff over Mark's replacement certainly produced conditions that only exacerbated the less-than-ideal communications between the field centers and headquarters.

Even when the full history of the O-ring charring and its causes was aired at the critical August 19 headquarters meeting with Marshall personnel, the deputy associate administrator for space flight, Michael Weeks, was the highest senior official in attendance. It was decided at this meeting that a new joint seal should be designed, but there was a decided lack of urgency in addressing it. When Graham was finally established as the acting administrator, nothing changed in regard to this safety issue. Graham's attention was devoted to mending fences on Capitol Hill, even on the actual day of the *Challenger* launch, because Beggs had been trying to convince certain senators that Graham had been a poor choice (Trento 1987, 285). As it was, for whatever reason, the third-ranking person in the organization's hierarchy, the general manager, Philip Culbertson, did not pass on to Graham what transpired at meetings during the day and at the infamous teleconference on the eve of the *Challenger* launch (284).

Missed Opportunities for Short-Term Learning

The leadership crises in the agency had a devastating effect on its learning capacity. Without strong top-level leadership to fight for resources and resist externally imposed launch schedules, agency midlevel managers believed they could not take the time to examine results from previous flights, consider causes, and allow the engineers to uncover solutions. As we saw in chapter 3, it was at the mid-management level that the waivers were authorized and the last-minute warnings about temperature's effect on the O-rings were blocked. Distracted agency leaders and pressures on NASA to live up to its promise that the space shuttle would be cost effective made it very difficult for NASA to admit that a problem existed. Operating under intense pressure to achieve promised launch rates, there were significant disincentives for agency leaders and political overseers to engage in "reality checks" that could trigger problem recognition. A senior space shuttle official or congressional committee member, for example, could have brought attention to the dangerous consequences of the agency's ambitious launch rate on the flight-readiness procedures of the shuttle program. Even the mild reprimand from political overseer Leahy served no purpose other than to place the agency leader, Beggs, on the defensive. These pressures, and the inability of the agency to resist them at the time, weakened NASA's capacity to acknowledge problems and search for solutions, basic steps in organizational learning.

PRESSURES FROM MEDIA COVERAGE

Nor did the media's coverage of NASA during the several months leading up to the *Challenger* accident provide an environment conducive to agency self-reflection and analysis, other vital ingredients in the process of organizational learning. Indeed, without these, there is no likelihood of drawing meaningful inferences and institutionalizing new solutions. The problem was, of course, that the agency was especially dependent upon the mass media for public support of human space exploration because it lacked sufficient clientele that would protect this particular aspect of its mission of space exploration and research. But this public organization, so highly vulnerable to changes in the public mood, was also bombarded with negative media coverage when its launches were delayed, seemingly endlessly. The media failed to provide a responsible analysis of the problems behind the launch delays. They might have, but did not, laud the agency for its patience and forbearance. Instead, they were only derisive and critical. For example, mission 61-C, the *Columbia* launch prior to the fateful *Challenger* launch, was subjected to relentless ridicule by the press and the television networks when NASA delayed its launch seven times. The delays were referred to as a "running soap opera," while network anchorpersons reported the delays with biting sarcasm. Dan Rather of CBS, for example, gave the following account of the aborted launch of January 10 to his evening viewers: "The star-crossed space shuttle *Columbia* stood ready for launch again today and once more the launch was scrubbed. Heavy rain was the cause this time. The launch has been postponed so often since its original date, December 18, that it's now known as mission impossible" (Ignatius 1986). Similarly, Tom Brokaw described another *Columbia* delay as follows:

> At Cape Canaveral today, mission commander Robert Gibson said, "We have a bad habit going here, a habit of delays." This time, the weather was bad at the Cape and two emergency landing sites. NASA decided the launch would be too risky. It's now aiming for Thursday of this week. These delays are becoming expensive as well. A NASA official said today that the agency loses as much as $300,000 every time there is a postponement. (Ignatius 1986)

Another example of media pressure arose on the eve of the *Challenger* launch when Dan Rather began his story on the latest launch delay with these words: "Yet another costly, red-faced-all-around space shuttle launch delay . . . Bruce Hall has the latest on today's high-tech low comedy" (Ignatius 1986).

What exacerbated media attention on the launch delays was the public relations campaign called the Teacher-in-Space, in which teacher Christa McAuliffe would give the nation's first science lesson in space while *Challenger* was on orbit. In addition, the stakes for a timely *Challenger* launch were raised even higher with the prospect of mention by President Ronald Reagan in his State of the Union message. Excited parents, schoolchildren, and teachers were watching each launch and were disappointed with each delay. The hold-up reported the day before the ill-fated launch by *NBC Nightly News* portrays a dejected public surprised and disappointed that an unduly stiff door handle and bad weather could thwart the ultimate "can-do" space agency:

> BROKAW: At Cape Canaveral today, the space shuttle *Challenger* ran into still more problems and that forced still another delay in efforts to put the first school teacher into space. The flight of Christa McAuliffe has been put off five times. And as NBC's Dan Molina reports tonight, there are worries that it might be put off again tomorrow.
> MOLINA: In the end, it was a stiff Florida wind that kept *Challenger* off the launch pad today. Winds like this would have made an emergency very dangerous. It all started out well. Teacher Christa McCauliffe and her crewmates marched up to the launch pad in the predawn hours. Up at Christa's school in Concord, New Hampshire, they crowded into the cafeteria to watch the big event on television.
> Then came the exasperating mishap. A handle attached to the outside of the shuttle hatch had to be unscrewed and removed before takeoff as usual. Today, the threads of one screw were stripped. The call went out for the

tools any home handyman would use, a big drill and a hacksaw. They went through two drills. They broke a drill bit. Finally, they got the handle on. But by then, the wind kicked up.

MAN: We are going to scrub for today, and we'll be getting the crew out of the orbiter, and they will go back to the crew quarters.

MOLINA: The crowd at the launch pad left. As to the students up in New Hampshire . . .

MAN: We're getting tired of it. We wanted her to go up, so, you know, we can find out what it's going to be like.

MOLINA: All this after NASA canceled yesterday's scheduled launch because the weather forecast looked bad but turned out fine. Now the plan is to press ahead with yet another try tomorrow but subfreezing temperatures are forecast and that could cause all sorts of problems. (*NBC Nightly News with Tom Brokaw*, January 27, 1986)

[Summarizing this period, we can see that diverse but relentless external pressures combined to produce a stressed organization struggling to meet the ambitious schedule of twenty-four launches per year by 1990. These pressures distracted the organization from recognizing and analyzing available information on the O-ring problem. The political battles with the White House, Congress's demanding launch expectations, the thinning of the top administrators, and media ridicule all conspired to push the agency to minimize the seriousness of evidence of problems with the joints of the solid rocket booster, a system that agency officials led themselves to think was fundamentally sound. Their minds were elsewhere. In this setting, most of the processes that make up agency learning were compromised. Agency administrators could not afford to recognize problems or take the time to reassess the causes of past launch anomalies. It took a catastrophic failure in the form of the *Challenger* accident to jolt the agency to undertake even some elements of learning about these technical and managerial problems.]

THE POST-*CHALLENGER* LEARNING PERIOD, 1986–91

During the five years following the *Challenger* accident, NASA appears to have learned several lessons about how to resist external pressures for unrealistic launch timetables. The Rogers Commission and the House committee reports provided external analysis of the schedule and resources problems, but there is also evidence that NASA's leaders themselves agreed with these assessments of the source of the problems and with the recommendations for solutions. It also seems clear that at least for a time these solutions were enlarged upon and institutionalized as work rules, safety procedures, and launch plans. Evidence about three kinds of lessons for NASA and its overseers can be found.

First, Congress and the White House supported the findings of the Rogers Commission with substantial funding increases. As we already know, NASA and its political overseers responded in a very positive manner to the Rogers Commission recommendation no. 8, which stated in part: "NASA must establish a flight rate that is consistent with its resources. A firm payload assignment policy should be established. The policy should include rigorous controls on cargo manifest changes to limit the pressures such changes exert on schedules and crew training" (Rogers Commission 1986, 201). Recognizing its own role in this recommendation, Congress funded the post-*Challenger* organizational and shuttle program reforms at $12 billion and included a new orbiter, *Endeavor*.

Second, based upon an assessment of NASA's resources and capabilities, flight-rate recommendations were presented to NASA by the U.S. National Research Council, established by Congress to provide independent assessments for government agencies. The Council projected eleven to thirteen flights a year with a four-orbiter fleet (GAO 1991), somewhat lower than the flight-rate projection by NASA's own Flight Rate Capability Work Group, which was sixteen a year, with four orbiters, commencing in 1991. The reason for the discrepancy was that the National Research Council believed that only three of the four orbiters would be in operation at any given time because of maintenance and inspection requirements and other unforeseen problems (GAO 1991, 13). In any case, NASA reduced its maximum projected annual flight rate from the pre-*Challenger* figure of sixteen down to ten, a goal that would only be achieved at the end of the 1990s.

Finally, NASA and its political overseers addressed the reasons for the launch-rate pressures: the requirements of the shuttle payload customers. The president directed NASA to adopt a new policy for a mixed space fleet in which expendable launch vehicles (ELVs) would carry most of the Department of Defense, foreign, and commercial payloads. Only in cases of national security or those requiring a human presence were payloads to fly on the shuttle. In addition, ground rules governing cargo manifests were compiled to minimize the possibility of last-minute changes that would exacerbate schedule pressures. In a letter dated September 26, 1991, in response to this GAO report, Assistant Deputy Administrator John O'Brien stated, "We find the report, for the most part, to be thorough, accurate, and objective, with conclusions that closely parallel our own. In fact, actions already under way within NASA anticipate some of its specific recommendations. Where we have differences, it is more a matter of point of view, not of disagreement on the facts or on the objectives we are trying to reach" (GAO 1991, 46).

O'Brien agreed that the goal of ten shuttle flights a year was a "realistic target" and that "the mixed fleet policy has been well integrated into [the agency's] flight assessment process" (GAO 1991, 46). In referring to their own analysis of the launch schedule and payload issues and to their agreement with the GAO findings, NASA and its overseers showed they were making a good-faith effort to learn from the catastrophic failure.

The new policies resulted in a number of changes in practice. During the almost three-year period between the first post-*Challenger* flight of *Endeavor* in September 1988 and June 1991, with a restored shuttle fleet of four orbiters, the agency achieved a flight rate of five in 1989 and six in 1991. The low flight rates were due in part to safety-based increases in the length of time devoted to the turnaround of each shuttle. As one 1991 GAO report noted: "Actual processing times have exceeded planned times by an average of about 45 days" (1991, 19). The reason, the report continued, was that during the three years following the flight of the *Endeavor*, agency decision makers exhibited a willingness to stop all shuttle processing until safety problems were resolved—a marked contrast to the pre-*Challenger* days, when "processing continued while problems were being resolved" (29).

Most importantly, real analysis and reflection of safety problems in the shuttle processing appeared to be taking place on the part of senior agency officials. In September 1990, for example, senior management appointed an agency team to examine the human errors that had produced safety "incidents" in shuttle processing (which had caused the delays mentioned above) and make recommendations. According to the GAO, the team found that the incidents were unrelated but recommended further analyses into the possible causes, such as worker fatigue, adequacy of procedures, and training. The team also urged that the mantra "Safety first, schedule second" must be continuously emphasized as an antidote to the "strong sense of schedule" during shuttle-processing activities (1991, 30). In addition, the GAO report recommended that:

> NASA reemphasize safety by (1) determining the underlying causes of incidents or mishaps, (2) increasing emphasis on reporting close calls, (3) developing a technique to measure overall quality improvement achievements and trends, and (4) improving management and worker awareness of the importance of quality and safety as job elements. (1991, 30)

The report also noted that an implementation plan to follow through on the team's recommendations had been established in July 1991, and as a result, "all of the 16 post-*Challenger* flights conducted through June 1991 were delayed on the launch pad because of safety concerns. For example, NASA delayed a planned February 1991 launch of *Discovery* for about 2 months because of cracks in the orbiter's fuel door hinges" (GAO 1991, 29).

The low flight rate and delays in shuttle processing noted by the GAO reflected the grounding of the entire shuttle fleet for several months in 1990 when leaks of explosive hydrogen on *Atlantis* (STS-35) and *Columbia* (STS-38) were discovered. In their 1991 annual report, the Aerospace Safety Advisory Panel, NASA's independent oversight body created under its authorizing legislation in 1968 and renewed in response to the Rogers Commission recommendations, commended the agency for these changes; in so doing, it offered strong evidence of organizational learning. As the panel stated:

> The commitment of NASA to seek and find the "leaks" on STS 35 and STS 38 is an excellent example of "safety first, schedule second." NASA was under tremendous pressure during the summer of 1990 to "get something off the ground" but they remained steadfast in their commitments and did not succumb. The launch rate is ever changing with the budget and times. NASA should maintain their posture of first being safe and allowing the schedule to follow. (Aerospace Safety Advisory Panel 1991, 27)

The GAO report also noted that the Kennedy Space Center management had addressed the safety problem of employee fatigue by placing limits on excessive overtime for those working on shuttle processing. In addition, the GAO found that NASA was indeed moving away from its pre-*Challenger* policy of "almost exclusive reliance on the shuttle to launch its payloads to one of using the shuttle when necessary." The GAO report concluded that it had

> found no evidence to suggest that NASA has compromised safety to increase the flight rate [since the *Challenger* accident]. Thus far, NASA flight schedules have been subordinated to safety concerns in launch decisions. NASA is taking action to prevent a recurrence of safety problems and it has implemented controls to help ensure that employees who are involved in shuttle processing are not fatigued by excessive overtime. (1991, 34)

At the same time, the GAO found that there was a strong desire on the part of NASA to improve its shuttle processing time in order to achieve its planned ten flights a year by the end of the 1990s. As a result of post-*Challenger* reforms, the space shuttle program found that it had three times as many safety-critical functions that needed to be checked and verified before each shuttle flight. To be exact, the number of critical items (as described in chapter 3) had increased from 1,350 to approximately 3,900. In addition, those items receiving failure analysis (which assesses the risk of failure) increased from 5,000 to approximately 15,000. These changes increased the processing time for the orbiter by approximately 192 work shifts (GAO 1991, 32). More detailed guidelines for inspection and maintenance were also issued. To cope with the added processing time, NASA did not hire more workers but rather reduced the frequency of maintenance and inspection requirements from after every flight to after every third or fifth flight. According to a GAO report at that time, officials from NASA's own safety organization maintained that these changes would not compromise safety since the agency's independent safety and quality control officials would participate in decisions regarding changes in maintenance and inspection requirements at headquarters and at the centers (34).

Thus, in the immediate post-*Challenger* years through the early 1990s, we see evidence that agency leaders and the NASA workforce recognized the disastrous effects of external pressures and responded in several ways. They adopted the recommendations of external bodies to reduce flight rates and worked with Air Force and DOD officials to offload much of the responsibility for military launches. They also successfully resisted pressures to launch with unresolved safety problems, or at least the conditions they recognized as problems. They generated solutions by creating more elaborate inspection and crosschecking systems adapted to the entrenched qualitative failure-modes-and-effects analysis, even as they reduced the frequency of inspection. All of these responses show an agency actively participating in the learning process and working to integrate lessons and institutionalize what it has learned. NASA could not control the administration or Congress indefinitely to fend off outside pressures, but it could and did adopt strategies for insulating the shuttle program from the most direct effects of those pressures. Nonetheless, by the end of the 1990s, we begin to see erosion in these lessons.

LEADERSHIP AND LEARNING AT NASA, 1986–90

Soon after the *Challenger* accident in May 1986, James C. Fletcher was appointed to oversee the agency's implementation of the Rogers Commission recommendations, so in a very real sense, Fletcher was appointed to lead the agency once again. The Rogers Commission submitted its recommendations in its report to the president on June 6, 1986. On June 13, Fletcher received a letter from President Reagan outlining Fletcher's responsibility to implement the recommendations of the commission as soon as possible and requesting a report in thirty days, indicating "how and when the Commission's recommendations will be implemented" (NASA 1986, preface). Fletcher responded with a document that laid out NASA's plan to implement the recommendations (NASA 1986), and a year later he submitted a detailed report on the steps the agency had taken (Rogers Commission 1987).

A year after that, in March of 1988, NASA's Aerospace Safety Advisory Panel submitted a report to Fletcher evaluating the agency's progress in implementing the recommendations of both the Rogers Commission and the U.S. House Committee on Science and Technology. In a letter to Fletcher that prefaced the report, Joseph F. Sutter, the panel chair, stated categorically that "NASA has followed scrupulously the recommendations laid out in the Presidential Commission Report on the Challenger Accident" (Aerospace Safety Advisory Panel 1988, i). The report covered the period between February 1987 and February 1988 and monitored NASA's efforts to achieve a "well-managed, risk-reduced restart of Space Shuttle flight activities" (i).

Although the implementation of each recommendation was still being completed, the Aerospace Safety Advisory Panel was confident that "the current endeavors of NASA will lead to Space Shuttle operations that are safer than those prior to the Challenger disaster" (Aerospace Safety Advisory Panel 1988, i). In particular, Sutter stated that risk assessment and management was still an ongoing challenge "and crucially important task" for the agency. He drew attention to NASA's efforts at installing its new assessment and management of risk policy, but acknowledged that, ultimately, NASA had to find a more "effective manner" of evaluating and reducing risk (ii). Sutter also was most explicit with regard to the dangers of launch pressures exerting an undue influence on the launch schedule. As he said: "The greatest source of risk will be the pressure to meet a specific schedule. The ASAP (Aerospace Safety Advisory Panel) reiterates 'safety first, schedule second.' We will continue to monitor the NASA effort to resist pressures to put fixed schedules ahead of achieving proper completion of the work" (ii).

Special consideration was also given by Sutter to the progress made in establishing the Office of Safety, Reliability, Maintainability and Quality Assurance independent of the line organization and whose head, the associate administrator of safety, would have direct authority for safety "throughout the agency" (ii) and would report directly to Fletcher. Sutter stated that the organization was "developing the ability to ensure that safety requirements are properly defined and are subsequently met. To say, however, that the organization is fully effective would be premature" (Aerospace Safety Advisory Panel 1988, ii). Sutter elaborated by saying that line management must develop a set of safety goals that are

> consistent with the Administrator's policy and which must be approved by him. Once established, these goals (and design precepts) may not be changed or violated by the line organization. The *now independent* SRM&QA (Safety, Reliability, Maintainability and Quality Assurance) function would actively monitor the program activities and ensure that all requirements are being met. (ii; emphasis added)

Most importantly, the Safety, Reliability, Maintainability and Quality Assurance organization would have the teeth to call line managers to heel in the event of any disagreement over the certification of any shuttle component. As noted in chapter 3, however, this organization did not operate long as a fully independent oversight body.

Another area of emphasis was NASA's ongoing safety review of the space shuttle program elements that included the failure-mode-and-effects analysis, the critical items list, hazard analyses, and waivers. The Aerospace Safety Advisory Panel was satisfied that NASA was fulfilling this requirement of the Rogers Commission by evaluating and making mandatory design changes before the first post-*Challenger* flight (STS-26) (Aerospace Safety Advisory Panel 1988, iii). Sutter's letter to Fletcher concluded the section that dwelt on the space shuttle program with the prescient remarks:

> Looking at the future, later programs could do well to reflect upon the Space Shuttle program. Continuing improvements in management, communications and quality assurance systems are necessary if future NASA programs are to develop satisfactorily. *The lessons learned on the Space Shuttle program must not be forgotten and must be applied for the guidance of future programs such as the Space Station.* The ASAP (Aerospace Safety Advisory Panel) understands that there are steps being taken by the Associate Administrator for Safety Reliability, Maintenance and Quality Assurance to do this now and in the future. (v; emphasis added)

The following year, in March 1989, in its report to Fletcher, the Aerospace Safety Advisory Panel emphasized that

> as the flight schedule picks up in FY 1989, there remains the clear and present danger of slipping back into the operating environment at KSC (Kennedy Space Center) that helped to contribute to the *Challenger* accident. At the same time,

wow mixed messages

the need to achieve greater efficiency and cost-effectiveness in turnaround procedures is clear. In this situation, NASA's commitment to the operating principle of "safety first; schedule second" must be retained. If experience of the past is a guide to the future, the pressures to maintain or increase flight rate will be intense. (Aerospace Safety Advisory Panel 1988, 5)

This report recommended that "NASA must resist the schedule pressures that can compromise safety during launch operations. This would require strong enforcement by NASA of the directives of governing STS (shuttle) operations" (Aerospace Safety Advisory Panel 1988, 5).

There were five shuttle flights in 1989, the year when Admiral Richard H. Truly (a former Navy vice admiral and space shuttle astronaut, and the associate administrator for space flight from February 1986) was appointed administrator. At that time NASA's annual budget was a respectable $9 billion and would grow steadily (allowing for inflation) to $14 billion by 1991. But this learning period was coming to an end for NASA as changing policy agendas at the White House once again began to exert a negative impact on the agency's budgetary fortunes. In fact, small cuts were already being made in early 1991. According to the CAIB, this decision was based on the belief that "the agency had overreacted to the Rogers Commission recommendations—for example, the notion that the many layers of safety inspections involved in preparing a Shuttle for flight had created a bloated and costly safety program" (CAIB, 107).

FORGETTING AT NASA: NEW LEADERSHIP, NEW VISION, AND THE RETURN OF TIGHT BUDGETS AND LAUNCH PRESSURES

By the early 1990s, the political climate was growing cooler for both NASA and Administrator Truly, who took over three weeks after the *Challenger* disaster. A confluence of forces seemed to be working against Truly. Setbacks with the *Galileo* project, problems with the Hubble Space Telescope and the Mars orbiter and lander spacecraft, and more shuttle delays were all very expensive and very visible failures at NASA. These embarrassing disappointments decreased public confidence, producing a climate of public distrust and skepticism regarding multibillion-dollar, large-scale missions. Added to this, major budget cuts made smaller, less-expensive missions, such as many of those in the planetary-science program, very enticing to the White House's National Space Council, established in 1989 and headed by Vice President Dan Quayle. Unfortunately for Truly, this new approach to space exploration, known in the agency as "faster, better, cheaper," jarred with his approach, which embodied the old NASA culture of large-scale human space missions with exorbitantly high price tags. In time of budget tightening, the typical NASA response was to make incremental cutbacks, reduce program redundancies, and damp down the program, thus slowing its pace and increasing its long-term costs before mission completion.

The Augustine Report and Faster, Better, Cheaper

The National Space Council had been impressed by the successful application of the "faster, better, cheaper" principles to the National Security Council's Strategic Defense Initiative during the early 1980s. The National Space Council believed such fast-response, low-cost missions were better than NASA's old way of doing things, and it hoped to revolutionize the agency along these lines (Roy 1998, 163–64). The Augustine Report of December 1990 echoed the National Space Council's philosophy. This report had been commissioned by the White House to evaluate U.S. space policy. Among its concerns was that NASA was overcommitted in its program obligations and organizational resources (NASA 1990, 3). In addition, the report cautioned against overly ambitious programs that "collapse under their weight" (3), and made it clear that space-science programs too often bore the financial loss "for problems encountered in larger (frequently manned) missions" (3).

The report also recommended that a fifth orbiter should be deferred or eliminated while steps should be taken to reduce dependency on the space shuttle system by developing an unmanned vehicle for routine space transport and by paring down plans for the space station. Among other things, these changes would reduce schedule pressures. In contrast, however, the report supported a far-reaching human space-exploration program, such as human exploration on Mars, that would evolve contingent on the availability of funds rather than on a rigid schedule. Most importantly, the report placed the highest priority for funding on the space-science program while avoiding oversubscribing to various programs that did not have the needed financial and personnel resources. Special note was also made of the fact that many useful, small, low-cost science projects could be undertaken for the price of a single large-scale project.

Changing Leadership at NASA

Though the Augustine Report, Vice President Quayle, and the National Space Council all strongly supported the idea of missions with shorter, faster timelines, smaller demands for hardware and personnel, and cheaper costs, Truly was never a believer in the approach. One chronicler of this period notes that the National Space Council saw Truly as "a former Shuttle astronaut, . . . too closely tied to the old way of doing business and a barrier to change" (Roy 1998, 164).

In addition, according to Quayle, NASA under Truly resisted the recommendations of the Augustine Report. Actually, even before the report was written, Truly resisted the Augustine Report's mandate, which was to examine every aspect of NASA's operations, including the space station and the space shuttle. Quayle had told Truly that "everything is on the table, and let the chips fall where they may" (Quayle 1994, 206). Although Quayle, the White House, and the Augustine Report supported the space shuttle and the space station on condition they be smaller and redesigned, by 1992 Quayle believed that Truly was not the man to bring about his new vision for the agency, and ultimately Truly was replaced.

Cutting Budgets and Downsizing

In his place, Daniel Goldin, a political outsider and formerly a vice president and general manager of TRW's Space and Technology Group, was appointed. Acting on the political cues of the vice president and the National Space Council, Goldin enthusiastically promoted a less costly and more targeted space-science mission, a direction that was carried over into the new Democratic administration of Clinton and Gore. In addition, Goldin resolved to implement the Clinton administration's government reinvention efforts by seeking efficiency through "downsizing" the shuttle program while aiming to "do more with less" by cutting costs, consolidating the contracts for the shuttle program (described in the previous chapter), and still undertaking an ambitious launch schedule.

One way to cut costs was to reduce personnel, based on the argument that safety would be assured with fewer bureaucratic layers and with the operators executing core tasks taking the responsibility for the quality of their work. As a result the space station program, set for completion in 2000, was to be accomplished with a pared-down budget and with a significant reduction in personnel. Altogether, from 1991–94, shuttle operating costs were cut by 21 percent. Budget-cutting through staff reduction continued through 1997, accompanied by the same assurances that the move would not compromise safety (CAIB, 107). In 2003, the CAIB concluded that even though the space shuttle program had always been "NASA's single most expensive activity"(104), it had at the same time suffered greatly from the budgetary belt tightening of the 1990s. A flat budget for NASA was the route chosen by Congress and the White House.

They would rather have NASA produce valuable scientific and symbolic payoffs for the nation without a need for increased budgets. Recent budget allocations reflect this continuing policy reality. Between 1993 and 2002, the government's discretionary spending grew in purchasing power by more than 25 percent, defense spending by 15 percent, and non-defense spending by 40 percent. . . . NASA's budget, in comparison, showed little change, going from $14.31 billion in Fiscal Year 1993 to a low of $13.6 billion in Fiscal Year 2000, and increasing to $14.87 billion in Fiscal Year 2002. This represented a loss of 13 percent in purchasing power over the decade. (CAIB, 102–3) (See table 5.1 and figure 5.1)

The flat budget, with only small, temporary increases in the direct aftermath of the *Challenger* accident, had serious implications for the shuttle and the space station. NASA had to reallocate its funds for the human space-flight program "from 48 percent of agency funding in Fiscal Year 1991 to 38 percent in Fiscal Year 1999, with the remainder going to other science and technology efforts" (CAIB, 103). Thus the financial problems of the shuttle program were compounded by a smaller NASA budget and by the harsh reality of having to divide

TABLE 5.1   NASA Budget, 1965–2004

Fiscal Year	Real Dollars (in billions)	Constant Dollars (in billions)
1965	5,250	24,696
1975	3,229	10,079
1985	7,573 .	11,643
1993	14,310	17,060
1994	14,570	16,965
1995	13,854	15,790
1996	13,884	15,489
1997	13,709	14,994
1998	13,648	14,641
1999	13,653	14,443
2000	13,601	14,202
2001	14,230	14,559
2002	14,868	14,868
2003	15,335	NA
2004	(requested) 15,255	NA

Source: NASA and U.S. Office of Management and Budget, CAIB 2003, 104

FIGURE 5.1　NASA's Budget as a Percentage of the Total Federal Budget

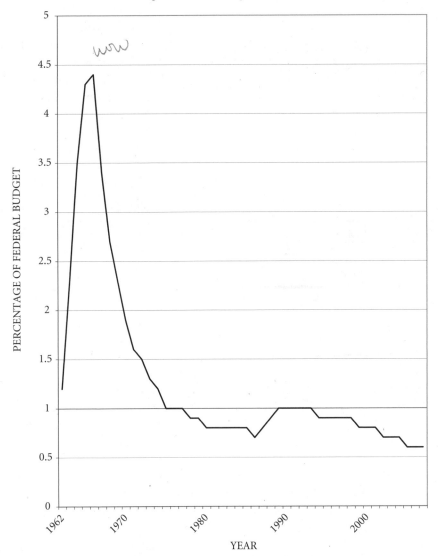

Source: Figure by the authors. Data from www.whitehouse.gov/omb/budget/fy2009/
sheets/hist04z2.xls

the smaller pie to meet the needs of more competing programs. In short, the International Space Station program was vying with the space shuttle's program for "decreasing resources" (104). Funding constraints were further exacerbated by the congressional practice of "earmarking," which required the agency to expend its budget in ways that drained funds away from its core task. Also, approximately $650 million was allocated for "Russian hardware and services related to U.S.–Russian space cooperation" (104). Agency leaders did not block these diversions. In fact, Goldin viewed himself as an innovative entrepreneur who could juggle these goals and reinvent the agency in line with the downsizing policies of the George H. W. Bush administration and then the Clinton–Gore administration (Lambright 2001, 15).

These serious budgetary constraints operating on NASA were accompanied by deep reductions in the workforce, including the contractor workforce. From 1991 to 1994, shuttle program operating costs were cut by 21 percent (CAIB, 107). According to the CAIB, "the Contractor personnel working on the Shuttle declined from 28,394 to 22,387 . . . and NASA Shuttle staff decreased from 4,031 to 2,959" (107). Further reductions in the workforce followed, accompanied by the agency's leadership's mantra of faster, better, cheaper that essentially conveyed the message of timely shuttle flights without compromising safety. By 1997, the civilian workforce at the agency had dwindled to 2,195 and contractor personnel to 17,281 (107).

Streamlining Safety Organization

Another development in November 1994 illustrates the significant effects of external pressures on the organization of the safety workforce. Goldin appointed a panel to review the space shuttle program to suggest where operating costs could be reduced while at the same time increasing efficiency. The Kraft Report described in the previous chapter addressed the opportunities for significant savings through consolidating the work of contractors under a single organization or prime contractor, the United Space Alliance. But this development was accompanied by other major changes in the management structure of the space shuttle program, based on the argument that the prime contractor, with the appropriate financial incentives, would be responsible for "safe and productive operations" as NASA oversight was greatly reduced (NASA 1995, 4).

According to the arguments advanced in the Kraft Report, bureaucratic layering at NASA had become wasteful. And a clear example of such waste was the parallel offices of the Safety, Quality, Maintainability and Reliability Assurance organization created after the *Challenger* accident. These offices were all to be part of a headquarters organization, independent of the centers they were to monitor. As noted in chapter 3, however, these offices retained their center ties and never became fully independent of the programs whose safety practices they were to oversee. The multiple center offices were originally designed to provide crosschecks and prevent gaps in tracking safety issues, but the Kraft report argued that the offices had become needlessly redundant, especially as the space shuttle program was now deemed a "safe and reliable system, and in terms of a manned rocket-propelled space launch system, is about as safe as today's technology will provide" (NASA 1995, 3). Consequently, there would be no need to maintain duplicative checks and balances. As the report states:

> Duplication and overlap have developed throughout the program. One of the most apparent examples in this regard is the area of SR&QA. As a result of the *Challenger* incident, a "safety shield" philosophy has evolved creating a difficult management situation. Managers, engineers, and business people are reluctant to make decisions that involve risk because of the fear of persecution. As a result, a parallel and independent SR&QA element has grown to large proportions. This is not only significant with respect to direct costs, but has an even greater impact when supporting efforts are included. (3)

Reducing the layers of bureaucracy was a virtue as far as the Kraft Report was concerned. Efficiency would be achieved without compromising safety.

And yet there was dissent in some areas. The Kraft Report stated that the space shuttle program was a mature operation, with sixty-five successful shuttle launches under its belt, thus "the current vehicle configuration" should be frozen, "minimizing future modifications" (NASA 1995, 4). But the Aerospace Safety Advisory Panel, NASA's independent oversight body created in response to the Rogers Commission recommendations, observed that the "assumption [in the Kraft Report] that the space shuttle systems was now 'mature' smacks of a complacency which may lead to serious mishaps. The fact is that the space shuttle may never be mature enough to totally freeze the design" (CAIB, 108). In addition, as noted in the CAIB report, there was a serious danger that cutting bureaucratic layers, especially those that were integral to the checks and balances necessary for a robust safety program, would bring the agency back to the pre-*Challenger* days of a silent safety program. As noted in chapter 4, a senior engineer at NASA was concerned enough about these cuts to write a letter to President Clinton on August 25, 1995:

> Historically NASA has employed two engineering teams at KSC [Kennedy Space Center], one contractor and one government, to cross check each other and

prevent catastrophic errors . . . although this technique is expensive, it is effective, and it is the single most important factor that sets the Shuttle's success above that of any other launch vehicle. (CAIB, 108)

In spite of reservations in certain quarters, NASA leadership, with White House support, accepted the recommendations of the Kraft Report, and in November 1995 the United Space Alliance was formed to implement the space shuttle operations contract (CAIB, 108).

Urging NASA to Remember

Still, some voices continued to urge the agency not to forget the lessons of the *Challenger*. The annual reports of the Aerospace Safety Advisory Panel show increasing concern about the effects of the cutbacks on shuttle program safety, even while acknowledging the increasing pressure that the construction of the International Space Station was placing on the program. During the 1990s the panel published annual reports on NASA's safety record for the operation of the space shuttle program and the construction of the space station. Even though the panel introduced each report with a statement commending NASA and its contractors for their commitment to safety, it usually followed the praise with examples of agency failures to place safety before cost and schedule.

A common theme in these annual reports was the dangerous consequences of budget cutting to the overall safety of space shuttle flight operations. In the 1996 report, the panel noted that although NASA enjoyed successes, such as the repair of the Hubble telescope, severe budget cutbacks and departure of key personnel, "particularly on labor-intensive operations such as Shuttle processing," compelled continual monitoring by the panel (Aerospace Safety Advisory Panel 1996, 3). Moreover, with the beginning of the Russian *Mir* space station missions, the panel made a particular point of saying it would track the potential for any increase in launch pressures, stating that: "NASA must renew efforts to resist pressures to assign a launch schedule priority so high that safety may be compromised" (3).

The next year, the acting director of the panel wrote a letter commending NASA on its prudent management in delaying a launch to transport the first International Space Station component (Aerospace Safety Advisory Panel 1997). But in the same letter he stated that "budget appropriations and their allocations are forcing continued staff reductions that have little relationship to workload," and that combined with hiring freezes, the reductions would "inevitably hamstring NASA's ability to monitor adequately the performance of Space Shuttle operations" (26). The panel report also noted deficiencies of certain skilled personnel in the Safety, Reliability and Quality Assurance office at Kennedy Space Center (26).

In 1999, the panel's annual report continued to raise concerns about the reductions in critical skills in the NASA workforce and its shrinking size. This report expresses particular concern for the projected increase in flight rate:

> Due to the unusually low recent Shuttle flight rate, the reduced workforce has been able to keep up with processing and short-term Ground Support Equipment (GSE) and facility maintenance demands. With future flight rates scheduled to rise to as many as eight per year, with surges equivalent to a rate of 12, this may no longer be the case. (Aerospace Safety Advisory Panel 1999, 16)

The same report indicated that with sufficient funding from its political overseers, these problems associated with the safe operation of the shuttle program would end: "Given appropriate funding and cooperative efforts among the Administration, the Congress and the various contractors, the Panel is convinced that safety problems can be avoided or solved resulting in lower risk for NASA's human space and astronautics programs" (Aerospace Safety Advisory Panel 1999, 5–6).

In subsequent years, these concerns increased. In the prefatory letter to the 2000 report, for example, Chairman Richard Blomberg wrote to Goldin applauding the vigor with which NASA was moving ahead with the "assembly and habitation of the International Space Station." Yet the letter almost immediately addressed Aerospace Safety and Advisory Panel concerns about the lack of planning for future resources that would be required for continued safe operation of the space shuttle program. In concrete terms, this planning involved spending money on important safety upgrades to an aging space vehicle system as well as its aging infrastructure. The report also argued that there was not enough staff for the increased flight rate associated with assembling the space station on orbit. Increasing productivity was not the answer, and even though NASA had resumed hiring, the dearth of critical skills and experience (partly from downsizing), had not been resolved. As the panel stated:

> NASA's recent hiring of inexperienced personnel, along with continuing shortages of experienced, highly skilled workers, has produced the challenge of training and integrating employees into organizations that are highly pressured by the expanded Space Shuttle flight rates associated with the ISS (International Space Station). There is no systematic effort to capture the knowledge of experienced personnel before they leave. Stress levels within the workforce are a continuing concern. (Aerospace Safety Advisory Panel 2000, 37)

)1 annual report continued to urge NASA to engage in long-term planning for safety improvements. Given the length of time needed to design and develop a new "human-rated space vehicle," it had become obvious that the space shuttle would be the primary means of transporting humans throughout the twenty years of the International Space Station's life (Aerospace Safety Advisory Panel 2001, 9).

Times had changed, however, as the report acknowledged. "The inauguration of a new administration and the events of September 11 have shifted national priorities. . . . Since last year's report was prepared, the long-term situation has deteriorated . . . budget constraints have forced the Space shuttle program to adopt an even shorter planning horizon in order to continue flying safely" (Aerospace Safety Advisory Panel 2001, 9). The panel also warned that "current and proposed budgets are not sufficient to improve or even maintain the safety risk level" (10) for either the shuttle or the space station. It would appear that the pleadings of the panel were heard because a letter in the 2002 panel report from its chair, Shirley McCarty, to the new NASA administrator, Sean O'Keefe, applauded NASA's decision to "extend the Space Shuttle service life" and noted that the decision "provides a planning horizon that facilitates safety improvements" (Aerospace Safety Advisory Panel 2002). The report was released just after the *Columbia* accident.

The redesign of the safety organization, greater reliance on contractors, and the shrinking of the workforce in the mid-1990s illustrate the gradual erosion of the lessons adopted after *Challenger*. No one set out to overturn the Rogers Commission recommendations or reinstitute the conditions that led to the *Challenger* disaster, but the sum total of the efficiency-based policy changes had that effect. The sizable resources devoted to oversight of safety now were characterized as wasteful in the era of reinvention and doing more with less. Earlier efforts to establish a safety presence independent of center or program-office interests were deemed needlessly redundant. Outside pressures that in many other agencies had benign effects here led to rolling back earlier lessons. We see these trends accelerated by the efforts of the Clinton administration to slash cost overruns and get the space station project back on schedule. Gains made in the first few years after *Challenger*, to resist pressures to launch before safety issues were resolved, now were jeopardized.

NEW SOURCES OF LAUNCH PRESSURES

During this period of fiscal and personnel reductions, launch pressures were reinstituted because constructing and servicing the International Space Station depended on the shuttle. In the words of the Columbia Accident Investigation Board's report:

> Tying the Shuttle closely to the International Space Station needs, such as crew rotation, added to the urgency of maintaining a predictable launch schedule. The Shuttle is currently the only means to launch the already-built European, Japanese, and remaining U.S. modules needed to complete Station assembly and to carry and return most experiments and on-orbit supplies. Even after three occasions when technical problems grounded the Shuttle fleet for a month or more, NASA continued to assume that the Shuttle could regularly and predictably service the Station. *In recent years, this coupling between the Station and Shuttle has become the primary driver of the Shuttle launch schedule. Whenever a Shuttle launch is delayed, it impacts Station assembly and operation.* (CAIB, 101; emphasis added)

In addition, newly appointed administrator Sean O'Keefe announced that completing the initial space-station assembly in 2004 was a test of the agency's capabilities and the fate of human space flight. In addition, meeting this deadline could position the agency for a presidential announcement in a presidential re-election year on the "next logical step": a Moon–Mars mission. O'Keefe took over from Goldin, who was identified with Clinton administration policies, at the end of 2001, just over a year before the *Columbia* accident. He moved from a position as deputy director of the Office of Management and Budget in the Bush administration, and he had impressed Vice President Cheney with his leadership of the Navy after the sexual harassment scandal known as Tailhook. His first year at NASA was devoted to coping with huge cost overruns in the space station program, which was at least $4 billion over budget (Lambright 2005, 14), and to re-establishing NASA's credibility (17). Part of that recovery effort was to get the International Space Station project, much behind schedule, back on track.

O'Keefe set February 2004 as the deadline for NASA to complete construction of the core of the station onto which European, Japanese, and other partners would add modules. This "U.S. Core Complete" milestone would be reached when a component called node 2 was constructed. According to the CAIB, this launch date "seemed etched in stone" (2003, 131). After all, NASA was "on probation" in terms of its ability to "meet schedules and budgets" (131). One could posit that the alternative would not bear thinking about: the serious loss of the already precarious political support from Congress and the White House. As a result, NASA was subjected to unending pressures to meet its launch date of February 19, 2004, for node 2 construction.

By late summer of 2002, it was clear that space-station assembly work and the shuttle flights had fallen behind the scheduled completion dates, meaning the agency had to operate without slack if it wanted to make the February 19 date. Deadlines for the shuttle missions and work on the space station assembly would have to become even more compressed:

> Meeting U.S. Core Complete by February 19, 2004, would require *preparing and launching 10 flights in less than 16 months.* With the focus on retaining support for the Space Station program, little attention was paid to the effects the aggressive Node 2 launch date would have on the shuttle program. . . . The high-pressure environments created by NASA Headquarters unquestionably affected *Columbia,* even though it was not flying to the International Space Station. (CAIB, 131; emphasis added)

This deadline, and the accompanying pressure, permeated the entire space-shuttle and space-station operations. A screen saver depicting a clock counting down to the U.S. Core Complete day, February 19, 2004, was given to the Human Space Flight program. However, although managers and workers alike were very well aware of the deadline, some were not necessarily happy with it, as illustrated by one employee's comments recorded by the CAIB:

> I guess my frustration was . . . I know the importance of showing that you . . . manage your budget and that's an important impression to make to Congress so you can continue the future of the agency, but to a lot of people, February 19th just seemed like an arbitrary date. . . . It doesn't make sense to me why at all costs we were marching to this date. (CAIB, 132)

The CAIB report continued by describing how the date was impressed upon the shuttle managers from the top down:

> The Space Station and Space Station Program Managers briefed the new NASA Administrator monthly on the status of their programs, and a significant part of those briefings was the days of margin remaining in the schedule to the launch of Node 2—still well over a year away. The Node 2 schedule margin typically accounted for more than half of the briefing slides. (132)

The ramifications were not lost to the workers assembling the space-station sections:

> While employees found this [the U.S. Core Complete day] amusing because they saw it as a date that could not be met, it also reinforced the message that

NASA Headquarters was focused on and promoting the achievement of that date. This schedule was on the minds of the Shuttle managers in the months leading up to STS-107. (CAIB, 133)

As this date became part of the working psyche of the space-shuttle and space-station operations, managers took note of the reduced time margins from program delays and sought ways to speed up work. With the space shuttle program work was authorized over the 2002 winter holiday, while other ways were found to hasten space-station assembly. Testing of space-station components was reduced and the number of work shifts for 2003 was increased (CAIB, 132–33). The terrible irony, of course, was that at the time of the accident, the *Columbia* was not directly engaged in the space-station-construction mission but was to have been modified to contribute to that effort after the completion of its disastrous flight (134).

It was in this environment that a particularly severe foam strike occurred but due to schedule pressures did not trigger a requirement to resolve the problem before future launches. As the CAIB reported, "For the first time in the history of the shuttle program, the Program Requirements Control Board chose to classify that bipod foam loss as an 'action' rather than a more serious In-Flight Anomaly. At the [next] Flight Readiness Review, managers accepted with little question the rationale that it was safe to fly with the known foam problem" (135).

In sum, years of downsizing and stagnant budgets for the shuttle program, along with schedule pressures to bring the space station to "U.S. Core Complete," created conditions much like those that existed before the *Challenger*. Both Goldin and O'Keefe were determined to prove that NASA could deliver on the promised flight schedules. This produced a set of circumstances that laid the groundwork for the *Columbia* accident. In a pattern too similar to the *Challenger* case, short-term learning from earlier foam incidents did not occur. Instead, the problem was categorized under new rules that did not require a remedy to continue launches.

NASA's political overseers played an important though indirect role in pushing NASA to abandon the post-*Challenger* lessons. They too seem to have forgotten the insights into their own role in NASA's environment that they articulated in the immediate post-*Challenger* period. The utterances of one congressional member during the *Challenger* recovery period could equally apply to the *Columbia*: "We have also taken considerable criticism for our role in this tragedy—for helping to create the environment that pushed NASA into taking the chances they did" (U.S. Congress, House Committee on Science, Space, and Technology

1987, 3). With other more pressing issues and events that had been thrust onto the policy agenda, the political branches forgot the lessons of *Challenger*.

Our principal concern is with learning at NASA, however, and here we see that lessons learned after the *Challenger* about how to resist external pressures by either cutting back on the scope of work or taking the time needed to resolve safety concerns were lost. Under extreme pressure, the agency leaders seemed to think they had no choice but to respond to the political cues that were coming down the pipeline from agency overseers. However, one could also argue that agency leaders could have tried to resist the pressures from Congress and the administration, challenging them with the reality of the consequences of such budget tightening. Indeed, the agency could have drawn from the concerns expressed in the annual reports of the Aerospace Safety Advisory Panel to buttress its arguments. But with externally appointed NASA leadership supporting outside launch pressures, the lessons were abandoned in favor of policies that would satisfy agency critics in Congress and the administration.

And so a resource-strapped shuttle operation that set unrealistic program expectations helped set the stage for the *Columbia* accident. The agency's focus was on completing the ambitious launch schedule. With such operational pressures, any attempt at even beginning the learning process by recognizing and analyzing the problem with the foam debris was easily labeled an unnecessary delay, because admitting that the foam debris constituted a significant safety problem would, under NASA rules, have required a moratorium on launches until the problem could be resolved. This scenario was not acceptable under the pressures of the space station deadline. In addition, it was unlikely that agency officials would find the funds to experiment with alternative designs or foam application when resources were simply insufficient. The agency had already been threatened because of cost overruns and shuttle delays in transporting materials to the International Space Station. They were under particular threat not to miss the schedule deadlines.

LAUNCH PRESSURES, FOAM LOSSES, AND DECISION MAKING AT NASA

Nonetheless, NASA management denied that the existence of excessive launch-schedule pressures clouded its judgment on the seriousness of the foam-debris events, especially the "event" that impacted the *Columbia* during its ascent on January 16, 2003. Members of the workforce of the space shuttle and the space station programs, however, told a different story. According to the CAIB:

"[They] thought there was considerable management focus on node 2 and resulting pressure to hold firm to that launch date, and individuals were becoming concerned that safety might be compromised. The weight of evidence supports the workforce view" (CAIB, 131). They pointed to pressures from the newly appointed NASA administrator, Sean O'Keefe, who established the node 2 complete date of February 19, 2005. Others believed that it was the budget that was equally important. In any case, hindsight allows us to see clearly the effects of these pressures on decision making by shuttle managers as they responded to the information of the foam-debris strike to the left wing of the *Columbia* during its descent on January 16, 2003.

During *Columbia*'s liftoff and ascent, film recorded that a large piece of foam broke off from the left bipod ramp of the external tank and hit the leading edge of the orbiter's left wing. As noted in chapter 3, photo lab engineers from the Intercenter Photo Working Group at Johnson Space Center, as well as contractor and NASA engineers, were worried about the potential damage from this strike and tried to acquire a more accurate evaluation of the potential damage of the strike while the *Columbia* was on orbit. In contrast, space shuttle managers were neither anxious about the matter nor did they try to investigate it further. The CAIB report takes note of these two distinctive perspectives of risk-taking:

> The opinions of shuttle program managers and debris and photo analysts on the potential severity of the debris strike diverged early in the mission and continued to diverge as the mission progressed, making it increasingly difficult for the Debris Assessment Team to have concerns heard by those in a decision-making capacity. In the face of the Mission managers' low level of concern and desire to get on with the mission, Debris Assessment Team members had to prove unequivocally that a safety-of-flight issue existed before the Shuttle program management would move to obtain images of the left wing. The engineers found themselves in the unusual position of having to prove that the situation was *unsafe*—a reversal of the usual requirement to prove that a situation is *safe*. (CAIB, 169; italics in original)

One explanation for this divergent pattern could be structural. Although everyone felt the urgency for making the node 2 complete deadline, working engineers were staff personnel and as such were much less directly susceptible to the schedule pressures than the space shuttle line managers. After all, line managers like Linda Ham, chair of the mission management team, Ron Dittemore, space shuttle program manager, and other senior managers had both the responsibility and the authority to move each shuttle mission further toward the launch deadline.

The effects of schedule pressures are clearly visible in the decisions made by the managers. Both managers and working engineers interacted and saw the same evidence, yet they drew very different conclusions about the risk to the mission posed by the debris event. In contrast to shuttle managers, one day after the launch, on Friday, January 17, engineers wanted a photo of *Columbia*'s left wing on orbit. However, in the words of the CAIB:

> *Already, by Friday afternoon Shuttle Program managers and working engineers had different levels of concern about what the foam strike might have meant.* After reviewing available film, Intercenter Photo Working Group engineers believed the Orbiter may have been damaged by the strike. . . . At the same time, high-level managers Ralph Roe, head of the shuttle program Office of Vehicle Engineering, and Bill Reeves, from United Space Alliance, voiced a lower level of concern. It was at this point, *before any analysis had started,* that shuttle program managers officially shared their belief that the strike posed no safety issues and that there was no need for a review to be conducted over the weekend. (CAIB, 142; emphasis added)

Though NASA and contractor engineers decided to conduct tests to calculate the potential damage over the Martin Luther King holiday weekend, the shuttle managers in the mission evaluation room thought otherwise. They communicated through various log entries and notes that the foam-debris impact was not serious enough to call a meeting over the holiday. The log entry dated at 4:37 p.m. for Friday, January 16, by the mission evaluation room manager, reads as follows: "I also confirmed that there was no rush on this issue and that it was okay to wait till the film reviews are finished on Monday to do a TPS [thermal protection system] review" (CAIB, 142).

It soon became apparent to the debris assessment team, however, that the only way to assess the exact damage that the debris had caused was to either conduct an actual on-orbit visual inspection by the *Columbia* crew or obtain on-orbit images of the orbiter's left wing. Neither of these actions was taken, as we know from earlier chapters. Instead, the mission management team remained focused on ensuring that the next shuttle flight launch (STS-114) was on schedule. Early on Tuesday, January 21, the debris assessment team briefed Don McCormack, the chief mission evaluation room manager. Later that morning, after other flight concerns were addressed; McCormack informed Linda Ham, the mission management team chair, that engineers were examining the debris impact and "planned to determine what could be done if *Columbia* had sustained damage" (CAIB, 147). Ham did not appear to be overly concerned with this issue as a serious safety concern, saying somewhat dismissively, "there is not much we can do about it" (CAIB, 147). Clearly, she did not believe the strike could seriously jeopardize the safe return of *Columbia*. As she stated, "What I am really interested in is in making sure our flight rationale to go was good," that is, that STS-114, the next shuttle mission for which she was the primary manager, would launch on time (CAIB, 147). Even so, minutes later, in an e-mail to Dittemore, she summarizes her unhappiness with the present rationale for future shuttle flights:

> The ET [External Tank] rationale for flight for the STS-112 [*Atlantis*] loss of foam was lousy. Rationale states we haven't changed anything, we haven't experienced any safety of flight damage in 112 flights, risk of bipod ramp TPS (foam) is same as previous flights . . . So ET is safe to fly with no added risk. Rationale was lousy then and still is. . . . (CAIB, 148)

Both of these comments communicate the preoccupation of the shuttle program managers in charge of the mission with schedule issues. Delays or an acknowledgment that the foam debris did pose a problem could put the schedule in jeopardy, as the CAIB report noted: "STS 114, due to be launched in about a month, would have to be delayed per NASA rules that require serious problems to be resolved before the next flight. An STS-114 delay could in turn *delay completion of the International Space Station's Node 2, which was a high-priority goal for NASA managers*" (CAIB, 148; emphasis added).

Additional evidence of Ham's worry about falling behind launch schedule was her lack of enthusiasm for imaging the left wing of *Columbia*. She balked both at taking the valuable time needed to maneuver the orbiter so that the left wing would be visible and at using other scarce agency resources. Also, as we noted in chapter 3, Ham cancelled several imagery requests to the Department of Defense for *Columbia* on-orbit. She defended the cancellations because the requests were not "official" and had not come from either the flight director or the mission evaluation room manager (CAIB, 153). However, she did not attempt to track down the source of the requests. What perplexed the CAIB was that although Ham was fully aware that the debris assessment team was analyzing the foam strike, "she never asked them directly if the request was theirs" (CAIB, 153). In addition, even though the engineers attempted to qualify their opinion that the foam strike probably would not cause a burn-through to the shuttle frame on re-entry, Ham and others on the mission management team did not inquire further about their uncertainty. Her concern for maintaining the schedule emerged again in the mission management meeting the next day when Don McCormick, the mission evaluation room manager, reassured Ham about the conclusions of the debris assessment team:

DON MCCORMACK: Also we've received the data from the systems integration guys of the potential ranges of sizes and impact angles and where it might have hit. . . . The analysis is not complete. There is one case yet that they wish to run, but kind of just jumping to the conclusion of all that, they do show that, obviously, a potential for significant tile damage here, but thermal analysis does not indicate that there is potential for burn-through. I mean there could be localized heating damage . . .

HAM: No burn-through means no catastrophic damage and the localized heating damage would mean a tile replacement?

DON MCCORMACK: Right, it would mean possible impacts to turnaround repairs and that sort of thing, but we do not see any kind of safety-of–flight issue here yet in anything that we've looked at. (CAIB, 161)

Importantly, Ham's focus was upon the conclusion of the debris assessment team's briefing from the previous day that would move the operational schedule along.

Clearly the aim of program managers was to justify their decisions to avoid investigations into the uncertainties associated with using the Crater computer model to predict possible damage to the wing and into the other assumptions embedded in the conclusions of the debris assessment team. Avoiding further inspection allowed them to maintain their rationale to continue flying with the foam-shedding problem and keep the shuttle program more or less on schedule. Their unanimous judgment was that there would be only minimal launch schedule delay due to longer turnaround time to repair the damage.

All of this points to the conclusion that in the months before the flight and during the flight itself, top shuttle managers avoided investigating a problem of potentially serious concern. In chapter 3 we described the series of flights before the *Columbia* on which critical foam-debris damage had been seen. Now we see how, during the flight, top managers also failed to make an effort to pursue the investigation of ambiguous results about the effects of foam strikes. In short, NASA managers could not afford to acknowledge that the foam debris was a significant problem that would disrupt the high-priority "U.S. Core Complete" deadline.

CONCLUSIONS

In this chapter we have set out the evidence that links agency decisions about launch criteria to external congressional and administration forces and the pressures they created on agency resources and schedules. These pressures in turn had significant and disastrous effects on the capacity of NASA to learn from its mistakes in the short term and hold on to the lessons it had learned over the long run. Lessons NASA seems to have learned in the aftermath of the *Challenger* about how to resist such pressures and maintain a rate of work commensurate with its resource base were eroded under new external pressures, magnified as well by the acquiescence of NASA's own leadership.

The similarities in the effects of strong external launch pressures in the two accidents illustrate the loss of post-*Challenger* organization knowledge. Efforts to speed the rate of launches to meet promised schedules, cutbacks in staff and materials, and increasingly lean budgets led to short-term learning deficiencies in the run-up to each of the shuttle accidents. Early indications of problems with the O-rings and foam losses were not given high priority despite concerns among some lower-level engineering staff in each case. Rules and procedures requiring NASA to solve problems before launch were ignored.

After the loss of the *Challenger*, a more searching analysis of the effects of these schedule and resources pressures led to real changes in NASA's organizational resources and its procedures involving safety restraints on schedule commitments. Forced by the loss of the *Challenger* to acknowledge problems caused by budget cutbacks and schedule pressures, both NASA and Congress changed their practices. But these lessons were soon supplanted by new post–cold war congressional priorities and new management practices associated with government reinvention and downsizing. In effect, NASA and Congress "unlearned" some of the lessons from the *Challenger*. Organizational problems with safety systems and procedures had been recognized, solutions had been evaluated and institutionalized, but they were displaced by new management ideas and other congressional needs.

CHAPTER 6

Organizational Culture

NASA's ORGANIZATIONAL CULTURE has been the subject of an enormous number of popular and scholarly works. Thomas Wolfe's 1995 *The Right Stuff*, and the subsequent film, observed the self-confident, can-do ethos of test pilots and its early influence on NASA and its astronaut corps. The 1995 film *Apollo 13* celebrated the dedication and ingenuity of NASA's engineers on the ground that were able to improvise a device to scrub carbon dioxide from the air and replot a return path for the crew of the badly damaged lunar landing craft in 1970. A darker view of the agency's culture is described by Diane Vaughan (1996), who traced the widespread acceptance of the increasingly clear evidence of faulty seals in the solid rocket boosters before the *Challenger* accident. Adams and Balfour in *Unmasking Administrative Evil* (1998) attribute what they see as the isolated and "defensive organizational culture" (108) of the Marshall Space Flight Center to its early management by a team of German rocket scientists with links to Nazi forced labor camps.

Cultural elements are also thought to have contributed to the two shuttle accidents. Both of the official investigations of the shuttle disasters identify culture as a cause. The Rogers Commission "found that Marshall Space Flight Center project managers, because of a tendency at Marshall to management isolation, failed to provide full and timely information bearing on the safety of flight 51-L to other vital elements of shuttle Program management" (Rogers Commission 1986, 200). Based on this finding, the commission indirectly recommended culture change as one remedy: "NASA should take energetic steps to eliminate this tendency at Marshall Space Flight Center, whether by changes of personnel, organization, *indoctrination* or all three" (200; emphasis added). The Columbia Accident Investigation Board went into much more detail about the failings of the shuttle program culture, identifying cultural issues behind several of the patterns of behavior that led to the accident. The board found that a "culture of invincibility" permeated the management (CAIB, 199), particularly as it used past successes to justify current risks (179). There were also "'blind spots' in NASA's safety culture" (184). Excessive hierarchy and formalization, intolerance of criticism, and fear of retribution kept those with concerns silent. The CAIB identified lapses in trust and openness, contributing to blocked communication across the shuttle organization, a finding that had also been identified in the Rogers Commission report and in 2000 by the Shuttle Independent Assessment Team (179). In both accidents, information and events had been interpreted though cultural frames of reference built up over years of experience (CAIB, 200).

In line with the approach taken in the previous three chapters, we will examine the evidence that similar patterns of cultural beliefs and assumptions contributed to both accidents. We then look at the efforts that were made to change these assumptions or learn to overcome their effects after the *Challenger* accident. Because underlying cultural assumptions tend to persist in organizations, we do not necessarily expect to find wholesale or rapid changes in the agency's culture, but rather some recognition that certain cultural beliefs contributed to the management patterns that led to the accidents. Finally, we search out the efforts that were made to understand the impact of cultural beliefs, to initiate changes when possible, or to make intelligent adaptations.

There are many characterizations of NASA's culture and subcultures. We cannot hope to track them all. Instead, we will consider the evidence surrounding four core cultural beliefs and assumptions about the work at NASA and the shuttle program particularly, each of which bears directly on the decisions and actions surrounding the accidents. They are, very briefly, the sense of rivalry and grievance that contributed to lapses in reporting and management isolation at Marshall, the dismantling of the hands-on laboratory culture at Marshall that left engineers without an effective means of judging reliability, the low status of safety work that contributed in both cases to a silent safety program, and the unwillingness to report unresolved problems based on what some have termed the "climate of fear" in the agency or, less elegantly, what contractors have called "NASA chicken" (Wald and Schwartz 2003).

INVESTIGATING THE CULTURE OF
THE SHUTTLE PROGRAM

All of the examples offered in the paragraphs above illustrate NASA's organizational culture, defined as the deeply held, widely shared beliefs about the character of work, the mission, the identity of the workforce, and the legacy of the

organization's founders. These kinds of cultural beliefs may not be overtly acknowledged by members. In fact, such beliefs may not be recognized as "the culture" but rather simply as the way things are done (Martin 2002). This "taken for granted" character of organizational culture makes it especially difficult to identify or to change, but it also means that the beliefs exercise a significant and lasting effect on the perceptions and actions of members. Culture is especially important to organizational learning because lessons learned across organization levels become embedded in culture as often-told stories, rituals, or tacit knowledge, as well as in new formal policies and procedures (Schein 1992; Levitt and March 1988). This link to learning also reflects the ways in which culture evolves as a product of the history of an organization. Van Maanen and Barley note that "culture can be understood as a set of solutions devised by a group of people to meet specific problems posed by the situations they faced in common" (1985, 33). Thus cultural meanings accrete over time and uniquely in response to the experiences of organization members.

There are many ways to conceptualize and study the culture of an organization (Martin 2002). Particularly useful here is Schein's (1992, 1999) approach that distinguishes the visible artifacts, behavior patterns, and articulated or espoused values from the underlying cultural beliefs and assumptions that may not be either visible or overtly articulated. These core assumptions describe the patterns of meaning in an organization (Martin 2002, 3), and they help account for how members think, feel, and act. Assumptions about the worth of the mission, the identity of members, and professional norms all inform the meaning of artifacts to organization actors. The overt manifestations of these underlying beliefs may include stories, architecture, and rituals, but also structures and policies (Martin 2002, 55). Public statements about the underlying beliefs may or may not be accurate. The tensions between core beliefs and the exigencies of the day may emerge in espoused statements of values that are clearly at odds with actions or with the actual operative beliefs about the organization and its members (Schein 1999).

INTERCENTER RIVALRIES AND GRIEVANCES

Rivalry among the centers, poor communication within the shuttle program hierarchy, and a reluctance to share information across centers emerged as patterns in both shuttle accidents, though much more strongly in the case of the *Challenger*. The Rogers Commission directly identified intercenter rivalries as a factor in communication lapses between the Marshall Space Flight Center in

Alabama and the Johnson Space Center in Houston. Marshall was criticized for management isolation and failing to provide "full and timely" information to other program offices (Rogers Commission 1986, 200). The CAIB found that one of the reasons that the mission management team failed to take vigorous action to acquire images of the orbiter wings was that Marshall and Langley engineers had been the first to identify the problem (CAIB 201), and "the initial request for imagery came from the 'low status' Kennedy Space Center" (201). In contrast, another member of the debris assessment team, who was without particular credentials on this issue but who had an office in the higher-status shuttle program office at Johnson, was instrumental in defining the problems as inconsequential early on (201–2). The implication is that the Johnson-based mission management team was unwilling to listen carefully to outsiders. While it appears that the rivalries between Johnson and Marshall were more directly implicated in the *Challenger* accident than in the *Columbia* disaster, struggles over status had impacts on communication and coordination in both cases.

The rivalry between the Marshall center and the Johnson center was of long standing and has been well documented. The centers had competed for resources and control of projects since at least the early 1960s, when they begin to plan for the lunar programs. The emerging proposals pitted Marshall's labs against the Manned Spacecraft Center in Houston, which became the Johnson Space Center in 1973, over whether a lunar landing craft would launch from an Earth orbit, favoring Marshall's heavy-propulsion systems, or would rely on new, lighter lunar orbital spacecraft designed at Houston. Lobbying by the Manned Spacecraft Center resulted in success for the latter plan, giving Houston the lead in the lunar program and setting up a pattern that was replicated many times in subsequent years (Dunar and Waring 1999, 56).

In the Apollo program, Marshall's role was to provide the propulsion systems, the Saturn rockets. Wernher von Braun, who was then center director, accepted this resolution so as not to jeopardize the project (56), but this was only one of many compromises. Marshall engineers were later given the *Lunar Rover* project as well, but they were required to design it to Houston's specifications. This was irksome to the engineering teams that had been successful in launching the first U.S. satellite, and it left them with a sense of grievance. Describing the arrangements that essentially made Marshall a contractor working for Houston, the *Lunar Rover's* project manager regretted that Marshall "'always seemed to get the short end of the string'" (102).

As noted in previous chapters, the funding for NASA projects diminished rapidly even before the lunar landing was achieved, as national attention began to focus elsewhere. To improve prospects for new projects to keep his team of scientists together, von Braun led efforts to diversify Marshall's capabilities and enlarge its mission. The center was able to secure initial work on space telescope projects for the Apollo astronomical observatories and later on the Voyager probes to Mars. Such strategies often put the centers in new competition as each jealously guarded its own project areas (Dunar and Waring 1999, 138). Dunar and Waring, for example, note that "Houston challenged any proposal from Marshall that related to operations, astronauts, or manned systems" (139). Rivalry intensified in planning for the post-Apollo projects. Marshall proposed a small space station based on reusing the spent rocket stage, making the best use of the center's own technologies, but Houston strenuously objected since this crossed the line into their province of manned spacecraft (181).

To clarify the division of labor and head off some of the increasingly bitter feuds, the headquarters associate administrator for manned space flight, George Mueller, brought these and other center staff to a retreat in 1966 to work out a formal division of labor (Dunar and Waring 1999, 139). It was here that the concept of lead center was formalized. The lead would have overall managerial responsibility and set hardware requirements for the support centers. In principle, Marshall and Houston would each be lead centers on different elements of the Apollo projects. But in practice the division between the modules was difficult to specify, and the sniping continued.

Rivalries also continued in planning for the shuttle, but by the mid-1960s, the centers had signed on to an agreement similar to that worked out for the Apollo project. Marshall would design and manage the contracts for the solid rocket boosters and, when it was added to the plan in 1971, the external tank, while Houston would management the orbiter project. This arrangement, however, effectively made Houston the lead center on the shuttle project. Commenting on this, a shuttle program developer noted, "There is a certain amount of competitiveness and parochialism between the Centers that makes it difficult for one Center to be able to objectively lead the other. . . . That was the real flaw in that arrangement" (282). In fact, Houston took firm control of the shuttle project management and disapproved some of Marshall's facility requests while filling its own. Again, Marshall staff agreed to this so as not to imperil the project overall (285), but it was another example of the center's "short end of the string."

In fact, relinquishing lead status to Houston was a blow to the sense of exceptionalism that was the hallmark of the engineering culture at Marshall. When von Braun and his 127 fellow engineers and scientists came to the United States in 1945 and later in 1950 to what was then the Redstone Arsenal in Huntsville (Dunar and Waring 1999, 11), they brought with them a team identity and a culture built upon German technical education and years together under his leadership in the German military rocket program. Others have described the moral and ethical issues surrounding their work on the American rocket program (Adams and Balfour 1998; Dunar and Waring 1999), but here we focus on the laboratory culture they established at Huntsville. Hands-on experience and the combination of theory and practice was part of their training and defined the culture they came to call the "arsenal system" (Dunar and Waring 1999, 19). They prided themselves on their capacity for "dirty hands engineering," which combined design and development work with the ability to execute and exhaustively test the project. They designed and built their own prototypes with a staff of technicians. In contrast, at most other centers, contractors typically did this work to the specifications of NASA employees. The hallmark of the arsenal system was conservative engineering. Engineers deliberately designed-in redundancy to improve reliability and performance, and would then "test to failure" (Sato 2005, 572; Dunar and Waring 1999, 43) to determine the limits of the design. The system was very successful. In the 1960s, no Saturn launch had failed, a remarkable record of reliability given the complexity of the technology (Dunar and Waring 1999, 92). This approach was also known for building in wide margins of safety and containing costs while still speeding the development of new designs. In one often-told story, to avoid delay and the $75,000 that a contractor wanted to charge for a rocket test stand, Huntsville engineers cobbled together their own stand for $1,000 in materials (20).

The technical strengths of the arsenal system as a whole also came under severe pressure as the resource-rich early years of the Apollo program came to an end. The hands-on lab culture eroded as reductions in force took first the younger engineers and then cut into the original team of German engineers. This was a particular blow to the Marshall workforce under von Braun, who

> believed that a good team did not work by a clear-cut division of labor. Rather, it depended on identity, honesty, mutual respect, and trust, which could develop only through a long period of collective effort . . . [and were] the prerequisites for any sound rocket-building organization. (Sato 2005, 566–67)

Von Braun's group was forced to move from its heavy reliance on in-house work to the more typical Air Force model of development by contracting its work. Using a wide array of contractors also helped NASA maintain its political base by creating constituency support at a time when the space exploration became a lower national policy priority. However, as a result, the Marshall team's ability to develop, manufacture, and test its prototypes was diminished. It lost its shops and technicians and with them some of the basis for its lab culture (Dunar and Waring 1999, 165; McCurdy 1993, 136). The cuts also compromised the ability of the engineers to closely monitor contractors' work and thus maintain their own quality and reliability standards. Earlier, 10 percent of the Marshall workforce had been on permanent assignment at contractor facilities to monitor the quality of the work, a system they called "penetration." Marshall managers felt forced to accept these changes even though they threatened their identity as an "exceptional workforce." As McCurdy summarized it: "The requirements of survival were simply more powerful than the organization culture during the period of decline" (1993, 138).

The management isolation cited by the Rogers Commission and the unwillingness of the Marshall managers to report unresolved problems thus emerge in the midst of a long history of competition and distrust between the centers. Recognizing the cultural context of their actions, the severe threats to Marshall's distinctive and successful lab culture adds to our understanding of Marshall's reluctance to acknowledge problems with the solid rocket booster joints or to delay launches to deal with the redundancy status of the seals. It helps explain Houston's sometimes dismissive responses toward Marshall's concerns about possible damage to *Columbia*'s wing. As the CAIB noted regarding both the *Challenger* and the *Columbia* cases, "All new information was weighed and interpreted against past experience" (2003, 200). Long-held cultural beliefs affected judgments about the launch and influenced the assessment and communication of information about risks.

The Rogers Commission recommendations for remedying the management isolation at Marshall included changes in personnel and in their training or "indoctrination" (Rogers Commission 1986, 200). While the commission's discussion of its findings appears to recognize the issues of competition and rivalry behind the charges of management isolation, NASA's response of the recommendations took a formal, structural approach. As noted in chapter 3, in the report on the implementation of recommendations issued a year after the Rogers Commission Report, NASA strengthened the shuttle program office at Houston's Johnson Space Center by making it a headquarters office and adding a shuttle project manager at Marshall to coordinate the Marshall elements and report on them to the shuttle program office. This solution addressed the formal communication issues, but not the underlying cultural beliefs that complicated the command and communication structures, because Houston was still the site of the "headquarters" office. By 1990 the Augustine Report on NASA's role in U.S. space policy noted internal and external evidence of continuing reluctance by "the various NASA centers to energetically support one another or take direction from headquarters," but also noted that "an intense effort by the current center and headquarters managements has been underway to redress these long-building trends, yet much remains to be accomplished in this most difficult of management challenges, a cultural shift" (NASA 1990, subsection "Institutional Aging"). In any case, the structure reverted back to the concentration of program authority at the Johnson center when the shuttle program office was repositioned under the control of that center in 1996. Reorganizations and downsizing also created overlaps between program management roles and safety functions. These changes were linked to efforts to improve the willingness of NASA employees and contract personnel to voice their safety concerns. We consider these issues below.

RELIABILITY AND RISK ASSESSMENT

Investigations of both shuttle accidents found that the shuttle program suffered from lapses in safety and reliability. The Rogers Commission found that NASA failed to track trends with the erosion of the O-rings and failed to act on the evidence they did have. The commission stated that "a careful analysis of the flight history of O-ring performance would have revealed the correlation of O-ring damage and low temperature" (Rogers Commission 1986, 148), and it concluded that "NASA and Thiokol accepted escalating risk apparently because they 'got away with it last time'" (148). The *Columbia* accident investigators found similar evidence of a willingness to assume that known hazards that had not produced a catastrophic accident did not require urgent action. As Vaughan found in the case of the *Challenger* (1996), the damage from foam debris had become "normalized" and was seen as simply a maintenance issue by program managers (CAIB, 181). The Board concluded, "NASA's safety culture has become reactive, complacent, and dominated by unjustified optimism" (180). But the assumptions about safety and how to judge safety were also rooted in the culture of the organization.

Reliability had been a central value of the arsenal system at Marshall under von Braun. The center's tradition of conservative engineering meant that engineers included wide margins of safety and reliability with built-in redundancies (Dunar and Waring 1999, 44, 103). Testing was done both on project components and on the assembled result, and the severity of test conditions was increased to allow engineers to find the point at which the design would fail. Then engineers would isolate and fix the problems (100). As noted, early results were impressive. Under this model, however, quantitative risk analysis was not seen as appropriate or feasible. Statistical analysis and random testing, while acceptable in a mass-production setting, was not appropriate in the zero-error environment of manned flight (45) in which failure was not permitted. Reliability assurance at Marshall thus rested on these premises, among others: a fundamental belief in engineers' vigilance, an emphasis on engineering judgment founded on broad experience, and a conservatism nurtured in a particular social structure (Sato 2005, 571–72). However, in the shuttle era, as resources were cut and the in-house arsenal system was dismantled, the "agency could no longer afford the conservative engineering approaches of the Apollo years, and had to accept risks that never confronted an earlier generation of rocket engineers" (Dunar and Waring 1999, 324). They did not do this willingly, holding instead to the importance of conservative engineering and the need for thorough testing even though they no longer had the resources to sustain that approach (McCurdy 1993, 150). The reliability of the arsenal system had been lost, but no culturally workable replacement was forthcoming.

The antipathy of shuttle program managers to statistical analysis has also been linked to the many frighteningly pessimistic figures about the shuttle's survival that had been circulated. Estimates of the reliability of the shuttle's rockets varied by source. A NASA ad hoc group put failure rate at 1 in 10,000, while a 1983 Teledyne study estimated failures at 1 in 100 flights (Dunar and Waring 1999, 399). Johnson Space Center managers offered figures of 1 in 100,000 flights, while Rogers Commission member Richard Feynman polled NASA engineers who put the rate at 1 in 200–300 launches (399). All these, of course, were inferences drawn from a very slim data base. Casamayou traces the low estimates by management to a desire to avoid publicizing unacceptable estimates of risk during the Apollo program (1993, 177). An estimated probability of overall failure of that spacecraft of 1 in 20 prompted a project manager to respond: "Bury that number, disband the group, I don't want to hear about anything like this again" (McKean 1986, 48). More recently, GAO reported that in 1995 a contractor offered a median estimate of catastrophic shuttle failure at 1 in 145 launches (GAO 1996, 10). NASA managers recognized that these numbers represent a level of risk that would be perceived as unacceptable by the public, but they did not consider the numbers to be accurate.

In addition, public tolerance of risk was diminishing with the increasing routinization of space operations (McCurdy 1993, 151), just as the complexity of the programs was increasing and the capacity of the agency to detect problems was declining. The greater ambitions of the shuttle and space station programs brought with them more complex and tightly coupled technologies with more parts and more potential interactions among flaws. Yet NASA generally and

Marshall in particular were cutting back on personnel and testing to reduce costs. They were also more dependent on contractors and less able to closely monitor them. This dependency was not entirely voluntary, but a result of repeated waves of personnel downsizing since the late 1960s. Nevertheless, it had the effect of reducing the close supervision and penetration of contractor facilities. The rapid decline in the arsenal system also meant that Marshall had a reduced ability to conduct its own tests and learn the limits of its designs. Where formerly individual components of rockets were tested before assembly, now much of the testing was "all up," reserved for the final product.

All these changes meant that engineers had become cut off from their traditional means of judging reliability, without being able to establish effective substitutes (McCurdy 1993, 150). While a probabilistic risk analysis was the method that hazardous program administrators typically adopted for risk management, NASA resisted using it. That approach was not well integrated into the agency culture generally, and it was especially inconsistent with the lab culture at Marshall. The Rogers Commission identified the absence of trend analysis as a factor in the loss of the *Challenger* and recommended improvements in documenting, reporting, and analyzing performance (1986, 201). But little was done to adopt these quantitative methods. In the mid-1990s GAO and the National Research Council faulted the agency for still using its qualitative risk-management method, based on engineering judgments to classify components based in their criticality and redundancy, instead of an integrated, quantitative risk-analysis system based on records of past performance (GAO 1996, 37). NASA maintained that such analysis was not appropriate because the shuttle flights were too few to offer a basis for probabilistic analysis, but the agency agreed to have contractors study the feasibility of such an analysis. After the loss of the *Columbia*, the CAIB found that despite external recommendations NASA still did not have a trend- and risk-assessment system for the components and the whole project (183, 188, and 193). The CAIB also criticized NASA's inability to integrate its "massive amounts of data" (180) about the shuttle into usable information for decision making. They noted, "The Space Shuttle Program has a wealth of data tucked away in multiple databases without a convenient way to integrate and use the data for management, engineering, or safety decisions" (193).

While there were strategic reasons for not publicizing risk estimates, it appears that there were also deeply held cultural reasons behind adhering to engineering judgments as a basis for assessing risk and reliability even in the face of changed lab conditions. The long-term evolution of the professional culture and significant losses of personnel had conspired to turn assumptions about professional engineering into an organizational liability.

was another path, too, by which reliability judgments were compromised. Anomalies seen in the erosion and charring of the O-rings and the debris shedding came to be considered acceptable because they did not lead to catastrophe (Casamayou 1993; Vaughan 1996). The absence of disaster, even as a result of deviations from specifications, became a rationale to continue. Standards for the O-rings changed from "no erosion" to "acceptable erosion" (Dunar and Waring 1999, 355), and debris strikes ceased being anomalies and became a maintenance or turnaround issue (CAIB, 135). Vaughan found that NASA decision makers would routinely define such data on anomalies as nondeviant by recasting their interpretation of the range of acceptable risk. Before the *Challenger*, the flight readiness reviews had become to some degree ritualized (Dunar and Waring 1999, 360), and they were not always carried out face to face with all the key participants. The CAIB similarly identified a "culture of invincibility" that permeated NASA management, particularly as it used past successes to justify current risks (179, 199). In each case, the deviations that became acceptable were part of systems that were, objectively, among the "least worrisome" in the program (353). But in the absence of cultural agreement on how to determine reliability, judgments were cut adrift and became subject to other imperatives.

THE STATUS OF SAFETY WORK

Another aspect of NASA's risk and reliability culture was the seemingly passive and underdeveloped safety system that was silent at crucial points in both accidents. After *Challenger*, the safety offices were found not only to be dependent on the programs they were supposed to monitor, but also to be significantly understaffed, with few resources to attract those most qualified for the painstaking safety work. Commenting on the lack of information on trends in seal erosion and the status of redundancy, the Rogers Commission found that "a properly staffed, supported, and robust safety organization might well have avoided these faults and thus eliminated the communication failures" (1986, 152). Reinforcing the safety organizations was not a priority in the shuttle program, particularly after it was declared operational. The number of safety and reliability officers across the organization was reduced after one shuttle was declared operational, and the offices were reorganized. Marshall's safety staff declined as the flight rate increased, and at headquarters only a few staff were detailed to the shuttle program (Rogers Commission 1986, 160).

But the safety officials who *were* in place also appear to have been ignored by the other actors. The Rogers Commission noted:

> No one thought to invite a safety representative or a reliability and quality assurance engineer to the January 27, 1986, teleconference between Marshall and Thiokol. Similarly, there was no representative of safety on the mission management team that made key decisions during the countdown on January 28, 1986. (1986, 152)

Within a year of the loss of the *Challenger*, NASA had established a goal for SRM&QA to "develop an SRM&QA work force that is manned with quality people who are properly trained and equipped, who are dedicated to superior performance and the pursuit of excellence" (Rogers Commission 1987, 45). But, as noted in earlier chapters, the changes in the independence and the scope of safety work were short-lived. The 1995 Kraft Report found, in fact, that the burden of safety checks since *Challenger* had grown excessive.

By the time of the loss of *Columbia*, safety organizations had again been downsized and reorganized. Mirroring the Rogers Commission findings, the CAIB found that the safety officers were "largely silent during the events leading up to the loss of *Columbia*" (192). As noted in chapter 3, both NASA and contract safety personnel were passive during the meetings of the debris assessment team, the mission evaluation room, and the mission management team (170). They did not press for more information, but "deferred to management" (170). The CAIB also points out repeatedly that the safety offices were no longer independent of program offices in the centers, so their ability to report critically might have been compromised.

While the pressures of schedules and budget reductions certainly explain the loss of safety personnel and the marginalizing of safety concerns, there is also evidence that safety work itself was not a valued assignment for NASA personnel. Safety monitoring in an operational shuttle program did not have the scientific or technical interest of testing the limits of new rocket designs. McCurdy's detailed study of NASA history and culture argues that NASA underwent a slow shift in its culture as its original technical, space-science identity was tempered by the management requirements of making the shuttle safe, routine, and operational (1993, 141). Steady funding and organizational survival became priorities. Governmental oversight, which had become more searching and less tolerant of failure, even in the name of scientific advance, led to a more conservative and preservation-minded NASA administration (McCurdy 1993, 163–72; Romzek and Dubnick 1987). Budget cuts had forced the agency to skimp on prototypes and flight tests, eroding NASA's capacity to pursue space research rather than routine operational missions.

But, McCurdy argues, these major changes in practice were not followed by changes in fundamental cultural assumptions. Engineers were reluctant to accept the changes in the character of their work identity that would go along with the administration's push for operational status, and a major cultural schism emerged between the engineers and scientists devoted to space exploration and the administrators (1993, 145). For space scientists, missions that did not test new ideas and take risks would not bring new knowledge but would be mere routine. At its core, the agency retained the assumption that cutting-edge research is inherently complex and risky and can be made safe only to a degree. Risk was justified as a means to ultimate reliability and, along the way, scientific advance. How the shift to the routine was viewed in the agency is exemplified in the comments of an executive from the earlier Apollo project who said that if the shuttle were becoming an operational rather than a research and development project, NASA "ought to paint the damn thing blue and send it across the river" (McCurdy 1993, 145) to the Air Force. As requirements for routine and efficient launches increased, the interest of engineering personnel in the program seems to have flagged. Marshall administrators appeared bored when briefed on the O-ring task force and devoted minimal attention to routine concerns about the solid rocket motor joints (Dunar and Waring 1999, 367). The Marshall director who came on after the shuttle accident noted, "When the Shuttle got operational, NASA 'got too comfortable'" and stopped looking for problems (Dunar and Waring 1999, 408).

After the *Challenger* accident, NASA clearly did make efforts to change the culture surrounding the safety function as well as increase the size and scope of the safety offices. NASA managers were to establish an open-door policy, and new formal and informal means of reporting problems confidentially were created. A campaign to promote reporting about safety issues by all was initiated. Posters were displayed, declaring "If it's not safe, say so." And some learning appeared to occur. A GAO study of NASA's safety culture in the mid-1990s, found that

> all of the groups reported that the shuttle program's organizational culture encourages people to discuss safety concerns and bring concerns to higher management if they believe the issues were not adequately addressed at lower levels. . . . NASA managers at the three field centers with primary responsibility for managing shuttle elements and at NASA headquarters reported having taken steps to create an organizational environment that encourages personnel at all levels to voice their views on safety to management. (1996, 19)

A full 90 percent of NASA employees responding to a survey by GAO in 1996 said "NASA's organizational culture encourages civil service employees to discuss safety concerns with management" (GAO 1996, 21).

However, such responses may be good examples of Schein's notion of espoused values: overt value statements of publicly acceptable values that do not actually reflect underlying cultural beliefs. Several events leading up to the loss of the *Columbia* suggest this to have been the case. The CAIB noted that NASA's testimony regarding its risk-averse culture stated that it encouraged employees to "stop an operation at the mere glimmer of a problem, " but this did not accord with reality (177). In fact, members feared retribution for bringing up unresolved safety concerns (192). Safety officials did not respond to signals of problems with debris shedding, and were again silent during key deliberations. As noted in chapter 3, Rodney Rocha, one of the cochairs of the debris assessment team, invoked the "if it's not safe . . ." slogan even as he declined to press further for images of the shuttle's wing. In 2004, a survey of NASA employees found that the agency had "not yet created a culture that is fully supportive of safety" and that workers were still "uneasy about raising safety issues" (David 2004).

All this suggests a confluence of factors that made the safety organizations weak. The founders, history, and mission of the organization led to a cultural bias for technological progress over routine operations and space science over safety monitoring. Given the training and background of NASA personnel and their contractors, concentrated ever more in the ranks of senior staff by repeated downsizing, safety was not as interesting as science. The organization was hard-pressed to make it so and keep the attention of qualified, respected personnel on these concerns. Even with ample outside attention directed to the problem of the safety culture, it is not surprising that the agency could not wholly shake its core professional identity. Moving the safety functions to contractors simply exacerbated the separation of safety from the core NASA technology.

Genuine cultural assumptions are often not recognized as such. Taken for granted, they are often not subject to analysis, which is partly why the absence of cultural change at NASA is not surprising. Core beliefs may also have been reinforced by the fear of recriminations for reporting delay-causing problems up the chain of command.

NASA CHICKEN

A fourth pattern of behavior linked to the culture of Marshall, and of NASA generally, was the unwillingness to report bad news. This reluctance seems repeatedly to have overcome engineers' and managers' concerns for safety. One part of this pattern was an intolerance for disagreement or criticism often seen in the responses of some NASA managers, and the unwillingness of some to listen to concerns of the working engineers. We see these behaviors in the events surrounding both accidents and in the intervening years.

Early on in the life of the shuttle, in 1978, two NASA engineers had observed the joint rotation and the problems with the O-rings in the solid rocket booster. They complained that Thiokol was "lowering the requirement for the joint" and should redesign it (Dunar and Waring 1999, 345). As we have seen, both Thiokol and Marshall managers rejected this contention. We have also seen how Marshall managers avoided acting on the unresolved problems with the joint and how Thiokol's concerns about temperatures on the eve of the launch were suppressed by Marshall managers. Intimidation and concern for preserving the chain of command also led to the suppression of information. Several engineers at Marshall had also been concerned about the temperature issues long before the accident, but they did not pass these doubts up to project managers. Nor were they heard by Hardy, Marshall's deputy director for science and engineering, the safety organization at Marshall. One of the concerned engineers stated he did not speak up himself because "'you don't override your chain of command'" (Dunar and Waring 1999, 377). Lawrence Wear, the director of the rocket motor project at Marshall, "admitted that at Marshall 'everyone does not feel free to go around and babble opinions all the time to higher management'" (377), though he acknowledged that the dissenters may have been intimidated by the Marshall management pronouncements about the seals. Lawrence Mulloy, manager of the solid rocket booster project at Marshall, revealed before Senate investigators that the seal decision had suffered from groupthink and that other participants censored themselves in the context of established management statements that the seals constituted an acceptable risk (377).

Excessive hierarchy and formalization were also seen also during the *Columbia* flight when the leadership of the mission management team, without probing into the reasons behind the requests for images of the shuttle's wing, cancelled requests because they had not been made through the correct channels. During the flight of *Columbia*, the debris assessment team cochair, Rodney Rocha, expressed serious doubts to colleagues about the decision of the mission management team not to obtain images of the wing: "In my humble technical opinion, this is the wrong (and bordering on irresponsible) answer from the SSP and Orbiter [managers] not to request additional imaging help from any outside source." But he did not press the matter further, noting that "he did not want to jump the chain of command" (CAIB, 157).

The leadership of the mission management team also stifled discussion of the possible dangers from the foam strike by rushing to the conclusion that the strikes did not pose safety of flight issues. As the CAIB reported, "Progr agers created huge barriers against dissenting opinions by stating preconceived conclusions based on subjective knowledge and experience, rather than on solid data" (192). The debris assessment team, too, admitted to self-censoring in failing to challenge these decisions (192). The CAIB reported that even members of the mission management team felt pressure not to dissent or challenge the apparent consensus. NASA contractors call this unwillingness to be the first to speak out "NASA chicken" (Wald and Schwartz 2003). One NASA engineer described the cultural basis for the phenomenon when he explained that "the NASA culture does not accept being wrong." Within the agency, "the humiliation factor always runs high" (Wald and Schwartz 2003).

The mission management team, like the Marshall actors before the *Challenger* launch, did not seek out information from lower-level engineering staff. They did not probe the reasons for the debris assessment team's requests, get frequent status reports on analyses, or investigate the preliminary assessments of the debris-strike analysis. The CAIB concluded that "managers' claims that they didn't hear the engineers' concerns were due in part to their not asking or listening" (170). Fear of criticism also affected the flow of information: "When asked by investigators why they were not more vocal about their concerns, debris assessment team members opined that by raising contrary points of view about Shuttle mission safety, they would be singled out for possible ridicule by their peers and managers" (169). In another instance, engineers reported that they had simulated the effects of a blown tire on the orbiter after-hours because they were reluctant to raise their concerns through established channels (192).

Ample evidence exists that many of the same kinds of failings of management openness and willingness to investigate possible hazards were factors in both accidents. This pattern was a major theme in the CAIB report, overall, and one reason the investigators questioned whether NASA could be characterized as a learning organization. It also raises questions about the cultural assumptions behind the management failings and what efforts NASA made to change these assumptions. Here we see some contradictory historical precedents in the agency.

Management in the Huntsville facility under von Braun in the 1950s and '60s was characterized by close teamwork and a nonbureaucratic ethos. Decentralization was essential for technical specialists to organize themselves to solve novel problems, but central control under von Braun served to resolve conflicts (Dunar and Waring 1999, 50). The Huntsville facility, which became the Marshall Space Flight Center in 1960, was organized into eight labs, each with its own test facilities and program management functions. The labs included such specialties as aero-astrodynamics, propulsion and vehicle engineering, and space sciences.

They constituted almost self-sufficient space agencies with duplicated administrative functions (40), leading Marshall historians Dunar and Waring to call them "imperial laboratories" (164). Another old hand described the German lab directors as having a "fiefdom philosophy where each one ran their own little kingdom" (197).

Von Braun himself was characterized as a reluctant supervisor, but stories told about him suggest he was held in high regard by most and seen as charismatic by some. This is illustrated in an account of him that evokes the classic founder story form:

> Center veterans recollected how von Braun had responded to a young engineer who admitted an error. The man had violated a launch rule by making a last-minute adjustment to a control device on a Redstone, and thereby had caused the vehicle to fly out of control. Afterwards the engineer admitted his mistake, and von Braun, happy to learn the source of the failure and wanting to reward honesty, brought the man a bottle of champagne. (Dunar and Waring 1999, 49)

He was also famous for his "weekly notes," summarized from lab directors' reports. He would circulate them around the Marshall labs, adding his handwritten comments and recommendations. They became a forum for considering technical problems and policy controversies and provided a way for Marshall managers to acquire a "holistic view of the Center" and learn how to coordinate their projects (51). Decades later the technique was still in use under William Lucas, who became center director in 1974 soon after von Braun left and who remained in charge until retiring after the *Challenger* accident.

Yet others gave von Braun mixed reviews as a supervisor, noting he was too autocratic, stifled criticism, was harsh on those who disagreed, and was too secretive (154). Adams and Balfour found that later, in the 1970s and '80s, even after the German team had largely left the top leadership positions, "Marshall was run like a Teutonic empire" (1998, 124).

Lucas, who worked in the structures and mechanics lab at Marshall for many years, may not have had von Braun's leadership skills, and he appears to have relied more on hierarchical control than teamwork. Only total loyalty led to advancement (McConnell 1987, 108). Under Lucas, "this autocratic leadership style grew over the years to create an atmosphere of rigid, almost fearful, conformity among Marshall managers. Unlike other senior NASA officials, who reprimanded subordinates in private, Lucas reportedly used open meetings to criticize lax performance" (McConnell 1987, 108). The aggressive management style at Marshall was said to have engendered an "underground decision making process" that prevented open discussion of problems (Dunar and Waring 1999, 312).

Many factors may have contributed to this authoritarian climate at Marshall. The pressures of adhering to a relentless launch schedule, the competition for project control, and resentments about Houston's role as lead center for the shuttle may all have pushed center leaders to show that they could successfully handle the challenges of the solid rocket boosters and the external tank. Vaughan describes these motives when she observes, "No manager wanted his hardware or people to be responsible for a technical failure" (1996, 218). But Lucas was also known for insisting on tight bureaucratic accountability and absolute conformity to the specifications of the preflight readiness reviews (218). Dunar and Waring quote an administrator at the Johnson Space Center saying, "Nothing was allowed to leave Marshall that would suggest that Marshall was not doing its job" (1999, 402). To admit that a step had been dropped or a problem was not resolved was to call down Lucas's scorn in open meeting (Vaughan 1996, 219–21). Lucas's subordinates "feared his tendency to 'kill the messenger'" (Dunar and Waring 1999, 403).

This aggressive management style also extended to contract management. Oversight of contractors was said to be harsh and excessive, though generally effective in the long run (Dunar and Waring 1999, 312). Marshall was very critical of Thiokol management, in particular, and blamed them for repeated problems with manufacturing safety and quality. Without their previous capacity to monitor contractor facilities, Marshall inspectors would wait until a problem surfaced and then impose heavy fees and penalties (312). The aggressiveness of their oversight reportedly made Thiokol project managers reluctant to open up to monitors, and the flow of information was blocked. A study of "lessons learned" commissioned after *Challenger* by the new safety organization, the Office of Safety, Reliability, Maintainability and Quality Assurance, found careless mistakes and other evidence of substandard contractor workmanship at the time of the *Challenger* launch. Some required quality verifications were not being conducted, and some inadvertent damage sustained during prelaunch processing went unreported. Workers lacked confidence in the contractors' worker-error-forgiveness policies, and workers consequently feared losing their jobs (NASA 1988, 13). In addition, they found that NASA's own error-forgiveness policy was harsh (Klerkx 2004, 242), so that even NASA's own technicians were "hesitant to report problems" (NASA 1988, 27). The report also offered suggestions for improving the morale and staffing of the safety functions, but the reaction of one agency safety representative did not bode well: "At the meeting where we presented the original version of the report, the safety guy in charge threw it in the waste basket. He said he was sick of hearing bad things about NASA. . . . This man was supposed to make sure these things didn't happen in the future, but he didn't want to hear anything had ever been wrong" (Klerkx 2004, 247).

While rivalry and budget and schedule pressures undoubtedly lay behind such management reactions, they also mirrored the management style of NASA administrator Beggs at headquarters and his top associate administrators. Years later, a similar pattern of pressure was seen under administrators Goldin and O'Keefe. In 2000, internal and external studies described a "workforce apparently paralyzed by a fear of displeasing their boss" (Lawler 2000b). Whistleblowers and public critics were not tolerated and fear of reprisals for criticizing the agency "was deeply engrained in the NASA culture" (Klerkx 2004, 243). Fear of the consequences of admitting delay-causing problems reportedly led to defensive decision making and a "'bunker mentality'" (Dunar and Waring 1999, 402). The result of these patterns was to block the upwards communication channels. One Marshall administrator explained:

> For a combination of semi-political reasons, the bad news was kept from coming forward. Contractors did not want to admit trouble; Centers didn't want Headquarters to know they had not lived up to their promises; and Headquarters staffs didn't want to risk program funding with bad news. (Dunar and Waring 1999, 312)

Efforts to change the culture to encourage upward information flows focused on trying to change the willingness of lower-level personnel to report problems rather than trying to alter the prevailing climate of aggressive accountability and resistance to seeking out or even listening to difficult news. Some of these efforts were summarized earlier in the chapter. Managers were coached to adopt the open-door policy and to establish alternative channels for critical information or safety concerns that personnel did not feel comfortable raising through formal channels. As noted in the CAIB, however, these changes were of questionable effectiveness.

LEARNING ABOUT CULTURE

Genuine culture change is a difficult and very long-range task, and it was not accomplished with the structural changes and short-term attempts at cultural intervention that followed the *Challenger* accident. Rocha's admission that he could not "say so" regarding what he saw as a seriously hazardous situation in the *Columbia* case demonstrates the limited success of creating alternative channels for safety information. It is not even clear how widely the direct and indirect recommendations about the need for culture change were accepted by NASA management. While safety was clearly espoused as a higher priority after the loss of the *Challenger*, we do not see actual changes in the cultural impediments to creating a more effective and aggressive safety organization. The 1996 GAO study does show that the agency was making structural adaptations to recognized cultural problems, but in the end, when immediate hazards appeared, the changes were not enough. Learning, as we are using the term, about how to change the cultural beliefs that affected shuttle management in dangerous ways occurred only very partially and temporarily.

These cultural patterns also influenced the kinds of learning that could have occurred about the structural, contractual, and political dimensions of shuttle management. Communication gaps among program modules created by the dispersion of program elements across separate centers were exacerbated by jealousies, grievances, and differences in laboratory styles. Reporting on hazards by contract management, already subject to perverse incentives, was made more difficult and less likely by the aggressive accountability practices and harsh treatment of violations. Even coping with external political and media pressure was complicated by the competitive stance among centers and the unwillingness of programs to admit to each other that the workload was putting an impossible strain on their capacities.

The effects of these and other long-lived cultural beliefs was to filter negative information about performance and hazards and offer interpretations of results that confirmed managers' inclinations and allowed them to pursue other priorities. The CAIB suggests that managers lost their wariness of the dangers and actually learned an attitude of risk acceptance (CAIB, 181). We next turn to what we can learn about organizational learning from the evidence collected in the past four chapters.

PART THREE

Institutionalizing Lessons about Public Organizational Learning

CHAPTER 7

The Challenges of Learning in Public Organizations

PART TWO EXAMINED THE EVENTS before each of the NASA shuttle accidents to search out evidence of learning or failure to learn in the space agency. In this chapter we examine what that evidence can tell us more generally about how and when learning occurred in the shuttle program and how we might refine the general information-processing theory of organizational learning to take account of the context of public sector agencies. This refinement, public organizational learning, identifies the conditions that were important in shaping the unreliable course of learning in the shuttle program and explains how the conditions affected the ability of shuttle program officials to undertake the processes that constitute learning. The events and conditions that facilitated or blocked each of the three processes of learning identified in chapter 2 are considered in turn to create hypotheses about learning and to draw conclusions about learning in public organizations particularly, but with implications for other organizations as well.

Overall, the NASA case shows that organizational learning was compromised because information needed to identify hazardous conditions and analyze their causes was misdirected, filtered, misinterpreted, and ignored. Standard operating procedures designed to identify hazards and resolve threats to successful flights had been allowed to deteriorate. Decision rules for identifying significant problems or granting waivers were inconsistently observed. The institutional setting for collecting, interpreting, and collating this information was troubled by conflicting political values and priorities, historical divisions, and cultural taboos. Knowledge about current procedures and past lessons were lost through multiple reorganizations and loss of personnel. Thus the organizational environment exhibited many unfavorable and few favorable conditions for the emergence of the contributing processes to learning. Learning is based on using information in ways that uncover new ideas about how to produce desired results. But institutional context shapes the understanding of this information and determines the willingness and ability of organizational actors to find, interpret, and use the information to dig out the causes of failure.

Above all, our analysis demonstrates the complexity of organizational learning, particularly in the public sector. Although the general theory of organizational learning invites us to consider the learning process as natural and almost automatic, this case demonstrates the variety of conditions—historical, political, and cultural—that can impede the course of learning. What emerges from this assessment is a view of learning as a set of complexly interlocking processes that touch almost all aspects of an organization.

EVIDENCE OF LEARNING

The shuttle accident investigations identified organizational contributions to the accidents in three areas: breakdowns in agency structures affecting communication, management control, and safety systems; compromises with professional safety practices brought on by the agency's response to outside pressure for cost-cutting and unrealistic launch schedules; and a culture of management isolation and inconsistent regard for raising safety concerns. To these we added perverse incentives in the management of relations with contractors. As the last four chapters have shown, NASA did learn some lessons about how to avoid these management failings.

The centralization of the shuttle management structure based on an assessment of the merits of the previous structure of the human flight program in the *Apollo* era was a relatively clear instance in which the agency followed a learning scenario, but these lessons were unlearned later under pressure from outside forces. Similarly, there was initial evidence that NASA had learned to resist schedule pressures. The agency delayed launches to deal with ongoing technical problems and made the decision to rely on the shuttle only when absolutely needed. But these lessons from the *Challenger* faded in the 1990s under severe budget constraints and new schedule pressures created by our participation in the International Space Station.

Other instances of learning were more permanent. The reduction of communication barriers between NASA and its contractors by again stationing NASA personnel inside contractor facilities is an example of the agency reflecting upon and drawing conclusions about the advantages of earlier systems. The creation of joint contractor–NASA problem-solving groups like the debris assessment team was another case of successful learning that persisted.

Less successful learning is exemplified by efforts to improve the tracking of potential technical hazards with the adoption of a cross-divisional problem-reporting system and the lessons-learned database. These systems were espoused by NASA after the *Challenger* accident but they were never fully institutionalized. Protection for those who raised safety concerns was also accepted as a valuable idea but was unevenly implemented. Some other changes, including some of those based on external recommendations, were never adopted. The move to improve the independence of the safety and quality-assurance program was actually done only at headquarters. Changes in pay and organizational location for safety work did not cope with the underlying cultural issues related to the low status of safety officers. Recommendations to integrate the distinctive subcultures of the centers through structural and personnel changes as made early on by the Rogers Commission were never adopted. Recommendations about matching realistic program goals to resources were accepted, especially in the early years of Truly's administration, but quickly were displaced under pressure from presidential and congressional forces and new agency leadership beginning in the early 1990s to reduce program redundancies and quicken the pace of launches. Special procedures for coping with emergencies that had been in place were forgotten in the repeated reorganizations and downsizing.

While each of the factors examined in the previous chapters adds to the explanation of the organizational failings in the shuttle program, their interaction was particularly lethal. For example, external budget and schedule pressures reduced the independence of the safety function by streamlining and outsourcing it. Long-standing cultural assumptions about the character of space-science work and the legacy of the early heroic advances in space exploration affected the status and aggressiveness of the relatively mundane work in the safety officers. The high value placed on the preservation of the individual centers and their professional staff influenced the willingness of agency directors to bargain for external support. The institutional history of the centers, especially the Marshall Space Flight Center, reinforced cultural barriers to sharing information across centers and isolated decision making about reliability and safety. The deterioration of the restructuring efforts that followed the *Challenger* accident exacerbated the sensitivity of those at Marshall to control from Johnson. The conditions that led to the accidents interacted in many perverse ways to make learning to solve the agency's administrative and organizational failings particularly difficult.

These positive and negative examples of learning at NASA can be used to refine the general theory of organizational learning to reflect conditions in public sector agencies. In chapter 2 we noted that the information-processing approach to organizational learning tells us that organizational performance and capacity are improved when members collect and analyze information about results to find solutions to problems and then find ways to share the solutions with others in the organization. Elaborating on this general theory, public organizational learning was defined as a three-part process of (1) problem recognition or acknowledging that results do not meet expectations, (2) analyzing or reflecting upon the results to make inferences about cause and effect to come to a new understanding of how to achieve better results, and (3) institutionalizing the new knowledge so that others in the organization can use it. These processes constitute an iterative cycle in which dissatisfaction with the present course spurs the creation of new solutions that are themselves later subjected to scrutiny and perhaps amendment. Inferences about the processes of organizational learning in public agencies generally are necessarily limited by our case study method. But the long case history does present a number of instances of successful and unsuccessful learning, and makes it possible to offer hypotheses about learning in public agencies that are applicable beyond the shuttle case.

PROBLEM RECOGNITION

A learning cycle begins with the realization among at least some organization members that there has been a significant failure to accomplish objectives or that results do not measure up to the organization's mission. NASA, of course, acknowledged the seriousness of the technical problems after the shuttle accidents. Before each accident, managers recognized specific problems as significant enough to warrant investigation, but they did not invoke emergency procedures to halt launches or insist that the task forces finish their work before continuing to launch. Similarly, there was some acknowledgment of managerial and organizational failings in the interval between accidents as evidenced by the number of internal and external investigations, many initiated by NASA. In some cases recommendations from these forums were adopted, in other cases they were not, and others as noted were adopted but displaced or lost.

Nonetheless, one key pattern repeated itself: at critical junctures the significance of problems with shuttle components was undervalued or ignored by key agency decision makers. The technical malfunctions that led directly to the accidents had been well documented. NASA and contract engineers had long experience with each set of problems. Each had been identified in numerous past flights as points of concern, but not enough concern to halt launches to resolve them.

Both problems were also the subject of investigation by engineering teams at the time of the accidents. But following through was a low priority even in these groups. Both Thiokol and NASA admitted that the research into the problems with the seals on the solid rocket booster was languishing, and in neither the *Challenger* nor the *Columbia* case were solutions to the problems with the components under investigation available by the time of the accidents.

There were also signals of management failings that were not designated as significant until after the accidents. Problems with coordination, chain of command, launch-review procedures, problem-tracking systems, the independence and aggressiveness of the safety organization, and the repressive culture were all managerial weaknesses that were identified in internal and external reviews after the *Challenger* and were still in evidence at the time of *Columbia*. Why were these weaknesses not recognized?

Part Two presented evidence of at least six reasons that top executives and midlevel managers in the shuttle program failed to acknowledge technical and managerial problems in need of urgent remediation: time pressures on shuttle processing, managerial turbulence, a weak safety organization, gaps in information processing, center rivalries, and lack of scientific or technological novelty in the failed systems. In addition, many of the organizational problems the program faced were to some degree self-reinforcing.

The external time pressures to cut costs and speed the launch cycle were unrelenting. Even before the shuttle was first launched, and certainly after the end of the cold war when foreign policy no longer justified an aggressive space program, Congress and several administrations created strong pressures to speed the launch cycle and to do more with less. Admitting that the O-ring problem was serious enough to halt launches would have exposed the shuttle program as being unable to maintain a cost-effective launch rate. Resolving the troubling foam-loss issues would have jeopardized the key completion date for the International Space Station, which was by then the principal justification for the expensive shuttle system needed, in the eyes of some at NASA, to preserve the human space-flight program. Continuing problems with the shuttle program technology and NASA management's accommodations to launch pressures meant that the staff became inured to some level of program failure and risk, especially in regard to hardware components that experience had suggested would be relatively unlikely to cause catastrophic failure. This led to cutting corners rather than resolving outstanding engineering problems (CAIB, 198).

A related problem was what the Augustine Report (NASA 1990) termed "managerial turbulence," defined as "continual changes in cost, schedule, goals, etc." that had "a way of cascading through the entire project execution system, producing havoc at every step along the way" (NASA 1995, 6). This turbulence was often the result of changes in the design of shuttle components, leading to calls to freeze the shuttle design. This proposal, of course, contradicted equally vocal criticisms that the shuttle had been prematurely designated as operational when in fact it was still experimental. Turbulence also resulted from numerous reorganizations and the loss of personnel and critical expertise through downsizing, which in turn led to understaffing the safety and quality-assurance offices and to the creation of dual roles for administrators to serve as managers and safety officers for the same projects. All of these situations compromised the ability and willingness of actors to identify problems as significant and to undertake time-consuming and expensive efforts to untangle the weaknesses in design and operations of the program.

A third factor contributing to the agency's unwillingness to flag technical and managerial problems as truly serious was the compromised position of the safety, reliability, and quality-assurance systems. This unwillingness was in part a structural issue as noted in chapter 3, but it was also a result of cultural assumptions about the status of work on safety systems in contrast to work on space science and technology. Even after efforts to shield workers who raised safety concerns and adjustments to create special safety reporting channels for contractors, GAO's culture survey found evidence of norms against reporting safety problems, a situation compounded by the common perception that criticisms of management would be met with reprisals. Just after the *Challenger* tragedy, safety offices were to have been removed from the control of project managers and given greater funding and visibility to entice highly qualified staff, but this plan was never implemented across the organization. The weaknesses of the safety organization reduced the likelihood that safety officers would challenge higher-status colleagues to insist that the problems with seals and foam debris be considered urgent. As we saw, in both cases the safety systems were silent.

A fourth factor that reduced the chances that serious problems would be recognized was the weakness of the problem-tracking systems that made it possible to ignore or diminish the importance of evidence of hazardous conditions. Though there is clear evidence that NASA managers at all levels had been made aware of the hazards of the O-ring technology, and perhaps of the connection between temperature and the performance of the seals, this news was only intermittently communicated. It could be and was ignored by key actors at key junctures. We are not the first to notice that unwelcome, inconvenient information is commonly discredited and ignored (Kaufman 1973; Perrow 1999). As we note in chapter 3, despite efforts to strengthen the problem-tracking systems and to create integrated, organization-wide systems for checking specifications and recording lessons learned after the loss of the *Challenger*, the information systems were compromised. In fact, recommendations for improvement were never fully implemented. Identifying serious problems was even more difficult because of the enormous technical complexity of the shuttle project and the inherent difficulties of maintaining an integrated information base with legacy data systems and a stove-piped organization. Without an ever-present, consistent record of incontrovertible information about dangers, NASA management solved its more immediate problems, maintaining the launch rate and holding down costs.

Next, admitting that serious problems with the shuttle had not been resolved was complicated by the rivalries among the centers and the programs they housed. Here, too, the organization's design, established to calm competition and preserve funding for the geographically dispersed centers, interacted with the cultural heritage of the centers to weaken the command structure and interorganizational communication. The implications of the Roger's Commission findings were that managers at Marshall were reluctant to report unresolved problems that could lead to time-consuming launch delays. To report failings to Houston was seen as impinging on Marshall's autonomy and threatening its reputation within the organization. Intercenter rivalries are not identified in the *Columbia* investigations as a significant contributor to the accident, but the persistent deficiencies of coordination among the centers over assigning responsibility for the foam-debris strikes clearly contributed to the lack of resolution of that fatal problem.

Finally, it is noteworthy that the failed components were relatively low-tech devices, unlike the shuttle's complex guidance or rocket motor systems, for example. In both cases there was abundant evidence of problems years before the accidents. The O-ring erosions and tile damage from foam debris on previous launches were recognized as problems and were under investigation, but they were not identified as significant enough to prompt immediate emergency procedures, such as a launch moratorium. They were familiar and lacked the scientific and engineering interest that other problems in the shuttle program offered. Their very familiarity seems to have reduced the perceived seriousness of the threat they posed. Vaughan's (1996) work on the decision to launch the *Challenger* describes in detail the processes that led to this state.

The fact that most of these factors identified as important in the *Challenger* cases were also evident in the years just before the *Columbia* accident attests to an absence of learning and helps explain why learning was so difficult for NASA. The very difficulties the agency faced with recognizing the seriousness of the launch system and managerial problems were self-reinforcing. Cultural templates

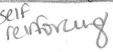

and external pressures made it unlikely the agency could acknowledge the problems that might have helped it learn to deal with the dysfunctional cultural elements or cope more effectively with external dependencies. The cultural bias against working in the safety organization made it less likely that safety information would be taken seriously or that safety officers would gain real authority. The tough cost and schedule pressures enforced by Congress and the White House led to reduced investments in project-management infrastructures to replace legacy data systems. Efforts to streamline management and outsource safety systems to cut costs thinned the flow of information across centers. All these problems blocked the feedback about results that would have made the recognition of the significance of the problems themselves more likely.

 Accounting for Problem Recognition

Under what circumstances were the problems later recognized to have contributed to the accidents identified as significant? Considering the whole series of learning cycles over the course of the case, problem recognition seems most often to have begun with front-line professionals and to have received high-level support when management could insulate itself from the ill consequences of admissions about failings. Experience with the problem first-hand, unfiltered and unmediated by cultural interpretations and influences, and clear, widespread knowledge of procedures for evaluating results seem to emerge as the key factors in problem recognition.

DIRECT EXPERIENCE

In the months and years before the accidents and in the immediate postaccident time frame, it was the engineering staff that raised the alarm most often and most vocally. Front-line professional engineers at NASA and at the contractor organizations were the first to identify the problems that caused both shuttle accidents. In the case of the *Challenger*, it was the engineers at Marshall's Structures and Propulsion Lab and contract engineers at Thiokol (Dunar and Waring 1999, 349). In the *Columbia* case, it was the debris assessment team composed of NASA engineers, USA contract engineers, and other engineers with whom they worked in the days after the launch. This pattern is particularly remarkable given the reports about the relatively few provisions for shielding contract employees from criticism for admitting or reporting mistakes.

Why should this have been the case? Three reasons are suggested. First, these were the personnel closest to the data. They conducted the bench research, ran the computer models, and made the direct postflight observations of the charring and erosion of the seals on the solid rocket boosters. They were the ones to inspect the tile damage on the orbiter. They saw the evidence first-hand. Given the limitations of the problem-tracking system, these actors observed the evidence of failed components more often than did upper-level officials. Not all engineers saw all of the evidence of component failures all of the time, but the first identification of significant problems seen in the *Challenger* case came from those with this direct knowledge of and experience with the problem.

In addition, upper- and midlevel managers had in some respects insulated themselves from the evidence of technological failures in order to keep the project running smoothly. The elaborate but unreliable problem-tracking systems and quality-assurance methods reduced direct experience to summary metrics that, as we saw in chapters 3 and 4, conveyed only a part of the information part of the time. The in-house qualitative problem-identification and risk-designation system rooted in the engineering culture of NASA's early years obscured the determination of more precise failure trends in the two launch vehicle systems that caused the accidents. Intercenter competition and fear of recriminations added to their insularity. The flight-readiness-review process, designed to identify and resolve problems from the last flight, had become "informally attended" and conducted by teleconference prior to the *Challenger* accident.

Finally, upper-level managers were conflicted about declaring an emergency in ways that front-line professionals were not. Such a declaration would threaten the precarious support for the shuttle program. Delays and public recognition of the continuing fragility of the shuttle system would not help garner support in Congress.

POLITICS OF PROBLEM RECOGNITION

When did top managers acknowledge technical and organizational problems? First, of course, they were forced to recognize both kinds of failings in the aftermath of the accidents. They did so at other times as well, though less publicly, when they initiated investigations and implemented recommendations to set up panels or commissions to review safety and management issues. They did not always act on the results of these investigations, however, as we will note in the next section. Some of the inquiries appear to have concluded just what the administration wanted to hear, as when the Augustine Report found that NASA should retain control of the shuttle program. Others, however, did not. The 1988 *Lessons Learned Report*, advising NASA to shield workers reporting safety violations or errors in processing, among other recommendations, was not well received, as noted in chapter 6.

These differences in reception suggest that problem recognition and definition can become a political process of negotiation and compromise among competing groups with different interests. The findings of outside panels may have been used as a resource or weapon in internal conflicts over the direction of programs or management strategies. The conclusions of the Kraft Report, for example, reinforced the wishes of top management and the White House for increased outsourcing and improved contract management at a time when the agency was downsizing. The report was not universally accepted, however, as evidenced by the internal disagreements over its recommendations to streamline the "unwieldy" safety structures by reducing crosschecks. Some of the reports and investigations brought with them new resources or a temporary reduction in external launch pressures and so were welcome to that degree. The 1988 *Lesson Learned Report* was not. We might, following Schattschneider (1960), expect that astute managers would differentiate between problems whose acknowledgment would bring in support and those that would generate increased criticism and even more constrained resources.

This analysis suggests that acknowledging the significance of a problem was not so much defined by objective engineering metrics as by internal agency dynamics or the potential for external benefit. Decisions about what was to be observed, researched, monitored, recorded, or tracked were thus not marginal technical issues. Rather, they were fraught with conflict over professional ideas about the work, how to negotiate with stakeholders, and how resources would be assigned. Only problems that were unusual enough to be consistently designated as out-of-family were identified as significant in the sense used here. But assigning that designation was itself contentious. The controversy among actors in the *Columbia* case about whether the foam strike was to be classed as an out-of-family event is an illustration of the friction that can occur in identifying the significance of problems and the need for further analysis. The case shows that gaining visibility for failures is not easy and requires a coalition of supporters who can garner the significant failure designation for their concerns. However, it is not clear that this calculative approach led to genuine learning so much as to the kind of strategic adaptation described in chapter 2. Only some of the problems identified by the panels and investigative bodies NASA commissioned led to implemented changes.

What can we learn from these conclusions about when managers do begin the learning process by acknowledging failings? When upper-level managers initiated internal investigations, they were putting resources behind recognizing problems even if they did not proceed to discovering solutions. The resulting analyses could, as we noted, be accepted or not, and so levels of threat and disruption could be controlled. Such studies thus could be used to control or depersonalize problems. Rather than revealing individual failings or loss of prestige, the problems become organizational conditions subject to further analytic processes.

PUBLIC EXPOSURE

Most of the instances of open acknowledgement of significant problems by upper levels of the shuttle program administration that did lead to the next stage of learning occurred in the immediate aftermath of the accidents. At that point, of course, the importance of the technical flaws had been publicly revealed. Soon, in the course of the investigations by Congress and the Rogers Commissions in the case of the *Challenger*, the organizational and managerial failures were made public. The same configuration of events unfolded after the loss of the *Columbia*.

Birkland (2004) found a similar pattern in policy learning after airliner disasters and the attacks of September 11, but he noted that the energy evoked by the sorrow and shock of the accidents inside agencies and among the public was likely to be short-lived. As shock wears off, the urgency to act diminishes. The shuttle accidents acted as focusing events (Kingdon 1995), spotlighting the resource and schedule pressures on the agency even as they revealed the flaws in the top management's decisions and the safety review systems. The time immediately after the accidents was also the time at which the reputation and the status of the agency were most threatened. Acting quickly to acknowledge problems and aggressively seek out solutions could make some constructive use of an event that was a tragedy for the astronauts, their passengers, the agency, and the nation. After the loss of the *Challenger*, public funding initially grew for staffing and safety systems, but the window of opportunity began to close again a few years later.

PROBLEM RECOGNITION, ACCOUNTABILITY, AND BLAME

The core of problem recognition is accepting responsibility or culpability for the failings of the organization. This is a difficult step for most individuals and organizations with implications for personal self-esteem, professional status, and organizational prestige. Almost no commentator suggests that NASA managers acted in bad faith in failing to invoke emergency procedures or failing to solve the problems with command structures and safety-tracking systems. Rather, other priorities, ultimately less important, crowded the safety issues off the management agenda. These were failures of decision making. However, it is possible that a sense of responsibility and accountability for maintaining external support might have shaped managers' perceptions of hazards as well as their managerial choices.

The weighty consequences of admitting failures and the high levels of oversight and accountability for performance may have affected NASA managers at the cognitive level. Research on the airline industry concerned with how pilots learn from close calls is instructive about the effects of organizational accountability. The problem, of course, in the airline industry is that if near misses are due to pilot error, and the pilot is held accountable and punished for the error, he or she will be less likely to report the error. But research by Morris and Moore (2000) goes further to suggest that even the thoughts and self-appraisals of those in high-accountability situations are affected by these levels of accountability, leading actors to shy away from recognizing opportunities for learning.

In a carefully designed study, commercial pilots who were held to account by the firm they worked for were compared to private, independent pilots. Data on errors were available through an industry-wide project to collect data on aviation incidents, ironically part of a NASA program to study aviation risk factors, in which legal liability would be waived if pilots reported their errors. Thus only the commercial pilots were accountable in an institutional sense to a firm. The study was designed to examine the relationship of accountability to counterfactual thinking in the pilots' detailed, postincident reports, including constructive counterfactuals (I might have avoided the incident if only I had done . . .) in contrast to comforting counterfactuals (it would have been worse if I had not . . .). The study found that the pilots accountable to their firms were just as likely as the private pilots to engage in counterfactual thinking, but the accountable pilots were only *half* as likely to engage in the kind of constructive counterfactual thinking that actually leads to improving performance in future difficult situations. The implications of these findings for interpreting the events of this case are that high levels of pressure for results could have made program managers less able to perceive or imagine how technical and organizational improvements might have been achieved.

Bearing responsibility could, in principle, motivate the search for remedies, but a serious continuing problem at NASA was the unwillingness to acknowledge failures, large or small, and to act to get at their sources. In the record of the accident investigations, there were few examples of top- or midlevel NASA managers accepting responsibility for failures. There were even fewer instances of the kind of constructive counterfactuals that lead to learning. An exception is the regret reported by Rocha, the NASA cochair of the debris assess team, that he had not been more forceful about getting images of *Colombia*'s wing (Wald and Schwartz 2003).

SHIFTING RESPONSIBILITY FOR PROBLEM IDENTIFICATION

The absence of clear and widely practiced standards for determining what constituted a hazard affected decisions at the top of the organization but also created difficult pressures for those at the bottom. Ambiguous standards for evaluating results from preflight tests, inconsistencies in determining criticality status, the ad hoc character of procedures for dealing with what might be a last-minute emergency, and the discrepancies in standards for waiving launch constraints all had the effect of shifting the responsibility for signaling problems from the institution as a whole to small groups of professionals.

Without clear agreement on what signals a significant risk, the burden of proof for determining what constitutes a danger falls on the professionals who are closest to the data, typically on the front lines, but who may not have the authority to declare an emergency on their own. In the days preceding each accident, lower-level employees struggled to make determinations about the severity of the hazard with incomplete data and ambiguous procedures for deciding whether an emergency existed. Problem recognition fell heavily on individuals who were aware of or suspected a hazard but could not fall back on the data, standards, or procedures needed to determine whether their fears were justified, forcing them to place their professional judgment on the line with little institutional support.

What made establishing widely observed standards and procedures so difficult? Several reasons are suggested by the events as they unfolded. First, a number of different centers and contracting units were involved, each with long histories, deeply embedded cultures, and different procedures and standards for coping with the problematic technologies. Integrating these distinctive standards and procedures, as well as their stove-piped data systems, was a management challenge. Also, some safety-assurance procedures were eliminated with streamlining but not replaced with procedures that became well entrenched. Finally, it appears that many NASA staff were not particularly interested in administration. Numbers of top administrators had graduated to those positions from engineering positions, and their focus was on a different set of issues. Von Braun's famous team-based systems substituted self-organizing professionalism for management procedures. The exception to this trend, of course, was provided by Administrator Goldin, who had a management background and who rapidly streamlined existing procedures—ironically contributing even more to managerial turbulence and loss of procedural knowledge. In the process, the standards, like those for waiving criticality ratings and defining out-of-family events, were compromised so that what clarity and uniformity there had been in their application was eroded.

ı recognition always depends on the professionalism of organizational
nd their ability and willingness to openly acknowledge signs of failure
and seek out alternatives even in the face of ridicule or loss of support. Without
widespread awareness of and agreement on standards for judging results, however, the identification of danger signs rests on the courage or stubbornness of
individuals who must make ad hoc cases. Instead of being able to rely upon the
kinds of institutionalized routines for identifying danger seen in highly reliable
organizations, shuttle officials who were concerned about the dangers of the cold
launch temperatures or the pattern of debris strikes were forced to try to justify
their concerns on the basis of personal credibility or professional opinion. Absent
clearly defined standards and procedures, the responsibility for admitting failure
or publicizing danger rests heavily on the judgment and determination of the
most committed professionals. When procedures for identifying hazards are cod-
ified and widely practiced, organizations may not have to rely so completely on
the self-sacrificing professionalism of its members.

Hypotheses about Problem Recognition

Based on these findings about problem recognition, several hypotheses can be
offered that generalize beyond the shuttle case to learning in other public organizations. The factors that affect problem recognition are closely linked to the
collection and interpretation of information about past results. Seven hypotheses
summarize the factors that are likely to foster or thwart the acknowledgment of
failures and the need for action:

- Those with direct experience with the failure, who see its effects unfiltered
  by long-linked communication channels, are most likely to be among the
  first to acknowledge problems.
- Those held most directly and severely accountable for program failure may
  be unable to imagine alternative outcomes or see results as unsatisfactory.
- Ambiguous or inconsistently observed procedures for evaluating results or
  declaring a hazard puts the burden of judgment on front-line professionals
  who may not have the power to declare performance flaws to be significant.
- Acknowledgment of significant performance flaws is most likely in the
  immediate aftermath of a public failure, when the failure cannot be ignored
  and when public sympathy may be high.
- Those who are insulated from the direct political or budgetary consequences of public recognition of a problem are more likely to acknowledge

the problem than those in the organization who must confront these effects.

- Acknowledgment of failure is most likely when the failure can be depersonalized as a system flaw or the concatenation of unforeseen factors.
- The size of a failure, in material or program terms, is not directly related to the willingness to acknowledge the problem.

Thus to succeed at problem recognition, especially in the absence of open failure or disaster, seems to require a high level of professionalism shielded from short-term accountability. It also depends on having a widely observed and well-entrenched basis for saying that performance standards are violated. These well-developed procedures are what are seen in highly reliable organizations. It is also what enables them to shift from routine operations to a more flexible, self-organizing hazard-response mode.

ANALYSIS AND INFERENCE

Learning organizations respond to acknowledged problems by analyzing or reflecting upon the sources of failures and drawing inferences about cause and effect. This represents the second defining process of public organizational learning. In examining the course of learning at NASA, we questioned at several points whether NASA officials themselves were actively engaged in analyzing the early warnings of engineering problems or the internal and external reports of organizational failings.

In previous chapters we looked at evidence of short-term, single-loop learning about the problems with the technical components that caused the accidents. We saw that while these problems were recognized to the extent that the shuttle management authorized task forces to study them, NASA and its contractors did not follow through to find causes and solutions for the problems that led to the accidents before proceeding with launch. Between 1986 and 2003, there were also long-term, double-loop learning opportunities to examine management practices, cultural assumptions about safety reporting and engineering, and strategies for maintaining external support. Some of these opportunities resulted in learning that altered, even if temporarily, the way the shuttle program operated, while others did not. These case findings suggest some of the conditions under which the second element of learning, analysis and inference, does or does not occur.

purposes of examining the patterns of analysis and inference in the case, we will separate the discussion of short-term, single-loop learning about the technical problems in the immediate run-up to each accident from the consideration of long-term, double-loop learning related to organizational and administrative problems.

Single-Loop Learning — technical problems

Efforts to remedy some of the troublesome technical problems or prevent their disastrous consequences were constrained by factors that limited the open debate of alternative causes and effects. These patterns illustrate missed opportunities for short-term learning. That is, early warnings of acknowledged technical problems could have led to finding explanations for the failings. These explanations in turn could have led to remedies or to the prevention of a launch under existing rules and procedures. This would have been an example of single-loop learning. In this pattern of organizational learning, recognized failures are examined within current rubrics to identify corrective actions. Ideas about how to analyze the situation are already present in rules, operating procedures, or professional research norms. We have noted, however, that existing methods for classifying critical elements were not reliably applied and that rules for resolving such problems before or after launch, imperfect and ambiguous as they were especially in the case of the *Columbia*, were not consistently observed.

Limited access to critical research and ambiguous or inconsistently applied procedures for classifying and treating problems blocked short-term, single-loop learning. The best examples of lost single-loop-learning opportunities appear first among front-line professionals, both those working as contractors and NASA employees. In the *Challenger* case, it was Thiokol employees who persisted in drawing inferences about the interaction between the cold temperatures and seal erosion on the eve of the launch, though NASA engineers had also identified the problems. Their efforts to pursue the problems were hampered, however, by the inconsistencies in the application of procedures for flight reviews, tracking the status of critical items, and waiving launch constraints. The rules were short-circuited.

A remarkably similar scenario emerges from the *Columbia* case. In the years before the launch, schedule pressures, reduced resources for testing, diffuse responsibility for the foam problem, and the "normalization" of the foam strikes all blunted the concern for resolving the situation. After the launch, front-line engineering staff identified the potential danger from the strike in informal discussions, again drawing inferences about how to remedy a potentially disastrous result using existing analytic techniques. But the procedures for tracking a crisis situation and gathering information were not followed. Many of the staff appear to have been unclear about what the correct procedures were. Drawing conclusions about the severity of the problem was hampered by the absence of data and by ambiguities in the application of rules for analyzing the situation.

Opportunities for Double-Loop Learning

organizational + administrative problems

The period after the *Challenger* accident brought with it an abundance of opportunities for analyzing and explaining both administrative and technical flaws in the shuttle program. The external and internal investigations that followed the loss of the *Challenger* offered many occasions for the kind of reflection and comparison that could have led to new explanations of the management failures. These explanations could in turn have guided improvements in coordination and reliability, including fundamental changes to integrate project oversight, restore the meticulousness of preflight reviews, and even alter the culture surrounding safety work and management openness. New strategies for negotiating realistic launch rates or acquiring resources might have emerged. The standards themselves for determining what would count as a critical problem could have been affected. Changes at this level exemplify what we described in chapter 2 as double-loop or turnaround learning, a type of learning that can lead to major organizational transformation and reform.

However, instead of overturning established ways of categorizing problems and arriving at new remedies, what emerged after the *Challenger* accident looked like a single-loop learning process with very few innovative options considered. Inference about cause and effect depends on having a variety of experiences to draw on, actual or vicarious, to figure out what goes with what. Here we see actors creating a causal explanation based on one known design alternative, to centralize the command structure.

Research by Haunschild and Sullivan (2002) on learning to reduce the numbers of close calls in the airline industry shows that organizational learning is more likely in a firm when the causes of the incidents it experiences are heterogeneous rather than homogeneous. They found that heterogeneity provokes more discussion as well as a wider range of interpretations of what caused the near-accident and a wider search for solutions. Even without direct experience, organizations can extend their range of cause–effect knowledge by observing similar organizations, or they can glean more from their own experience by creating scenarios based on actual incidents (March, Sproull and Tamuz 1996). NASA's sample of actual accidents was, thankfully, small, but there had been multiple near-accidents, including, of course, incidents of seal erosion and debris strikes. Analyzing these incidents by probing and inviting alternative interpretations could have extended their experience base of administrative solutions for tracking hazards and coordinating project elements. Analysis that extended to underlying organizational, political, and cultural causes might have opened up the possibility of other, novel remedies. There is no evidence in NASA's implementation reports following on the Rogers Commission recommendations that these tactics were used (NASA 1986; Rogers Commission 1987).

The time pressures under which the actors operated may also have interfered with the creation of alternative explanations, not only for solving the technical problems, but also for contriving administrative remedies. Experimentation or comparisons outside the agency might have delayed the return to flight. NASA and its stakeholders wanted assurance that the problems had been remedied and the organization could proceed, justifying the higher levels of support promised in the aftermath of the *Challenger* disaster. This pattern of "premature closure" is not unique to this case. In general, the pressure to codify program regulations to satisfy outside investigators or legislators often leads to truncated experimentation and unverified or uncertain solutions (Landau and Stout 1979).

Another factor limiting the capacity to investigate alternative explanations for technical or administrative failures may have been a resistance to adopting solutions created elsewhere, especially if they did not match internal management priorities. Even though NASA's own experience with forms of command structures and safety reporting systems was limited, the agency could have made use of vicarious learning. But both GAO and the Columbia Accident Investigation Board comment on this lapse, the latter specifically citing the availability of high-reliability organizational models. The absence of vicarious learning, along with the intolerance for dissent and outside pressures, meant that opportunities for double-loop learning were not realized. A slightly different pattern accounts for the imposition of changes by the presidential appointees who supported a downsized mission and a lean organization. These changes were, of course, institutionalized, though not learned. Their effect was to displace the earlier learned changes.

Finally, we do see a successful analysis of the problems with poor communication across contractor–NASA lines that exhibits some of the characteristics of double-loop learning. The changes adopted altered both the incentives and the structure of coordination and communication between contractors and contract managers at NASA. Perverse incentives for contractors were addressed by removing the contract officers from the chain of command. New communication routes were created so that crisis-response teams such as the debris assessment team were cochaired by NASA and contract personnel. NASA staff were again assigned to contractor facilities to provide closer liaison with the contractors and to identify problems and to improve contract management and cost controls. These changes replaced the formerly hierarchical control relationship between the contractor and NASA with a teamwork approach. They were consistent with the increases in contracting and with the public management reform movements of the 1990s. The NASA–contractor divide that had been an issue in the *Challenger* case was not seen as a significant problem in the *Columbia* case.

Accounting for Analysis and Inference

Three conditions in the case of the shuttle program account for much of this pattern of success and failure in analyzing and drawing new inferences about acknowledged problems. The first is the strong internal pressure for orthodoxy that appears to have squelched the exploration of alternative interpretations of events. Multiple interpretations are what lead to new inferences about the causes of problems. The second, linked to the first, is the absence of a "requisite variety" of organizational practices to allow for comparisons of results and inferences about what practices lead to what outcomes. Finally, the shifting and uncertain standards and procedures embodied in the flight-readiness-review process, with its many variations, exceptions, and waivers and the confusing and inconsistently observed procedures of in-flight monitoring and review, made it unlikely that actors could discover which technical fixes or management patterns might lead to which program improvements.

MULTIPLE INTERPRETATIONS

Investigations into both organizational and policy learning have noted the importance of considering alternative interpretations of past results and program information in drawing new cause–effect associations. Confrontation and moderate conflict have been shown to enhance this effect (Brown and Duguid 1996; Hutchins 1996; Jenkins-Smith and Sabatier 1993; Bouwen and Fry 1991). But at NASA the consideration of alternative versions of events was inhibited by time pressures, management hostility toward criticism, uneven access to data about results, jealously guarded center autonomy, and a culture that had come to accept deviant launch results (Casamayou 1993; Vaughan 1996).

While only a few of the kinds of internal discussions that illustrate NASA's approach to analyzing problems can be documented, those few instances demonstrate a clear lack of openness to considering alternative interpretations. In the meetings between Thiokol engineers and managers and officials at NASA, engineers' efforts to include the consideration of temperature were suppressed. With a clear reference to time considerations, NASA managers argued that such a discussion would introduce a new launch constraint and delay the program. During the flight of the *Columbia*, we see a similar unwillingness to consider whether the dominant "mental model" of shallow damage to the tiles could have been wrong, despite the reservations of engineers and the requests from several quarters for more information about the effects of the impact. Again, the principal concern behind these refusals was a concern for future flight schedules. Admitting that foam debris could cause serious damage would have challenged the characterization of foam strikes as turnaround issues rather than out-of-family issues requiring resolution.

There is also evidence from the postaccident investigations as well as studies authorized by NASA and GAO that staff feared reprisals for criticizing management decisions and that reports of errors and safety violations were severely dealt with. A key GAO study of the functioning of the safety culture in 1996 offered evidence that a willingness to identify unsafe practices was espoused but was not reliably honored in practice. Staff reported that raising questions about safety was still considered to be evidence of poor performance. A protester of increased outsourcing of the shuttle program and the loss of the long-standing system of crosschecks stated openly that others would object too if not for fear of punishment. The post-*Challenger* study of lessons learned, commissioned by NASA in 1988, revealed a reluctance by technicians to report problems because of the absence of an "error forgiveness" policy. Testimony from participants after the *Columbia* accident indicated that actors believed that it would be inappropriate to go over the heads of reluctant mission managers to get images of the damaged shuttle. All these instances point to the pressure for orthodoxy or conformity to management policy, making it extremely difficult to achieve an open exchange about alternative interpretations of events.

The rivalry between the centers and the culture of autonomy and distinctiveness that characterized management at the Marshall Space Flight Center also contributed to the difficulty of achieving an exchange of ideas and interpretations about the technical problems that were accumulating. At Marshall, the legacy of the management practices of the von Braun team of early rocket scientists shaped habits of independence, decentralized, center-based decision making, and an ethos of personal rather than institutional accountability (Rogers Commission 1986; Adams and Balfour 1998; Sato 2005; McCurdy 1993), which seems very like the postaccident characterizations of center actors as noncollaborative and likely to make decisions in isolation. This is inconsistent with an open, vigorous pursuit of alternative views on how to resolve the problematic launch-system elements.

REQUISITE VARIETY

A second condition that appears to have repressed the analysis of causes is the absence of "requisite variety" of organizational practices to allow for comparing results and making inferences about which actions lead to which outcomes (Levitt and March 1988; Morgan 1986). In NASA's case, several factors limited the variety of experience. The constant pressure of launch schedules truncated the research of task forces to come up with explanations for failures of components. Perennially scarce funds reduced experimentation and bench-testing and eliminated the costly but generally successful redundant program development processes of the *Apollo* era. The shuttle, as well as the original Hubble Space Telescope and other projects, were affected by these cost-cutting tactics.

The uneven capacity to retrieve information about results and the absence of an integrated problem-tracking system also made it difficult to pull together a record of events in enough detail and across enough cases to make it possible to analyze causes in the periods before each of the accidents. Even though the relevant technical information about the seals and the foam debris existed somewhere in the system, because it was not present in an accessible and meaningful form throughout the organization, it was easily disregarded by those who found it a threat to other priorities. In general, feedback is cut short when past results cannot be linked to present circumstance or remembered and retrieved. Lebovic (1995) found that as a problem or subject of learning becomes more complex, with irregular, nonlinear shifts, learning becomes more difficult. Past trials of learning may be forgotten when key actors leave with a change of administration (Etheredge 1985). It becomes difficult to re-establish even approximately what the consequences of particular changes were. Learning in government organizations under these conditions is inevitably a daunting task.

The clearest instance of comparing information about events and making inferences about causes occurred in the aftermath of the *Challenger* accident. In response to the Rogers Commission recommendations, a former *Apollo* program director was brought in to chair the study group working on remedies for the failings of the command structure and the lack of coordination among the centers. In the face of undeniable failure, analysis and comparison with past program designs did lead to an explanation for the failure: the decentralized structure. From this emerged a plan to revert back to the more centralized structure from the *Apollo* era in which program elements would answer to NASA headquarters managers directly or indirectly.

There may have been more robust and suitable designs possible, however. We do not know what alternatives were considered by the group. But we do know that a lack of tolerance for criticism was "deeply ingrained in the NASA culture" (Klerkx 2004, 243). We also know that the implementation of the Roger's Commission findings, including the design of new management structures, was under the command of Lt. General Samuel Phillips, the former *Apollo* program director. The resulting plan looked very much like the centralized structure of that program. That structure was later "unlearned," however, and the return of project management leadership to the centers meant a return to internal battles for autonomy and control. The underlying problems of shuttle program management had not been permanently remedied.

UNCERTAIN STANDARDS AND PROCEDURES FOR ANALYSIS
Finally, the absence of clearly defined and reliably applied standards for analyzing results made it difficult to make inferences about the causes behind the accidents and predecessor incidents. Because standards for evaluating results, whether from bench tests or from postflight analysis of shuttle hardware, were not clearly defined and widely shared, determining which events or conditions led to hazardous outcomes was not possible. If effects are inconsistently classified as unsatisfactory and thus subject to further scrutiny, their underlying causes cannot be dependably identified over time. The record appears muddled. Similarly, if procedures for reviewing pending problems from past flights or in-flight concerns are ambiguous or unevenly enforced, the weaknesses of these procedures remain hidden. The effect of this pattern on analysis and inference was to create apparent discrepancies in the record about what causes led to what effects.

A number of examples of this problem appear over the years covered by our study. The evidence of charring and blow-by at the joints of the solid rocket booster both in the laboratory and in recovered segments was inconsistently interpreted by Thiokol and NASA engineers from the earliest days of the shuttle. What constituted a margin of safety was the subject of much disagreement. Flight readiness reviews became increasingly casual prior to the *Challenger* accident, and full reports were not always made from one level to the next. The standards for determining criticality, and worse, the basis on which a finding of criticality 1 could be waived, were either not widely known or not reliably practiced. The burden of proof for approving launch in the face of unresolved problems was not clearly established before either of the accidents. The procedures for investigating in-flight anomalies were not followed or even apparently recalled by many of the key actors during the *Columbia* mission. These uncertainties and inconsistencies affected both single-loop learning about the problems with the joints and the foam debris, and the chance for double-loop

learning about program management. All of these ambiguities st
of the learning process because they make it impossible to de
current structures, policies, and procedures led to unsatisfactory
trast, highly reliable organizations devise well-defined, widely known, and regularly practiced procedures for evaluating the state of the system and the
adequacy of the preprogrammed procedures.

Hypotheses about Analysis and Inference

Based on NASA's pattern of learning, unlearning, and forgetting, five hypotheses
can be offered about the circumstances under which an agency is likely to analyze
its failures, find causal explanations for them, and create solutions based on these
explanations:

- Single-loop and double-loop learning are most likely when actors have
  widespread access to data about past results and when existing procedures
  for evaluating results are widely known and practiced.
- New explanations of failures and remedies based on them, a hallmark of
  double-loop learning, are most likely to appear when officials are able to
  compare a variety of past experiences or are able to observe the effects of
  alternative solutions.
- The consideration of multiple interpretations of a past experience, one element of single- and double-loop learning, is most likely when the participants are able to voice alternative views and when the outcome is not
  predetermined by the priorities of funding sources, stakeholders, agency
  executives, or by deeply embedded cultural assumptions.

These hypotheses are concerned with the core of the learning process: the
inference about improvements based on past results. But the basis for inference
is weakened if the analysis of the organization's direct or indirect experience does
not offer hints about what might work better. Similarly, if past performance is
not consistently evaluated and the policies and structures that were associated
with it are not observed, learning is compromised.

INSTITUTIONALIZING LESSONS LEARNED

The final requirement for the organizational learning process is that lessons and
new inferences become institutionalized as rules, policies, standard operating

procedures, or artifacts of organizational culture. This process makes the new knowledge, learned by some in the organization, available to all or most members. Conclusions based on a performance analysis may be established formally as new case-management procedures, for example. Alternatively, new knowledge may be embodied in information-bearing stories or rituals, professional norms, tacit work knowledge, or mental models of how the organization's technologies are supposed to work. In this way, formally and informally institutionalized knowledge informs the next round of learning.

Institutionalizing organizational learning appears to have been particularly difficult in the NASA case. There are several instances in which changes agreed to by NASA management dissipated as new launch pressures, cultural constraints, technological impediments, competing program priorities, and new management orthodoxies overtook the agency. Over the whole case, five institutionalizing patterns emerge: Learning did not occur, so there were no lessons to institutionalize; lessons were learned but not institutionalized; they were institutionalized but later forgotten; they were institutionalized but later unlearned; or they were institutionalized and remained in force.

In some instances learning did not really occur, thus lessons were never put into action. The Rogers Commission recommended, for example, that NASA managers reduce the number of critical items and review those remaining. GAO and the CAIB, however, reported that in the years following the loss of the *Challenger*, the number was as large as or larger than ever. Lessons about resisting external schedule pressures by adopting a policy of strategic refusal were, not surprisingly, never adopted since the White House made the top agency appointments and Congress set funding based on launch milestones. Even if top shuttle-program managers had wanted to resist these milestones and organizational streamlining, it would have been difficult to do under these circumstances. Preserving the core mission of human space flight was simply too important.

In other instances, new solutions or lessons were accepted but never institutionalized. Some newly discovered solutions clashed with entrenched cultural values. The 1996 GAO report on the reporting of safety information revealed the tensions between the overt support for a heightened safety program, the embedded cultural assumptions about the low scientific status of the safety program, and the tacit belief that raising safety concerns was indicative of weak performance. Despite efforts to improve pay and attract more qualified officials to the safety-monitoring organization, professional norms were against it. We also saw evidence of cultural impediments to efforts to achieve better coordination with the Marshall Center, more collaborative readiness reviews, and better communication of reservations about the status of outstanding launch problems. The power of NASA's culture, its pride and devotion to human space exploration, were not only strengths of the agency but also sources of inflexibility that make adopting alien or novel professional values difficult. The implication for learning was that, though the agency agreed in principle with the changes in command structure and safety priorities, it was difficult in practice to implement them as working routines.

Other lapses seem to have resulted from the unintentional loss of previously established lessons with the disruption of organizational memory. That is, some lessons were the learned result of agency analysis and inference, and they were implemented. But they were then forgotten, becoming unintentionally lost in a muddle of half-remembered procedures and policies. Such losses followed the downsizing of the shuttle program, and they accelerated in the 1990s under the privatization and reinvention initiatives eagerly carried out under Goldin's faster, better, cheaper management transformation, affecting the ability of agency members to recall lessons to apply to present conditions. We see the effects of these dislocations in the efforts of several midlevel managers to obtain images of the possible wing damage. The lessons-learned database and the post-*Challenger* efforts to create an integrated information system, once highly touted, were weakened when they collided with structural and technological barriers. Legacy data systems and multiple reorganizations splintered communications patterns so that efforts to make substantial improvements in problem tracking and data sharing in the period between the accidents were lost.

Some of the lessons that were learned in the aftermath of the *Challenger* accident were not forgotten but were "unlearned" in the 1990s. That is, they were discarded as the agency established other, incompatible, priorities. Lessons about coordination and communication that had been institutionalized after the *Challenger* accident were supplanted by leaner command structures and outsourced safety-monitoring systems. The principles behind this suite of management reforms were consonant with new principles in public administration generally, but they were not crafted to mesh with the particular management and technological challenges of the shuttle program. This is a deficiency in generic management reform movements. While lessons learned elsewhere, such as new models of management, may contribute to vicarious learning, in NASA's case the reforms were imposed to reduce costs and adapt to the loss of public interest in space exploration. The eventual effect of the reforms, however, was that insider objections to the loss of redundancies in engineering and safety systems were ignored. Thus the lessons of the *Challenger* were supplanted by management transformations that were not so much learned as strategically adopted from among the larger sphere of public management reforms. The preservation of institutional memory was not a priority.

Finally, some lessons were learned, they were institutionalized, and they were in place at the time of the *Columbia* disaster. The best example of this is the new patterns of communication and joint decision making between NASA and its contractors. While concerns remained about the contractor accounting issues, the oversight of contractor work and the teamwork between contractor and shuttle personnel during the *Columbia* flight suggest that the learning cycle was completed, and the lessons were not subsequently displaced.

Reliability and Institutionalized Lessons

The failures to institutionalize the lessons that had been learned and the loss of those that were forgotten or discarded had immediate and important implications for the reliability of the organization. In high-reliability organizations, formal and informal lessons about work procedures in urgent, crisis, or emergency situations are practiced and reinforced. Upper management supports these procedures. In contrast, in the shuttle program, the readiness reviews, the prelaunch equivalent of up-tempo work for the *Challenger*, did not take up the issues that caused the accidents. Further, the late-night review of the interaction between temperature and the seals by Thiokol engineers, managers, and NASA officials was not initiated as a result of any formal, emergency work procedure. It was an ad hoc process attempting to supplement the weak links in the formally established procedures.

As the CAIB noted, the practices of high-reliability organizations were not seen in the management responses during the *Columbia* flight. Indeed, up-tempo and crisis responses do not appear in the record of events leading up to the *Challenger* or the *Columbia* accidents. Instead, in an almost complete reverse of the pattern seen in highly reliable organizations, the relations between managers and working engineers became *more* rule-governed, *more* hierarchical, and *more* focused on "normal" managerial issues of schedules and chain of command. In the case of *Columbia*, we see some evidence of procedures for an emergency-response team, the famous "tiger team." But that designation never materialized, and the debris assessment team never had access to the information collection or management attention that could have made it a more successful emergency responder. Reactions to concerned engineers during the *Columbia* flight were confused and characterized by miscommunication and lack of current procedural knowledge. Much of the knowledge for dealing with the problems seems to have resided in old hands like Wayne Hale, but his advice was ignored an efforts to initiate requests for images were squelched. This situation is particularly inexplicable given that NASA had experienced crises in the *Mercury* and *Apollo* programs: System failures could not have been unexpected. Models for crisis-response patterns, seen most often in dangerous military and aviation settings, were certainly known to NASA management. The kind of experience-enlarging exercises that March, Sproull, and Tamuz (1996) identify might have substituted for limited experience with emergency situations. In the end, however, a practiced, dependable way to identify a genuine crisis and respond to it was not in place. The mission evaluation room was supposed to troubleshoot engineering problems with the flight, and the mission management team was to direct and coordinate the mission overall. But neither performed as designed, and procedures for information gathering by other actors were not reliably carried out.

Accounting for Lost Institutional Knowledge

NASA offers several lessons about preserving lessons learned and provides positive and negative evidence of the institutionalization process. Both cultural and political factors help account for the patterns seen here.

LOSS OF ORGANIZATIONAL MEMORY

Research on learning in firms supports the idea that high personnel turnover saps organizational memory and reduces the capacity for learning (Carley 1996). Etheredge (1985), examining foreign policy learning, shows that the loss of institutional memory from changes in administration actors and agency appointees has the effect of reducing the capacity of officials to recall precedents and make choices calculated to avoid problems experienced with past policy decisions. Informal lessons or tacit knowledge can diminish with the loss of institutional memory. Stories buried in the culture recall how similar problems were solved in the past (Brown and Duguid 1996), and so the loss of members reduces an organization's capacity for recall. Vigorous downsizing, loss of key engineering personnel, and reorganizations that dislocated staff from settings relevant to their knowledge were all ways that organizational memory at NASA was lost, and with it, formally and informally institutionalized knowledge. Even formal procedures become inoperative if restructuring dislocates those who have been trained in the procedures. Awareness of this dynamic lay behind the cautions regarding "managerial turbulence" offered in the Augustine Report (NASA 1990).

THODOXY

ing management orthodoxy in the agency described in the
ight have worked in favor of preserving organizational mem-
onalize long-term lessons learned. Unwillingness to challenge
management decisions might have had the effect of making it easier and faster
to institutionalize solutions that emerged from the post-*Challenger* investigations
and harder to displace them. But orthodoxy changed with the top administrators. After Administrator Truly left, the new agency administration initiated its
own version of the national administration reform movement and initiated a
new set of projects for the agency in which the shuttle program was only one
component. The lessons that became embedded were not the ones that had
emerged from previous analysis. Those had been discarded.

COMPETING CULTURAL ASSUMPTIONS

Another impediment to institutionalizing solutions and lessons that emerged
from internal and external investigations was deeply embedded cultural assumptions. Two assumptions in particular seem to have affected the institutionalization of lessons learned: organizational norms about the status of safety functions
in contrast to other scientific and engineering work in the organization, and
assumptions about the chain of command. These assumptions limited the implementation of solutions that had emerged in the aftermath of the *Challenger*,
including the design of the newly reconstituted safety and quality-assurance
offices. These offices were to have had more autonomy, more positions, and
higher pay. But the relatively low status of the safety function made staffing the
offices difficult even immediately after the loss of the first shuttle. Officials in the
newly organized offices were not accorded the status they needed. Theirs was not
the work for which the organization is famous.

Widespread reluctance to report problems or express criticism also worked
against the reform of preflight and in-flight procedures for monitoring safety.
The "NASA chicken" phenomenon described in chapter 6 indicates some of the
sources and depth of this disinclination. Cultural prohibitions against challenging management also made it very difficult for actors to jump the chain of command to protest the inaction in getting images during the *Columbia* case, even
though, in principal, there was a procedure for doing so. The effect of these
cultural norms was to prevent the newly designed safety program from operating
as intended. It existed on paper, but did not have the status informally to challenge project-management decisions. In the investigations after each accident,
safety offices were found not to have intervened.

COMPETING POLITICAL PRIORITIES

Finally, several solutions to the shuttle program's organizational and management problems that had been adopted lost out to competition from higher-priority political requirements. New solutions that fell into this category included the recentralization of the command structure and efforts to coordinate program elements across the centers through integration offices in each. Over much of the period between the two accidents, agency leadership had other priorities. The dominant coalition directed resources to meet these leader priorities, a pattern Montjoy and O'Toole (1979) found in other settings. There were strong pressures to reduce costs and simplify preflight reviews by eliminating redundant safety and quality-assurance structures. These priorities conflicted with making major investments in updating and integrating incident-reporting systems; thus a genuinely integrated problem-tracking system and a lessons-learned database never materialized. The separate legacy data systems of the many shuttle components made these improvements a more costly undertaking than the agency was willing to accept.

In the immediate aftermath of the *Challenger* accident, NASA clearly agreed to make these kinds of changes. However, the safety structures were streamlined and contracted out in the 1990s and in the aftermath of the 1995 Kraft Report. That report, the product of an independent review commissioned by NASA leadership, offered a rationale to eliminate the redundancies in the system that had been created after the *Challenger* accident, providing a solution to a newly defined set of problems that displaced the post-*Challenger* solutions.

Hypotheses about Institutionalization

These patterns in successful and unsuccessful institutionalizing of new solutions suggest four hypotheses about the process of learning:

- Successfully institutionalized changes are likely to be lost to the accessible, functioning knowledge of organizational personnel when large numbers of long-time members leave or when repeated reorganizations do not re-establish knowledge in its new location for the new personnel.
- Previously institutionalized lessons are likely to be displaced and unlearned over time as continuing political and cultural patterns re-exert pressure to return to a previous state of affairs.
- New lessons are most likely to be institutionalized when they are in harmony with dominant cultural assumptions so that they are perceived to be

professionally respectable changes that mesh with existing doctrines and agency technologies.

- New lessons are most likely to be institutionalized when they are in harmony with political priorities within the agency because resources to implement them are more likely to be available.

THE CONTEXT OF AGENCY LEARNING

The NASA case demonstrates how it is that public agencies can, but often do not, learn. We have seen the ways in which a relatively small set of key organizational and political factors blocked or diverted learning. Organizational fragmentation, the responses to external pressures on the agency to cut costs and stay on schedule, ambiguities in the evaluation of results and in procedures for monitoring mission safety, multiple iterations of reorganization and downsizing, internal cultural assumptions about the status of safety work, and management intolerance of criticism all affected learning at many points. Each of these causal factors rippled across the post-*Challenger* organization to reduce the chances that the learning cycle would unfold and solve the problems that had come to light. External political, administrative, and legal trends, the oversight of Congress, and the appointment powers of the president were also important features of the case.

We can draw several conclusions about the learning cycle in public organizations from the positive and negative evidence of learning at NASA. Foremost is that organizational learning is not so much a single organizational event or activity as the result of many other processes and conditions that shape the understanding, capacity, and willingness of members to undertake the sometimes discomforting and costly course of learning. The general information-processing theory of organizational learning as a more or less rational process emphasizes the collection, analysis, and retrieval of organizational information, but in practice public organizational learning depends on a range of contextual factors as well. Our study demonstrates that at NASA the rationality and the learning capacity of actors were bounded in major ways by technological, cultural, political, and professional forces. In this chapter we have seen how these factors affected the core activities that comprise learning and thus how organizational learning is shaped by its institutional context in complexly interrelated ways. The agendas of administration appointees, the personal management styles of founding scientists, the decline in national interest in expensive, astronaut-led space exploration, and myriad other events and institutional characteristics shaped the capacity for learning at NASA. In the end, successful learning in public organizations appears to be dependent on the many conditions that allow members to admit the existence of program flaws, to sanction experimentation with alternative solutions, and to support these solutions over the long run.

Second, the case demonstrates how complex interactions between an agency's political setting and its culture affect the course of learning. Culture has long been recognized as a likely impediment to learning (Mahler 1997; Schein 1992), but this case shows a more complex set of connections than is generally acknowledged. Institutional loyalties and the desire to keep the human space-flight program intact led officials to accept compromises with staffing levels and program control just as von Braun had in the earliest days of the shuttle program. The survival of the institution and of its particular missions became a guiding principle overriding even entrenched engineering standards among organizational leaders. Openness to learning was replaced by strategic adaptation. In contrast, lower-level engineers at NASA and its contractors, who were insulated to some degree from direct accountability and the close oversight exercised by Congress and top administration appointees, showed greater openness to learning. Those with the actual authority to advance the learning processes believed they could not afford to do so.

The capacity of all the actors to declare an emergency or to make inferences about the causes behind technical and administrative failings was also hampered by the absence of clear, consistent performance standards and evaluation procedures. Again, strong outside pressures and conflicting cultural predispositions interfered, with the result that increased pressure was placed on front-line professionals to make and defend judgments about these failings on their own.

The implication of all this for explaining learning in public organizations is that agencies inhabit a particularly difficult environment for learning. Especially important in that environment is the oversight of external political actors who are able to constrain or countermand professional judgments. By setting cost and schedule requirements unconnected to the technology of human space flights, these external actors limit the choices that professionals can make to achieve a mission. We take this dynamic to be the normal and intended effect of accountability, but it has unintended effects as well, and constrained learning is one of them. The task then becomes separating these effects so that learning and accountability can coexist. We take this issue up further in the next chapter.

Finally, the case also reveals the evolving and cyclical nature of public organizational learning. Learning may take years, not weeks or even months, to be realized. Sabatier notes that policy learning is a process that unfolds slowly over years or decades (1993), and the same is true of public organizational learning.

To see the pattern of events that comprise the learning process, the fate of the lessons learned, and their transformation into a basis for subsequent learning requires a long-term view of agency development. The process is also iterative or cyclical so that core organizational weaknesses appear again and again to be redefined and reanalyzed and resolved. Furthermore, these processes are ongoing, and the results are not permanent. Lessons learned at one time may be forgotten or lost, they may be displaced by new lessons of greater or lesser value, or they may be usurped by more current orthodoxies or management fashions. Advances or losses at one time affect later developments, and we can observe how under changed circumstances, different results can emerge. The cyclical character of the process reveals its essential similarity to structuration models in which individuals enact the patterns and structures that in turn constrain them (Berends, Boersma, and Weggeman 2003).

The learning cycle appears then both as a possible process of change in an institutional context and as the prisoner of that context. While historical and institutional frameworks emphasize strong tendencies toward stability and the preservation of established patterns of action, relationship, and choice (March and Olson 1984; Scott 1995, 26; Immergut 1998, 16), organizational learning offers a potential means to account for change. Learning moves actors to challenge established rules, procedures, policies, tacit knowledge, and cultural beliefs in an effort to uncover the sources of failure and implant more effective regimes. The NASA case demonstrates that success in challenging the embedded structures of cultural and political expectations does occur, though only rarely. The *Challenger* accident offered enormous incentives to undertake an essential reexamination of the shuttle program management. This process could have meant moving beyond the centralized *Apollo* management model of recent experience or reconsidering the priority given to preserving the center structure. It might have led to reassessing the qualitative engineering hazards-analysis methodology and raising the status of safety analysis. But combined internal and external pressures based on tradition, culture and both political and economic survival resulted in uneven and impermanent learning.

We have identified the learning cycle as comprising three elements, but we suspected, and the shuttle case supports the suspicion, that the three elements are not necessarily chronological steps or stages. Recognizing and defining a problem may follow from counterfactual speculations about the causes of an event. Acknowledging a problem and seeking out its causes may be more or less simultaneous activities. But this simultaneity may not be an advantage because identifying the cause of a failure and assigning responsibility for it may be too easily confounded. It may also be easy to scapegoat a person or office as a way of minimizing the pain of acknowledging failure, a fact that may partly explain why midlevel managers and their failures of communication were identified as the factors chiefly responsible for the events that led to the *Challenger* accident, even though the real causes were multiple and complex (U.S. Congress, House Committee on Science and Technology 1986; Vaughan 1996, 11).

This examination of the learning that occurred in the period between the shuttle accidents does offer some suggestions about what conditions or actions might foster learning. While the case is in too many ways a chronicle of lost opportunities for learning or holding onto lessons that were learned because of the rich record of actions, events, and agency research, we have been able to reconstruct some of the learning cycles and what they reveal about learning in public organizations. We next turn to what this rich record suggests about how to foster public organizational learning or at least avoid those conditions that seem incompatible with it.

Lessons from NASA about Organizational Learning

MANY HAVE ASKED whether government organizations can learn. That is, can actors in large state bureaucracies make inferences from experience to avoid the mistakes of the past and reliably share this knowledge with other members? In principle at least, learning offers a model for a self-correcting, self-designing organization that can address concerns of reform-minded public administrators to decentralize and deregulate agencies without detaching them from their missions. Learning also represents a change in focus about how agencies improve, from a view that meaningful change only results from external intervention to the view of change that rests on indigenous, knowledge-based enhancements in administrative and policy ideas. Learning looks at the way that new ideas about how to manage or how to achieve program objectives are discovered and how they evolve to prominence or diminish to obscurity. Change occurs against the shifting backdrop of resource restrictions, changes in law and policy, and political demands, but learning looks at the effects of these demands on the ideas the emerge from considered experiences, new analysis, and professional developments in the field.

The NASA case offers a rare opportunity to examine learning over a multi-decade period in a large, complex organization with a relatively clear-cut record of successes and failures. NASA is also unusual in the variety and depth of the record of organization events and organization actors' views and perceptions. As noted in chapter 1, the many histories and popular accounts of the agency, journalistic and scholarly reports of events, and thousands of hours of testimony, all readily accessible, provide a particularly detailed record of what happened at NASA and why. NASA may not be so unusual, however, in its record of missed opportunities for learning, learning the wrong lessons, or forgetting the important ones. Current investigations of the failures surrounding the intelligence before September 11 and the inadequate response to Hurricane Katrina offer similar examples.

In one sense we expect that learning in governmental organizations will be natural and common. Learning in some form is built into the very idea of modern public administration. The progressive view of administration assumes that public bureaucracies will improve the quality, efficiency, consistency, and effectiveness of their work over time based on professional knowledge, public scrutiny, and self-evaluation. Of course, this does not always happen. Yet continuous assessment is assumed to underlie what we mean by rational administration, both traditionally and in its most recent evidence-based incarnation in various models of performance measurement. The questions must then be: Why does it not occur? What blocks this "normal" process and what can we learn from the NASA case to help us foster knowledge-based change?

The previous chapter offered a refinement of the general theory of organizational learning that focused on the effects of the agency's political and cultural context on communication, coordination, and decision making. A series of hypotheses derived from the case study summarized the conditions that fostered or thwarted learning. They described the constraints on learning imposed by institutional pressures and concluded by noting the ways in which these factors created complexly layered and interactive impediments to learning. In this chapter we make inferences from those findings about NASA to offer lessons about learning that may be useful beyond the shuttle case, for other public organizations or organizations in general. While most organizations cannot radically alter their political or cultural environments, they might be able to cope more successfully with the constraints imposed by them.

Six lessons about what is required for learning emerge from studying NASA: establish clear procedures and standards; integrate disparate sources of information; inject imagination and skepticism into the interpretation of results; link learning and accountability; invest in memory; and practice learning. While the universal applicability of these lessons cannot be proved by one case, however complex and revealing, it appears that all of them act together to make learning possible; they are not fully independent or separable in their effects. They interact to enable the processes of learning, as summarized in table 8.1.

Overarching all these factors, however, is time. Learning is an iterative process, so that inferences are examined in light of experience with their consequences to provide a basis for the next round of analysis and inference. More time and more iterations afford an organization a succession of opportunities to reflect on past results and to make the best inferences. Successful one-trial learning in the kind of complex, layered problems that governmental organizations

TABLE 8.1 Relationships between Lessons and Learning Processes

Lesson	Effect on Problem Recognition	Effect on Analysis and Inference	Effect on Institutionalization
(1) Learning requires widespread knowledge of present standards and practices.	When members are aware of and use formal standards and procedures, they are not forced to rely on other justifications or personal courage to declare the existence of a flaw or problem.	Analysis of the sources of inadequate results rests on knowing which program procedures and which work standards led to inadequate results so they can be changed.	Inadequately institutionalized lessons from the past may make the next round of learning more difficult or force members to relearn lessons.
(2) Learning requires more than information.	When information is not shared or integrated, results are not visible to those who might be best able to understand their significance.	Analysis and inference requires the comparison of various combinations of cause and effect based on experience or shared knowledge of practices elsewhere.	Participation in forums where interpretations are compared also serves to pass on new inferences and institutionalize new knowledge.
(3) Learning requires imagination and skepticism.	Support for imagination and skepticism helps counter the typical reluctance in organizations to alter patterns of action or cultural assumptions, or to accept blame for failure.	Skepticism forces us to challenge entrenched mental models that no longer fit emerging events, results, or experiences. Multiple interpretations increase the chances for new inferences.	Well-entrenched and institutionalized practices from the past can block the acceptance of new lessons

TABLE 8.1 Continued

(4) Learning requires an investment in memory.	When organizational memories fade, old problems may not be recognized for what they are and may be ignored or misunderstood.	Institutional memory makes it possible to compare actions and outcomes experienced over time.	Institutional memory and accessible databases preserve lessons from the past.
(5) Learning requires that accountability includes professional standards.	Accountability standards influence what members pay attention to and what will be classed as a problem. If these standards are incompatible with agency mission, learning may not enhance the core technology.	Accountability constrains the alternatives that members can imagine or afford to examine. Including professional accountability standards provides space for learning.	Lessons may be more readily institutionalized if they are responsive to professional standards and judgments.
(6) Learning requires practice.	Without practice, lessons fade from memory and departures from desired results will be less likely to be detected.	When lessons deteriorate, hard-won knowledge about causal relationships behind program technologies is lost and reasons for present success or failure become difficult to comprehend.	Reliable application of past lessons requires they be taught, practiced, and used.

face is very unlikely. Like policy learning (Sabatier 1993), public organizational learning appears to be a multi-decadal process. One of the most tragic aspects of the NASA case is that at critical junctures, actors believed they did not have the time to do the research, recheck the results, or reinterpret their experiences with their own managerial technologies. These actions constitute the core of public organizational learning.

ESTABLISHING CLEAR PROCEDURES AND STANDARDS

In the previous chapter the relationship between learning and the lack of widely observed standards and procedures was described. This pattern affects learning in two ways. First, problem recognition becomes a more precarious process. Absent such standards, the onus of declaring an emergency falls to professionals who must defend and justify their call on other grounds, perhaps personal, historical, or external practice, against internal opposition. This dynamic makes the professionals vulnerable and puts the burden of proof on them to demonstrate that the situation is a dangerous one or that results are otherwise inadequate. Lower-level professionals, who are often the first to see hazards or unsatisfactory results, are particularly susceptible to pressures to "duck" or to bend standards. Whistleblowers and dissenters withstand such pressures, sometimes heroically (O'Leary 2005), but they are not the organizational norm. More typically, as we see in the NASA case, actors may be unable to resist the pressure to follow the path of least resistance, leaving the problems formally unacknowledged.

Analysis and inference are also compromised in the absence of well-defined and reliably practiced standards and decision rules because actors cannot know what actions have led to what outcomes. When procedures are vaguely recognized and often violated, linking procedural cause and effect is not possible. Linking shifting structures and their consequences is similarly difficult. In some ways this situation is a weak form of organizational anarchy, a condition also known for interrupted learning cycles (March and Olsen 1976). Both of these patterns appeared in the history of the shuttle accidents. Lower-level engineers were put on the spot to declare an emergency in the face of shifting criteria for safety margins. Administrative actions after the *Challenger* accident illustrate an absence of alternative interpretations of cause and effect regarding administrative arrangements other than to revert back to the centralized structures of the pre-shuttle era.

NASA's history also makes clear that devising clear standards for identifying hazards and establishing procedures for coping with possible emergencies is only a first step. New procedures must be culturally acceptable, as illustrated by the resistance to the hierarchical reporting relationships among agency centers and the unwillingness of officials to jump the chain of command within centers. The procedures must also be widely known and practiced. There may also be political impediments to creating performance standards that contradict or delay externally defined goals, for example, the pressures for scheduling the shuttle. But the lesson here is that clear and widely observed standards and procedures make it easier to identify real problems and to analyze their causes.

INFORMATION IS NOT ENOUGH

Information is universally identified as a requisite for any kind of learning, including public organizational learning. But the availability of information in itself does not generate learning in complex organizational settings. By definition, in multidivisional organizations, different kinds of information about program actions and their results are available in separate offices or bureaus and at different levels of hierarchy. If these sources cannot share the information they have in some reasonably open forum, warning signs of problems can be missed and opportunities to design responsive changes will be lost.

Information sharing and coordination are core management problems. NASA is far from unusual in not putting together key pieces of information regarding the seal-erosion problems or the potential for significant damage from foam debris. In Kettl's 2007 portrayal of the coordination lapses that preceded September 11, he describes the failure to integrate information about the terrorists and the intentions of terrorist groups by the various intelligence, law enforcement, border security, and State Department agencies. Comfort, Ko, and Zagorecki (2004) simulated complex disaster systems to show the role of information linkages in making even willing, cooperative systems effective. They found that cooperation without information does not improve effectiveness, and the loss of only a few key information nodes affects the capacity of the entire network.

The NASA case teaches us the importance of providing a forum, actual or virtual, in which participants can compare notes, openly and without fear of censure or ridicule. The four-level flight-readiness-review process, starting at the contractor levels and ending with the headquarters' determination that any problems have been resolved, was designed to be just such a process. But the actors at each level sometimes failed to convey critical information for a number of convoluted and self-reinforcing reasons, and sometimes that was enough to derail the process. In the *Challenger* case, intercenter rivalries and status conflicts prevented officials at Marshall, especially, from admitting that the seals on the joints in the solid rocket boosters had unresolved problems. Thiokol, the manufacturer of the rockets, was similarly unmotivated to act decisively on the engineers' concerns about the seals. Several NASA engineers and managers, including Hardy, the director of Marshall's safety organization, testified after the fact that they would have made a different decision about the launch had they known what the engineers knew about the seals. Of course, NASA engineers were at the same time successfully tracking and resolving many other problems that appeared to them more likely to cause problems. But the one that did cause the loss of the *Challenger* was not caught, in part because key pieces of information were not presented to the right people at the right time.

In the case of the *Columbia*, the absence of information integration before and during the flight led directly to the loss of the shuttle. Before the last *Columbia* flight, information about the foam problem was inconsistently collected and classified by the several offices sharing responsibility for the problem. During the flight, NASA and contractor engineers who were concerned that the foam strike may have caused serious damage were isolated and largely ignored by mission managers. The forums that could have served to integrate key information about the potential for damage to the wing and the correct procedure to obtain images did not meet or were not created.

Hierarchical divisions also thwarted the integration of information. In both the *Challenger* and *Columbia* accidents, front-line engineers were shut out of discussions at key points. In the case of the *Challenger*, engineers at Thiokol and Marshall spotted the increasingly clear evidence of seal erosion but were reluctant to report on a problem that could jeopardize their contract or subject them to criticism. In the *Columbia* case, the concerns of front-line engineers and mid-level managers were shunted aside, and inputs were barely acknowledged, much less sought out, by mission managers. In each case front-line professionals brought bad news that could delay launch schedules and disrupt program plans. They constituted an unwelcome interference with the smooth operations of the shuttle on which outside support rested. In high-reliability organizations, discussed below, experienced front-line employees often play key roles in crisis situations, but they were not given those responsibilities at NASA.

While not a solution on its own, the creation of forums in which actors are free to present information and express reservations in the prelaunch and in-flight stages of a mission might have improved NASA's ability to forestall disaster. These forums could be face-to-face exchanges in open meetings. Such gatherings were, in fact, held at the centers and were to be the basis of flight readiness reviews, but did not exhibit an atmosphere of open exchange. Forums could also be virtual, however, so that some measure of distance or anonymity might be created to cope with cultural conditions that discourage dissent. Online forums such as the organization's intranet chat room, virtual meeting sites, or even e-mail lists offer a way to access a wide, informal network of interested participants across the organization and a place to assemble and share information. Externally hosted blogs created as forums for current and former employees also offer a place for remarkably candid and open discussions about agency practices and decisions (Mahler and Regan 2007, 2008).

McAfee (2006) especially champions joint-authoring tools such as blogs and wikis because "the intranet platform shifts from being the creation of a few to being the constantly updated interlinked work of many" (24). He cites the experience of Wikipedia to suggest that such forums can offer highly reliable information. However, these forums are not immune to management oversight and interference, and McAfee cautions managers not to castigate employees for the inevitable criticisms of management and policies that arise in virtual spaces. Adopting virtual forums may not always be necessary, but they offer a reasonably well-developed approach to breeching organizational and hierarchal boundaries for interested participants. The result could be to embolden isolated organization members and encourage or legitimate further action.

Had managers been listening to the concerns of lower-level professionals, expressed in e-mail traffic among some front-line actors during the flight of the *Columbia*, they might have pressed harder for the resolution of questions about the safety of the flight. More effective physical or virtual forums might have prompted problem recognition across the agency and initiated a learning process. Jenkins-Smith and Sabatier (1993) find that professional forums away from public scrutiny, in which there are moderate levels of conflict among contending views, are the most conducive to policy learning. It is not enough that information exists somewhere in the organization. It must be shared, interpreted, argued over, and reinterpreted to tease out trends and understand the link between actions and results.

INTERPRETING RESULTS WITH IMAGINATION AND SKEPTICISM

Collating experience in an open forum is a first step in understanding programs and operations well enough to improve them, but interpretation—making sense of experience—is also essential for learning. Situations or conditions must first be interpreted as problems before they can be acted upon (Barzelay 1992), and the features of a situation that are responsible for the problem must be distinguished or discerned before the connections and inferences that constitute learning are possible. But in the NASA case, many of the potentially dangerous situations were not identified as high-priority failures. The belief that the consequences of these failings would be benign was widely accepted among the upper levels of managers, especially. This view was not shaken despite the uncertainties of the engineers providing the data. Generating multiple interpretations of the problem and its possible causes is one way to challenge entrenched assumptions associated with present outcomes. Comfort (2002) illustrates the value of cultural openness to new concepts of operation and organization for self-organizing and learning in the aftermath of September 11. Breaking out of these conventional, and in the NASA case, expedient mental models requires imagination and skepticism.

Skepticism forces us to challenge entrenched mental models that no longer fit emerging events, results, or experiences. Most organizations are conservative institutions that hold on to action patterns and cultural assumptions. This characteristic gives them their admirable stability, but it also means that members' loyalty to key ideas behind programs and policies sometimes lasts longer than experience justifies. Skepticism may be the province of a key actor, a visionary or iconoclast, or as in the NASA case, some of the working engineers. Their professional training did not allow them to ignore troubling evidence about the connections between temperature and seal erosion or the uncertainties associated with the estimates of damage to the wings. When they were being asked to put aside their doubts about the seals on the eve of the *Challenger* launch, they were asked to put aside their professional engineering role and put on their "management hats" to attend to the administrative aspects of the situation.

Imagination allows us to piece the evidence together in new ways. It makes it possible for us to conceive of alternative futures and unusual or unexpected consequences. In the post–September 11 world, we know that we did not "connect the dots," but the dots typically do not lie in a straight line (Kronenberg and Khademian 2007). Moving from one to the next requires us to at least look in several unaccustomed directions. At key points NASA managers did not acknowledge, much less seek out, evidence of unexpected effects of the cold temperatures or debris strike. Perhaps more important, over the long term, in the years before each of the accidents when there was time to consider the unusual or the unlikely, the risk-assessment technology and the management accommodation to scarcity and launch pressures seem to have led organization members to imagine only the most likely scenarios. There is little evidence of the use of constructive counterfactuals (Morris and Moore 2000) to spur analysis of administrative forms in new directions. During the *Columbia* flight, the mission officials operated under significant pressures to accept conventional mental models, to avoid messy and complicated investigations, and to maintain the launch schedule to which they were deeply committed. They had many opportunities to imagine the worst and to practice skepticism about the assurances offered by a record of successful flights. Had they done so, it is possible that outcomes would have been different.

Contemporary public administration has identified a wide variety of techniques for fostering skepticism and imagination. Models of decision making and strategic planning typically include elements of "brainstorming." March (1976) urges us to appreciate the "technology of foolishness," a consequence of organizational anarchy in which propositions that could not be floated in a genuinely rational decision setting can emerge in the course of garbage-can decision making. Foolish or imaginative proposals have the advantage of bringing fresh ideas with unexpected value to the table. Janis (1982) offers a number of remedies for "groupthink" such as ensuring group diversity, creating multiple independent groups to work on a problem, and installing a devil's advocate, all designed to foster alternative interpretations of events and projected consequences. Designing forums that include members from different divisions with different interests and ideas may achieve these ends. Though the flight-readiness-review process had been designed to do many of these things, cultural and political pressures overwhelmed the forum meant to produce professional scrutiny. Our analysis makes the case for reinvigorating these kinds of forums and recognizing their truly essential role in learning and improving.

INVESTING IN MEMORY

Particularly in the case of the *Columbia*, the loss of knowledge about procedures was costly. Problem-solving procedures at NASA were considered by the CAIB to be among the best of their type (180). But at key points they were abandoned in favor of expedited decisions to speed the launch process and maintain a smoothly functioning mission. For some actors, key procedures could not be recalled because they had never been fully learned or had been forgotten after years of downsizing, multiple reorganizations, or job realignments. In the years before the *Challenger*, preflight procedures were slighted, in some instances apparently out of boredom with the overly familiar.

Organizational memory resides in people and in the information systems the organization maintains. When an agency downsizes it loses the knowledge of procedures and of past events that former employees possessed. Learning has been shown to be affected by the loss of personnel (Epple, Argote, and Rukmini 1996), and NASA experienced wave after wave of downsizing. All of the centers lost civil service personnel over the forty years covered in this study. With them went some of the agency's formal and informal knowledge of how past crises had been handled, which lines of communication were reliable, and which actors constituted a working group of problem solvers. Tacit knowledge in particular is lost when key personnel leave. Well-rehearsed formal crisis-response procedures are the backbone of high-reliability organizations, but in NASA's case the formal procedures were slighted and the information network of knowledgeable members had been undermined by loss of personnel and multiple task realignments.

The inability to summon up procedures is not the only important kind of lapse in organizational memory. Because learning depends on comparing outcomes and making inferences about what actions led to improved results, the capacity to remember past events and retrieve information about consequences is essential. Here again, we see that the shuttle program was handicapped by its inability to assemble and integrate information across the organization and over time. The dispersed center-based structure, the antiquated, stove-piped data systems, the sharing of monitoring responsibilities between NASA and its contractor, and the complex, qualitative hazard-analysis systems all made a unified, accessible organizational memory more difficult to create. In some instances described in chapter 3, access to requirements and specifications for components was not available outside the center with the primary responsibility for them so that following up problems was extremely difficult. All these weaknesses limited the capacity of the system to track and compare results. The weakness of garbage-can decision making in just this regard is why March and Olsen (1976) link it to an interrupted learning cycle.

The importance of memory in learning suggests that organizations that want to foster learning should invest in organization memory. When personnel are lost or reassigned, it is important to preserve their familiarity with procedures, their knowledge of how to assemble information for comparison, and their recollection of trends in performance improvement. Their expertise may be formally available in reports or research documents or preserved though a formal transition process, but trends and insights at early stages of verification may be only available informally in the form of speculation, stories, or even gossip. Much of the critical intelligence in organizations resides in the tacit knowledge of members and in evolving "communities of practice" (Brown and Duguid 1996).

Passing on this information should be a priority for agency managers as they cope with the loss of personnel and the introduction of new staff members. Important procedural information for dealing with crises might be "backed up" by passing on to new officeholders the lore of the office. This goal is often accomplished through lengthy conversion periods or more rapidly with stories of disaster averted or crises survived told at retirement parties or informal gatherings. Both formal and informal means of preserving knowledge of procedures and of trends in results take time, but they constitute critical investments in future organizational improvements.

LEARNING AND ACCOUNTABILITY

By any telling, the history of the shuttle program reflects an almost incessant scramble for resources to keep the shuttle and the human space-flight program alive. Congress and the White House pushed NASA for lower costs and a launch rate fast enough to help pay for the program and support the International Space Station. The aerospace industry contractors pressed for greater scope and size of contracts, and Congress supported the use of broad geographically distributed contractors. Even the media and the public demanded glamorous and ambitious accomplishments from the agency. These pressures were a result of a number of factors, immediate and distant: the design history of the shuttle and the International Space Station, U.S. foreign policy, the end of the cold war, the administrative-reform movements of the Clinton–Gore administration, and congressional impatience with NASA's performance. This list is long. But the consequences were that NASA was continually under scrutiny by a large number of actors who wanted a faster, cheaper, and more hard-working space program. We have seen what some of the impacts of these pressures were on launch decisions and the functioning of internal safety systems.

The effects of the pressures, however, were indirect as well. Research from the airline industry described in the previous chapter suggests that multiple sources of accountability may have influenced the inability of shuttle program actors to even contemplate how different decisions might have led to different outcomes. To exercise counterfactual thinking is to admit that other procedures or other decisions might have avoided a disastrous outcome. It is clear that acknowledging a problem is a first step in learning to overcoming it, but under strict accountability, actors are less likely to allow themselves to imagine what they might have done to avoid a threat. It is simply too dangerous, psychologically and strategically, to do so. Cognitive dissonance, too, accounts for inability to face having made a mistake, leading to the linguistic evasion "mistakes were made" (Tavris and Aronson 2007). All of this research helps explain the resistance of NASA managers in the post-*Challenger* period to consider a wide range of alternative structural and procedural arrangements for the shuttle program.

What lessons about accountability can be drawn from this situation? Eliminating accountability for agencies is obviously not an option. Accountability is the cornerstone of modern, progressive public administration. But was NASA held accountable for the right kinds of results? Romzek and Dubnick (1987) raise a related question when they examine the appropriateness of the accountability structures under which NASA operated. They argue that different systems of public accountability, all legitimate, are more or less appropriate contingent upon the institutional setting of the agency. Traditional hierarchical accountability to internal agency leaders can coexist with political accountability or responsiveness to external legislators, executives, and constituencies. In both these cases front-line operatives are held to account for conformance to means and ends established by other actors, internal or external to the agency. Under the legal accountability model also, the controlling source is outside the agency and able to enforce legal sanctions or contractual obligations for performance (228).

Only in the case of the professional accountability model are an agency's technical experts the ones to make authoritative decisions about means and, sometimes, ends. Physicians and scientists have traditionally operated under this form of accountability, college professors and legal practitioners less so. Needing the results that the experts can only achieve by exercising judgment based on training and insight, lawmakers and top administrators defer to these professionals. Under Perrow's contingency theory (1967), these actors require a measure of autonomy, and this in turn shapes the structures and power relations of organizations that operate under this model. Romzek and Dubnick suggest that in the run-up to the *Challenger* accident, NASA was inappropriately forced to shift from the professional accountability model of the Mercury and early Apollo years to the bureaucratic and political accountability models. This had the effect of suppressing technical engineering judgments and replacing them with decisions based on ease of control, cost efficiency, and political expediency. Inappropriate accountability thus contributed to the accident.

Radin (2006) makes a complementary case about the accountability of professionals under the performance-measurement rubric. She argues that efforts to subject professional decisions and actions to uniform measurement have had the unintended effect of compromising professional judgments. Because it is very difficult to construct quantitative and qualitative output measures of the real contributions that scientists, physicians, teachers, and other professionals make to society, various unsatisfactory systems of proxy measures have evolved. Cost may be used in place of more precise rating schemes. Measures may be put to very different uses than intended; for example, performance-improvement measures may in the end be used for personnel evaluations. Too often, over-reliance on performance measurement has led some to game the system while obedient professionals, pressured by governmental requirements, distort their work to comply. Radin notes that even when professionals are involved in creating the measures they may not have enough control over the process to insist upon more sensitive measures. Participants may also be chosen for their political rather than their professional credentials. The public status of the profession in society can also explain why some groups, notably physicians, have been able to control more successfully the terms under which their professional work is scrutinized.

Applied to the NASA case, these arguments suggest that as other national priorities replaced the space race, the publicly perceived value and status of space exploration eroded, and NASA actors lost the ability to act as professionals. They became increasingly subject to the kinds of bureaucratic and political controls more typical of routine government tasks. Performance came to be measured not in terms of discoveries made or national status preserved, but in the more standard administrative metrics of cost, on-time work, compliance, and predictable results. We see this pattern in the lead-up to both accidents. After the *Challenger*, Congress initially increased funding and relieved NASA of some routine military-satellite-launch responsibilities to allow it to focus on continuing development work on the shuttle and other space-science missions. But by the early 1990s external pressures returned for both leaner organizational structures and a faster-paced schedule, this time associated with the construction of the International Space Station. Historically and culturally, NASA has been a research and development organization, but to continue to function, it had to adopt externally defined goals for an operational program to shuttle material to the space station, with the political and bureaucratic accountability patterns that went with the new role.

What effects did inappropriate accountability have on NASA's capacity to learn? The most direct impact was to distract the agency from its main work in order to satisfy incompatible objectives. In general, it is more difficult to identify performance gaps and analyze their causes when the results for which the agency will be held to account are different from those defined by its mission, technology, and culture. In NASA's case this led to inattention and low morale, and a form of goal displacement in which meeting external benchmarks had to take precedence over the engineering and science work for which the agency was created. Agency actors were only partly successful in learning to adapt to the new political and bureaucratic realities of their situation. Their genuine commitment to the mission and the culture of the agency made it impossible to relinquish work on human space flight and space science, but the realities of their political situation made it necessary to compromise these goals repeatedly because of reductions in funding and changes in national priorities and popular interests. This pattern appeared even in the 1960s as political support for the agency waned. Under these circumstances, the learning cycle was often interrupted and truncated.

Learning and accountability are linked in complex ways. Most agencies can learn to be more politically responsive, adept at working with lawmakers and serving their clients. Many can also learn to function more efficiently and consistently and to create effective and progressive management practices. But learning makes its greatest contributions in the realm of knowledge work. Public organizational learning comes most fully into its own when its object is *ideas* about the work of the agency. In some agencies, like NASA, these are ideas about how to explore the cosmos, while for human service agencies, discoveries are concerned with new understandings of clients or the design of programs. Thus a professional accountability model, under which agency actors are able to carve out some of the discretion they need to pursue promising ideas and develop a "requisite variety" of experience, offers the best opportunity for learning.

LEARNING TAKES PRACTICE

Finally, the NASA case reveals the relationship between learning and reliability. An argument sometimes offered to explain why organizations like NASA fail in emergency situations is that because genuine emergencies are rare, the organization has not experienced a variety of outcomes and so has not had an opportunity to learn how to mount an effective response. Crises in shuttle flights have, thankfully, been uncommon. But experience with crises is not the only way to learn about them, as we noted in chapter 2 in describing research on organizational reliability. One of the most interesting findings shows how, in high reliability organizations, work relations that are normally centralized, routine, and rule-governed shift to a collegial, self-organizing pattern in which the expertise of front-line workers is respected when the work becomes fast-paced and dangerous. Yet another largely preprogrammed and highly coordinated emergency response takes over if a complex, unstable situation deteriorates toward disaster (LaPorte and Consolini 1991).

These routines are, however, learned over time as a result of experience with the normal work routines, practice in successfully handling up-tempo work, and training with scenarios about predicted, if not actually encountered, situations that can cascade toward disaster. Experience and practice lead to uncovering workable procedures. Emergency responses are programmed and subject to well-developed SOPs that are dependably initiated. Self-organizing responses in the fast-paced, dangerous settings are not programmed, but still depend on well-established and reliable tacit or overt agreements about the circumstances under which the shift to collegial relations occurs. Even if the most dangerous conditions are rare, organizations that are highly reliable practice their responses to scenarios about possible, expected threats. March, Sproull, and Tamuz (1996) note how organizations can expand even limited learning opportunities when experience with a variety of outcomes is rare.

At NASA, reliable crisis-response practices were not in place for a variety of reasons including structural divisions, political pressures, and the cultural history of the agency. Funding had always constrained NASA's actions, but it is far from clear that if greater funding had been available it would have been devoted to improvements in the safety- and quality-assurance systems or the development of more dependable up-tempo and crisis-response programs. Finally, the shuttle technology presents an exceedingly large and complex set of critical elements whose failure could cascade into disaster. In chapter 6 we discussed how culturally informed assumptions inured shuttle program managers to the dangers of some commonly encountered, low-technology elements, and this too seems to have worked against the creation of the kind of multimode crisis responses described by research into high reliability. All these factors contributed to the absence of dependable safety-response systems.

The eventual test of learning, and its value to any organization, is that it improves performance and that those improvements, the lessons learned, are dependably practiced throughout the organization. This is what it means in the end to institutionalize new inferences and solutions to problems. High-reliability theory underscores the importance of institutionalizing the new lessons dependably by making them part of the tacit or formal knowledge of the organization members. Even if emergency routines are admirably designed, if they are not widely known and practiced, they will not be useful. Within the shuttle program, there is evidence that elements of an emergency response system were in place, but they were not functioning as designed. There were some procedures, but they had been superseded, never fully implemented, or discarded. For learning to foster reliability, lessons must be widely known and practiced (see table 8.2).

TABLE 8.2   Putting Lessons into Practice

Lessons	In Practice
Learning requires widespread knowledge of present standards and practices.	Clarify formal standards for core organizational technologies, ensuring that all members from the top to the bottom of the hierarchy understand and take them seriously. Take stock of procedures, including procedures for routine as well as fast-paced or emergency work. The current emphasis on outputs and outcomes need not lead to ignoring work process. Tacit knowledge may alert members to problems but may not be a legitimate basis for criticizing unsatisfactory practices or results.
Learning requires more than information.	Create real or virtual forums for integrating information and comparing interpretations of events. Make sure someone is listening to reports of problems and that others are listening to her.
Learning requires imagination and skepticism.	Make room for competing evaluations of results and interpretations of causes. Open the door to discussions of competing professional standards for performance and technologies. Find ways to include dissenters, iconoclasts, or devil's advocates.
Learning requires an investment in memory.	Find ways to disseminate or pass on organizational memory of past events, especially crises, "workarounds," and unsolved problems. Make information in databases accessible and interoperable, but do not neglect ways to circulate information about tacit organizational practices that are too complex or subtle for rules or too confusing to record. Use social settings and team-based problem solving to pass on this kind of knowledge.
Learning requires accountability to professional standards.	Opportunities for learning about how to improve core mission technologies are enhanced when professionally defined standards are among those for which agencies are accountable.
Learning requires practice.	Disperse new conclusions about how to improve performance widely in formal standard operating procedures but also through timely online forums and socializing opportunities. Find ways to preserve the tacit knowledge of those leaving the organization. Practice old routines with reorganized personnel. Review established procedures and determine which are still useful and which have been superseded and why.

CONCLUSIONS

We began by asking whether it was true that NASA was not a learning organization. We found that NASA did in fact learn important lessons after the *Challenger* disaster, but that only a few of those lessons survived by the time of the loss of the *Columbia*. Some were intentionally displaced or unlearned, and others were forgotten. Still other lessons, responses to persistent cultural and political challenges, were not learned. So the answer to the question of whether NASA could be considered a learning organization is that it could, in some cases, at some times, about some things.

In focusing on the accidents that destroyed the *Challenger* and the *Columbia*, we have concentrated on the weaknesses of the shuttle program as a learning organization. Has this condition changed in the aftermath of the *Columbia*? The evidence is mixed. Even after extensive work on the foam covering the external tank, technicians have not been able to prevent all debris shedding at launch. However, the orbiter is now subject to minute examination for damage by cameras on the external tank. It performs an elegant backflip as it approaches the International Space Station for another inspection. Experiments to repair some kinds of tile damage in space have proved generally successful. The shuttle is scheduled to be retired in 2010, when a new expendable launch vehicle (ELV) is to come on line, smaller and simpler in design but without the capacity of the shuttle to ferry supplies to the space station. However, NASA is still short of the funds it needs to carry out its current programs in space science. The space station and even more ambitious plans for a lunar base and Mars exploration continue to put pressure on the other programs. Administrator Griffin, who took over from Sean O'Keefe in 2005, initiated new rounds of layoffs, prompting one journalist to declare the "climate of fear has returned to NASA" (Hudson 2005). Whether NASA has learned how to be reliable remains to be seen. The complexity of its projects, the tensions among its cultures, and the organizational and technical impediments to collating information may pose continuing threats to learning.

This investigation of the events leading up to the loss of the shuttles offers many lessons about how public organizations learn. Learning in public organizations is not one process but several, and it is more complex and contingent than typically recognized. Its core dynamic depends on the resourcefulness, professionalism, and intellectual honesty of agency members. Because it is driven by the ideas of agency professionals about how to be more effective, it offers the possibility of building on their deep institutional understanding of the agency's programs, its workforce and culture, and the environment it inhabits. In many cases, learning is short-circuited by internal conflicts or external constraints, but recognizing its potential and the importance of efforts to collate and compare program and management experience is a first step in enlarging the potential for public organizational learning. These lessons about knowledge-based agency change can only become more important as we move ahead to build unique and complex organizations to handle the hazards of providing security against hostile action and natural disasters.

Notes

Chapter 1

1. All citations are to volume 1 of the *Rogers Commission Report* (1986) unless otherwise noted.

2. Other works in this genre are David Baker, *The History of Manned Space Flight* (1981), Andrew Chaikin, *A Man on the Moon: The Voyages of the* Apollo *Astronauts* (1985), David Harland, *How NASA Learned to Fly in Space: An Exciting Account of the* Gemini *Missions* (2004a), *The Story of the Space Shuttle* (2004b), and *Exploring the Moon: The* Apollo *Expeditions* (1999).

Chapter 2

1. Another set of distinctions focuses on the arena for learning. Here the concern is organizational learning, but related work characterizes learning in policy coalitions and in larger political settings. Jenkins-Smith and Sabatier note, "Policy-oriented learning involves relatively enduring alterations of thought or behavioral intentions that result from experience and which are concerned with the attainment or revision of the precepts of the belief system of individuals or collectivities (such as advocacy coalitions)" (1993, 42). Emphasizing the importance of experience, Bennett and Howlett define policy learning to mean "that states can learn from their experiences and that they can modify their present actions on the basis of their interpretation of how previous actions have fared in the past" (Bennett and Howlett 1992, 276). Other specialized forms of learning include political learning (Heclo 1974; May 1992), governmental learning (Etheredge 1985), and social learning. Rose (1991) also uses the idea of learning as "lesson drawing" in his comparative research on the diffusion of policy ideas.

2. Organizational development practitioners have also built upon theories of organizational learning to create a new family of models that integrate learning and prescriptions for change based on humanist values and applied behavioral research. In developing one such model for public agencies, Dilworth notes that "the learning organization involves both natural and planned synergy between mission accomplishment and opportunities for both professional and personal growth of employees at all levels in the organization"

(1996, 407). Though prescriptive organization-development models of learning have become important in consultancy practice (Easterby-Smith, Snell, and Gherardi 1998), the emphasis here is on the descriptive approaches to learning.

3. Perrow himself apparently did not view the *Columbia* accident as "normal" in his terms. Speaking of the technical elements of the accident, he noted, "it's odd and almost embarrassing, but this may be a case of a single point failure, not a complex interaction of multiple failures" (Beam 2003).

Chapter 3

1. The U.S. House of Representatives permanent committee that oversees science and technology has changed its name with some regularity. It has gone by the Committee on Science and Astronautics (1958–74), the Committee on Science and Technology (1975–86); the Committee on Science, Space and Technology (1987–94), and the Committee on Science (1995–2006). In 2007, it was officially renamed the U.S. House of Representatives Committee on Science and Technology (see U.S. House Committee). This text identifies the committee by the name in use at the time of the events discussed.

2. Morton Thiokol Inc. (known before 1982 and after 1989 as Thiokol) was the Utah contractor that provided the solid rocket boosters in the period directly before and after the *Challenger* disaster. The contract was managed from Marshall Space Flight Center, which directed the elements of the propulsion systems for the shuttle. In this chapter and throughout, risking some confusion for the sake of brevity, we use the name Thiokol as the short form for Morton Thiokol.

3. At the time of the *Challenger* disaster, the program was headed by the Office of Safety, Reliability and Quality Assurance. In the immediate aftermath of the Rogers Commission implementation report and in an effort to highlight the agency's commitment to maintaining safety, NASA changed the name to the Office of Safety, Reliability, Maintainability, and Quality Assurance. Over time, the agency reverted to using the original name.

4. The commission was named for its chair, Norman Augustine, who was then chairman and CEO of Martin Marietta Corporation and a former undersecretary of the Army. He had also been assistant secretary of the Army for research and development and assistant director of defense research and engineering in the office of the secretary of defense (NASA 1990).

5. The report was the product of an independent review team chaired by Christopher Kraft, a former director of the Johnson Space Center. The team included Col. Frank Borman, a retired astronaut and former CEO of Eastern Airlines; George Jeffs, former president of Rockwell International's North American Aerospace Operations; and Robert Lindstrom, the former senior vice president and general manager for space operations at Thiokol Corporation and retired manager of the space shuttle projects office at the Marshall center (NASA 1995).

References

Adams, Guy B., and Danny L. Balfour. 1998. *Unmasking administrative evil.* Thousand Oaks, CA: Sage.

Aerospace safety advisory panel, (ASAP) annual report. March 1987. Washington, DC: NASA Headquarters.

Aerospace safety advisory panel, (ASAP) annual report. March 1988. Washington, DC: NASA Headquarters.

Aerospace safety advisory panel, (ASAP) annual report. March 1991. Washington, DC: NASA Headquarters.

Aerospace safety advisory panel, (ASAP) annual report. March 1996. Washington, DC: NASA Headquarters.

Aerospace safety advisory panel, (ASAP) annual report. March 1997. Washington, DC: NASA Headquarters.

Aerospace safety advisory panel, (ASAP) annual report. March 1999. Washington, DC: NASA Headquarters.

Aerospace safety advisory panel, (ASAP) annual report. March 2000. Washington, DC: NASA Headquarters.

Aerospace safety advisory panel, (ASAP) annual report. March 2001. Washington, DC: NASA Headquarters.

Aerospace safety advisory panel, (ASAP) annual report. March 2002. Washington, DC: NASA Headquarters.

Argyris, Chris. 1991. The use of knowledge as a test for theory: The case of public administration. *Journal of Public Administration Research and Theory* 1 (3): 337–54.

Argyris, Chris, and Donald Schön. 1978. *Organizational learning: A theory of action perspective.* Reading, MA: Addison-Wesley.

Associated Press. 2006. Official: Genesis pre-launch test skipped. Space.com, 7 January, 2006. http://www.space.com/missionlaunches/ap_060107_genesis_update.html (accessed March 8, 2008).

Baker, David. 1981. *The history of manned space flight.* New York: Crown Publishers.

Barzelay, Michael. 1992. *Breaking through bureaucracy.* Berkeley: University of California Press.

Beam, Alex. 2003. *Columbia:* A "normal accident"? Bostonglobe.com, 4 February, 2003. http://boston.com/news/packages/shuttle/globe_stories/Columbia_a_normal_accident_+.shtml (accessed April 25, 2008).

Bennett, Colin, and Michael Howlett. 1992. The lessons of learning: Reconciling theories of policy learning and policy change. *Policy Sciences* 25:275–94.

Berends, Hans, Kees Boersma, and Mathieu Weggeman. 2003. The structuration of organizational learning. *Human Relations* 56 (9): 1035–56.

Berinstein, Paula. 2002. *Making space happen: Private space ventures and the visionaries behind them.* Medford, NJ: Plexus.

Birkland, Thomas. 1997. *After disaster: Agenda setting, public policy, and focusing events.* Washington, DC: Georgetown University Press.

———. 2004. Learning and policy improvement after disaster: The case of aviation security. *American Behavioral Scientist* 48 (November): 341–64.

Bouwen, Rene, and Ronald Fry. 1991. Organizational innovation and learning. *International Studies of Management and Organization* 21 (4): 37–51.

Bromberg, Joan Lisa. 1999. *NASA and the space industry.* Baltimore, MD: Johns Hopkins University Press.

Brown, John, and Paul Duguid. 1996. Organization learning and communities-of-practice: Toward a unified view of working, learning, and innovating. In *Organizational learning,* eds. Michael Cohen and Lee Sproull, 58–82. Thousand Oaks, CA: Sage.

Brown, Mary Maureen, and Jeffrey L. Brudney. 2003. Learning in the public sector? A study of police agencies employing information and technology to advance knowledge. *Public Administration Review* 61 (1): 30–43.

Burrell, Gibson, and Gareth Morgan. 1979. *Sociological paradigms and organizational analysis: Elements of the sociology of corporate life.* London: Heinemann.

Byrnes, Mark E. 1994. *Politics and space: Image making by NASA.* Westport, CT: Praeger.

Cabbage, Michael, and William Harwood. 2004. *Comm check . . . The final flight of shuttle Columbia.* New York: Free Press.

Carley, Kathleen. 1996. Organizational learning and personnel turnover. In *Organizational learning,* eds. Michael Cohen and Lee Sproull, 230–66. Thousand Oaks, CA: Sage.

Casamayou, Maureen Hogan. 1993. *Bureaucracy in crisis.* Boulder, CO: Westview.

Chaikin, Andrew. 1995. *A man on the moon: The voyages of the* Apollo *astronauts.* New York: Viking Penguin.

Columbia Accident Investigation Board. 2003. *Columbia Accident Investigation Board Report.* Washington, DC: GPO.

Comfort, Louise. 2002. Managing intergovernmental responses to terrorism and other extreme events. *Publius* 32 (fall): 29–49.

Comfort, Louise, Kilkon Ko, and Adam Zagoreki. 2004. Coordination in rapidly evolving disaster response systems: The role of information. *American Behavioral Scientist* 48 (November): 295–313.

Cook, Scott, and Dvora Yanow. 1996. Culture and organizational learning. In *Organizational learning,* eds. Michael Cohen and Lee Sproull, 430–59. Thousand Oaks, CA: Sage.

Cooper, Henry S. F. 1987. *Before lift-off: The making of a space shuttle crew.* Baltimore, MD: Johns Hopkins University Press.

Cowling, Keith. 2003. An astronaut's perspective on NASA culture. Spaceref.com, March 5, 2003. http://www.spaceref.com/news/viewnews.html?id = 76 (accessed January 3, 2006).

Daft, Richard, and George Huber. 1987. How organizations learn: A communications framework. *Research in the Sociology of Organizations* 5:1–36.

David, Leonard. 2004. NASA's fear of flying: What if the shuttle never flew again? Space.com, April 16, 2004. http://www.space.com/news/ (accessed July 17, 2007).

Dilworth, Robert. 1996. Institutionalizing learning organizations in the public sector. *Public Productivity and Management Review* 14:407–21.

Dixon, Nancy M. 1992. Organizational learning: A review of the literature with implications for HRD professionals. *Human Resource Development Quarterly* 3 (1):29–49.

Douglas, Mary, and Aaron Wildavsky. 1982. *Risk and culture: An essay on the selection of technological dangers*. Berkeley: University of California Press.

Dunar, Andrew, and Stephen Waring. 1999. Power to explore: A history of the Marshall Space Flight Center. Washington, DC: NASA History Office.

Easterby-Smith, Mark, Robin Snell, and Silvia Gherardi. 1998. Organizational learning: Diverging communities of practice? *Management Learning* 29 (3): 259–72.

Epple, Dennis, Linda Argote, and Rukmini Devadas. 1991. Organization learning curves: A method for investigating intra-plant transfer of knowledge acquired through learning by doing. *Organization Science* 2 (1): 58–70.

Etheredge, Lloyd. 1985. *Can governments learn?* New York: Pergamon.

Freudenberg, William R. 1992. Heuristics, biases, and the not-so-general publics: Expertise and error in the assessment of risks. In *Social theories of risk*, eds. Sheldon Krimsky and Dominic Golding, 229–49. Westport, CT: Praeger.

GAO. 1991. *Space Shuttle: NASA faces challenges in its attempt to achieve planned flight rates*. GAO/NSIAD-92–32, December 6, 1991. http://archive.gao.gov/d31t10/145567 .pdf (accessed April 25, 2008).

———. 1994. *NASA: Major challenges for management*. GAO/T-NSIAD-94–18, October 6, 1994. http://archive.gao.gov/t2pbat5/150119.pdf (accessed July 27, 2007).

———. 1996. *Space Shuttle: Need to sustain launch risk assessment process improvements*. GAO/NSIAD-96–73, March 26, 1996. http://www.gao.gov/archive/1996/ns96073.pdf (accessed April 25, 2008).

———. 2001a. *Major management challenges and program risks: National Aeronautics and Space Administration*. GAO-01–258, March 7, 2001. http://www.gao.gov/new.items/ d01492t.pdf (accessed April 25, 2008).

———. 2001b. *NASA: Status of achieving key outcomes*. GAO-01–868, July 31, 2001. http://www.gao.gov/new.items/d01868.pdf (accessed July 27, 2007).

———. 2002. *NASA: Better mechanisms needed for sharing lessons learned*. GAO-02–195, January 30. http://www.gao.gov/new.items/d02195.pdf (accessed July 27, 2007).

———. 2003. *Business modernization: Improvements needed in management of NASA's integrated financial management program*. GAO-03–507, April 30, 2003. http://www .gao.gov/new.items/d03507.pdf (accessed July 17, 2007).

Golding, Dominic. 1992. A social and programmatic history of risk research. In *Social Theories of Risk*, eds. Sheldon Krimsky and Dominic Golding, 23–52. Westport, CT: Praeger.

Graber, Doris. 2003. *The power of communication: Managing information in public organizations*. Washington, DC: Congressional Quarterly.

Grandori, Anna. 1984. A prescriptive contingency view of organizational decision making. *Administrative Science Quarterly*. 29:192–209.

Gugliotta, Guy. 2006a. Discovery's goal: A quiet trip. *Washington Post*. June 29, 2006: A1.

———. 2006b. Underfunded, panel reports; ambitious plans coming at the cost of science missions. *Washington Post*, May 5, 2006: A3.

Halperin, Morton H., Priscilla A. Clapp, and Arnold Kanter. 2006. *Bureaucratic politics and foreign policy*. Washington, DC: Brookings Institution Press.

Handberg, Roger. 2003. *Reinventing NASA: Human spaceflight, bureaucracy, and politics*. Westport, CT: Praeger.

Harland, David M. 1999. *Exploring the moon: The Apollo expeditions*. Chichester, UK: Praxis Publishing.

———. 2004a. *How NASA learned to fly in space: An exciting account of the Gemini missions*. Ontario, Canada: Apogee Books.

———. 2004b. *The story of the space shuttle*. Chichester, UK: Praxis Publishing.

Haunschild, Pamela R., and Bilian Ni Sullivan. 2002. Learning from complexity: Effects of prior accidents and incidents on airlines' learning. *Administrative Science Quarterly* 47 (4): 609–45.

Heclo, Hugh. 1974. *Modern social politics in Britain and Sweden*. New Haven, CT: Yale University Press.

Hedberg, Bo. 1981. How organizations learn and unlearn. In *Adapting organizations to their environments*. Vol. 1 of *Handbook of organizational design*, eds. Paul Nystrom and William Starbuck, 3–27. New York: Oxford University Press.

Heimann, C. F. Larry. 1993. Understanding the *Challenger* disaster: Organizational structure and the design of reliable systems. *American Political Science Review* 87, no. 2 (June): 421–35.

Huber, George. 1991. Organization learning: The contributing processes and the literatures. *Organizational Science* 2 (1): 88–115.

Hudson, Audrey. 2005. "Climate of fear" returns to NASA, watchdog says. *Washington Times*, June 28, 2005.

Hutchins, Edwin. 1996. Organizing work by adaptation. In *Organizational Learning*, eds. Michael Cohen and Lee Sproull, 20–57. Thousand Oaks, CA: Sage.

Ignatius, David. 1986. Did the media goad NASA into the Challenger disaster? *Washington Post*, March 30, 1986.

Immergut, Ellen. 1998. The theoretical core of the new institutionalism. *Politics and Society* 26, no. 1 (March): 5–34.

Janis, Irving. 1982. *Groupthink*. 2nd ed. Boston: Houghton Mifflin.

Jenkins-Smith, Hank, and Paul Sabatier. 1993. The dynamics of policy-oriented learning. In *Policy change and learning*, eds. Paul Sabatier and Hank Jenkins-Smith, 41–56. Boulder, CO; Westview Press.

Jensen, Claus. 1996. *No downlink: A dramatic narrative about the* Challenger *accident and our time*. New York: Farrar, Straus and Giroux.

Kaufman, Herbert. 1973. *Administrative feedback: Monitoring subordinates' behavior*. Washington, DC: Brookings Institution.

Kay, W. D. 2005. *Defining NASA: The historical debate over the agency's mission*. Albany: State University of New York Press.

Keeney, Ralph. 1983. *Acceptable risk*. New York: Cambridge University Press.

Kettl, Donald F. 1994. Managing on the frontiers of knowledge: The learning organization. In *New paradigms for government*, eds. Patricia W. Ingraham and Barbara S. Romzek, 19–40. San Francisco: Jossey-Bass.

———. 2007. *System under stress: Homeland security and American politics*. Washington, DC: CQ Press.

Khademian, Anne M. 2002. *Working with culture: How the job gets done in public programs*. Washington, DC: CQ Press.

Kingdon, John W. 1995. *Agendas, alternatives and public policies*. 2nd ed. New York: Harper Collins.

Klerkx, Greg. 2004. *Lost in space: The fall of NASA and the dream of a new space age*. New York: Pantheon.

Korten, David. 1980. Community organization and rural development. *Public Administration Review* 40 (5): 480–511.

Kronenberg, Phillip, and Anne Khademian. 2007. Linking the lightening under contingent ambiguity: Strategic managing of organizing at DHS and DOD. Paper presented at the meeting of the American Society for Public Administration, Washington, DC.

Lambright, W. Henry. 1995. *Powering* Apollo: *James E. Webb of NASA*. Baltimore, MD: Johns Hopkins University Press.

———. 2001. *Transforming government: Daniel Goldin and the remaking of NASA*. Washington, DC: IBM Center for the Business of Government. http://www.businessofgovernment.org/main/publications/grant_reports/details/index.asp?GID = 82 (accessed April 25, 2008).

———. 2005. *Executive response to changing fortune: Sean O'Keefe as NASA administrator*. Washington, DC: IBM Center for the Business of Government. http://www.businessofgovernment.org/pdfs/LambrightReport4.pdf (accessed April 25, 2008).

Landau, Martin. 1969. Redundancy, rationality and the problem of duplication and overlap. *Public Administration Review* 29, no. 4 (July–August): 346–58.

Landau, Martin, and Russell Stout. 1979. To manage is not to control: Or the folly of type II errors. *Public Administration Review* 39 (2): 148–56.

LaPorte, Todd R. 1987. The self-designing high reliability organization: Aircraft carrier flight operation at sea. *Naval War College Review* 90 (Autumn): 76–90.

————. 1988. The United States air traffic system: Increasing reliability in the midst of rapid growth. In *The Development of Large Technical Systems*, eds. Renate Mayntz and Thomas P. Hughes, 215–44. Boulder, CO: Westview Press.

LaPorte, Todd, and Paula Consolini. 1991. Working in practice but not in theory: Theoretical challenges of "high-reliability organizations." *Journal of Public Administration Research and Theory: J-PART* 1, no. 1 (January): 19–48.

Lawler, Andrew. 2000a. Reports will urge overhaul and delays to NASA's Mars missions. *Science* 287, no. 5459 (March 10): 1722–23.

————. 2000b. "Faster, cheaper, better" on trial. *Science* 288, no. 5463 (April 7, 2000): 32–34.

Lebovic, James. 1995. How organizations learn: U.S. government estimates of foreign military spending. *American Journal of Political Science* 39 (4): 835–63.

Levine, Arthur. 1992. NASA's organizational structure: The price of decentralization. *Public Administration Review* 52 (2): 198–203.

Levitt, Barbara, and James March. 1988. Organizational learning. *Annual Review of Sociology* 14:319–40.

Lipshitz, Raanan, Micha Popper, and Victor J. Friedman. 2002. A multifacet model of organizational learning. *Journal of Applied Behavioral Science* 38, no. 1 (March): 78–99.

Lowrance, William W. 1976. *Of acceptable risk: Science and the determination of safety.* Los Altos, CA: William Kaufman.

Mahler, Julianne. 1997. Influences of organizational culture on learning in public agencies. *Journal of Public Administration Research and Theory* 7 (4): 519–40.

Mahler, Julianne, and Priscilla M. Regan. 2007. Active and passive leadership in virtual collaboration networks. Paper presented at Leading the Future of the Public Sector: The Third Transatlantic Dialogue, University of Delaware.

————. 2008. Agency-related blogs as policy network forums. Paper presented at the annual meeting of the American Political Science Association, Boston, MA.

Malik, Tariq. 2004. Investigators find preliminary cause of Genesis crash. Space.com, October 15, 2004. http://www.space.com/scienceastronomy/genesis_update_041015 .html (accessed March 8, 2008).

March, James. 1976. The technology of foolishness. In *Ambiguity and choice in organizations*, eds. James March and Johann Olsen, 69–81. Bergen, Norway: Universitetsforlaget.

March, James, and Johan Olsen, eds. 1976. *Ambiguity and choice in organizations.* Bergen, Norway: Universitetsforlaget.

March, James, and Johan Olsen. 1984. The new institutionalism: Organizational factors in political life. *American Political Science Review* 78, no. 3 (September): 734–49.

March, James, Lee Sproull, and Michal Tamuz. 1996. Learning from samples of one or fewer. In *Organizational Learning*, eds. Michael Cohen and Lee Sproull, 1–19. Thousand Oaks, CA: Sage.

Martin, Joanne. 2002. *Organizational culture.* Thousand Oaks, CA: Sage.

May, Peter. 1992. Policy learning and failure. *Journal of Public Policy* 12 (4): 331–54.

McAfee, Andrew. 2006. Enterprise 2.0: The dawn of emergent collaboration. *MIT Sloan Management Review* 47 (3): 21–28.

McConnell, Malcolm. 1987. Challenger: *A major malfunction.* Garden City, NY: Doubleday.

McCurdy, Howard E. 1990. *The space station decision: Incremental politics and technological choice.* Baltimore, MD: Johns Hopkins University Press.

———. 1993. *Inside NASA : High technology and organizational change in the U.S. space program.* Baltimore, MD: Johns Hopkins University Press.

———. 2001. *Faster, better, cheaper : Low-cost innovation in the U.S. space program.* Baltimore, MD: Johns Hopkins University Press.

McDougall, Walter A. 1985. *The heavens and the earth: A political history of the space age.* New York: Basic Books.

McKean, Kevin. 1986. They fly in the face of danger. *Discover* (April): 48–54.

Miner, Ann, Paula Bassoff, and Christine Moorman. 2001. Organizational improvisation and learning: A field study. *Administrative Science Quarterly* 46:304–37.

Montjoy, Robert, and Lawrence O'Toole. 1979. Toward a theory of policy implementation: An organizational perspective. *Public Administration Review* 39, no. 5 (Sep.–Oct): 465–76.

Morgan, Gareth. 1986. *Images of Organization.* Thousand Oaks, CA: Sage.

Morris, Michael, and Paul Moore. 2000. The lessons we (don't) learn: Counterfactual thinking and organizational accountability after a close call. *Administrative Science Quarterly* 45 (4): 737–71.

Naeye, Robert. 2000. Mars exploration: The sounds of silence. *Astronomy* 28 (March): 24–25.

NASA. 1986. *Actions to implement the recommendations of the presidential commission on the space shuttle challenger accident.* July 14, 1986. http://history.nasa.gov/rogersrep/actions.pdf (accessed April 26, 2008).

———. 1988. *Lessons learned from challenger* (Dahlstrom Report). NASA Office of Safety, Reliability, Maintainability and Quality Assurance. http://www.internationalspace.com/pdf/LessonsLearnedFromChallenger-1988.pdf (accessed April 29, 2007).

———. 1990. *Report of the Advisory Committee on the Future of the U.S. Space Program* (Augustine Report). December 1990. http://history.nasa.gov/augustine/racfup4.htm# Management (accessed May 1, 2007).

———. 1995. *Report of the space shuttle management independent review team* (Kraft Report). http://spaceflight.nasa.gov/shuttle/reference/green/kraft.pdf (accessed April 17, 2008).

NBC Nightly News with Tom Brokaw. 1986. Transcript. January 27.

O'Leary, Rosemary. 2005. *The ethics of dissent: Managing guerrilla government.* Washington, DC: CQ Press.

Perrow, C. 1967. A framework for the comparative analysis of organizations. *American Sociological Review* 32(2): 194–208.

———. 1999. *Normal accidents.* Princeton, NJ: Princeton University Press.

Quayle, Dan. 1994. *Standing firm: A compelling portrait of the politician and the man*. New York: Harper Collins.

Rabinow, Paul, and William Sullivan, eds. 1987. *Interpretive social science: A second look*. Berkeley: University of California Press.

Radin, Beryl. 2006. *Challenging the performance movement*. Washington, DC: Georgetown University Press.

Raynor, Steve. 1992. Cultural theory and risk analysis. In *Social theories of risk*, eds. Sheldon Krimsky and Dominic Golding, 83–115. Westport, CT: Praeger Publishers.

Rogers Commission. 1986. *Report of the presidential commission on the space shuttle* Challenger (Rogers Commission Report, vols. 1–5). Washington, DC: GPO. http://science .ksc.nasa.gov/shuttle/missions/51-l/docs/rogers-commission/table-of-contents.html (accessed April 26, 2008).

———. 1987. *Implementation of the recommendations of the presidential commission on the Space Shuttle Challenger accident* (Vol. 6 of the Rogers Commission Report, June). Washington, DC: Government Printing Office. http://history.nasa.gov/rogersrep/v6 index.htm (accessed April 26, 2008).

Romzek, Barbara, and Melvin Dubnick. 1987. Accountability in the public sector: Lessons from the *Challenger* tragedy. *Public Administration Review* 47, no. 3 (May–June): 227–38.

Rose, Richard. 1991. What is lesson drawing? *Journal of Public Policy* 11:3–30.

Roy, Stephanie. 1998. The origin of the smaller, faster, cheaper approach in NASA's solar system exploration program. *Space Policy* 14:153–71.

Sabatier, Paul 1993. Policy change over a decade or more. In *Policy change and learning*, eds. Paul Sabatier and Hank Jenkins-Smith, 13–39. Boulder, CO: Westwood.

Sagan, Scott. 2004. Learning from normal accidents. *Organization and Environment* 17 (1): 15–19.

Sato, Yasushi. 2005. Local engineering and systems engineering: cultural conflict at NASA's Marshall Space Flight Center, 1960–1966. *Technology and Culture* 46 (July): 561–83.

Schattschneider, E. E. 1960. *The semisovereign people: A realist's view of democracy in America*. New York: Holt, Rinehart and Winston.

Schein, Edgar. 1992. *Organization culture and leadership*. 2nd ed. San Francisco: Jossey-Bass.

———. 1999. *The corporate culture survival guide: Sense and nonsense about cultural change*. San Francisco: Jossey-Bass.

Schön, Donald A. 1975. Deutero-learning in organizations: Learning for increased effectiveness. *Organizational Dynamics* 4 (1): 2–16.

Scott, W. Richard. 1995. *Institutions and organizations*. Thousand Oaks, CA: Sage.

Senge, Peter. 1990. *The fifth discipline: The art and practice of the learning organization*. New York: Doubleday.

Sietzen, Frank Jr., and Keith L. Cowling. 2004. *New moon rising: The making of America's new space vision and the remaking of NASA*. Ontario: Apogee Books.

Slovic, Paul. 1992. Perception of risk: Reflection on the psychometric paradigm. In *Social theories of risk*, eds. Sheldon Krimsky and Dominic Golding, 117–52. Westport, CT: Praeger.

Starbuck, William. 1996. Unlearning ineffective or obsolete technologies. *International Journal of Technology Management* 11:725–37.

Starbuck, William, and Moshe Farjoun, eds. 2005. *Organization at the limit: Lessons from the* Columbia *disaster*. Malden, MA: Blackwell Publishing.

Starr, Chauncey. 1969. Social benefit versus technological risk: What is our society willing to pay for safety? *Science* 165 (3899):1232–38.

Tavris, Carol, and Elliot Aronson. 2007. *Mistakes were made (but not by me): Why we justify foolish beliefs, bad decisions, and hurtful acts*. Orlando, FL: Harcourt.

Trento, Joseph. J. 1987. *Prescription for disaster*. New York: Crown.

Tufte, Edward. 2003. *The cognitive style of powerpoint*. Cheshire, CT: Graphic Press.

Tversky, Amos, and Daniel Kahneman. 1988. *Judgment under uncertainty: Heuristics and biases*. Cambridge, MA: Cambridge University Press.

United Space Alliance. 2006. About USA. http://www.unitedspacealliance.com/about/his tory.asp and http://www.unitedspacealliance.com/about/default.asp (accessed April 15, 2007).

U.S. Congress. House Committee on Science and Technology. 1986. *Investigation of the Challenger Accident*. 99th Cong., 2nd sess..

U.S. Congress. House Committee on Science, Space, and Technology. 1987. *Hearings before a subcommittee on space science and applications of the Committee on Science, Space and Technology*. 100th Cong., 1st sess.

U.S. Congress. Senate Committee on Appropriations, Department of Housing and Urban Development, Independent Agency Appropriations for Fiscal Year 1986. 1985. *Hearing before a subcommittee of the Committee of Appropriations*. 99th Cong. 1st sess.

U.S. House Committee on Science and Technology. History of the committee. http://science.house.gov/about/history_committee.shtml (accessed Nov. 10, 2008).

Van Maanen, John, and Stephen Barley. 1985. Cultural organizations: Fragments of a theory. In *Organization Culture*, eds. Peter Frost, Larry Moore, Meryl Reis Louis, Craig Lundberg, and Joanne Martin, 31–54. Beverly Hills: Sage Publications.

Vaughan, Diane. 1996. *The* Challenger *launch decision: Risky technology, culture and deviance at NASA*. Chicago: University of Chicago Press.

von Braun, Wernher. 1952. Man on the moon: The journey. *Colliers* (18 October): 52–59.

Wald, Matthew, and John Schwartz. 2003. Shuttle inquiry uncovers flaws in communication. *New York Times*, August 4, 2003.

Walsh, James, and Geraldo Ungson. 1991. Organizational memory. *Academy of Management Review* 16 (1): 57–91.

Washington Post. 1986. Did the media goad NASA into the Challenger disaster? March 30.

Weick, Karl. 1979. *The social psychology of organizing*. 2nd. ed. Reading, MA: Addison-Wesley.

Weick, Karl, and Karlene Roberts. 1993. Collective mind in organizations: Heedful inter-relating on flight decks. *Administrative Science Quarterly* 38 (Sept.): 357–81.

Wikipedia. NASA budget. http://en.wikipedia.org/wiki/NASA_budget. Based on data from the NASA Procurement Management Service Online Query at http://prod.nais.nasa.gov/cgi-bin/npms/map.cgi (accessed May 8, 2008).

Wildavsky, Aaron. 1988. *Searching for safety*. New Brunswick: Transaction Publishers.

Wilson, James. 1989. *Bureaucracy*. New York: Basic Books.

Wolfe, Tom. 1979. *The right stuff*. New York: Bantam Books.

Index

Note: Page numbers followed by "f" or "t" represent figures and tables.